PORTUGUESE STUDIES

Volume 32 Number 2
2016

Authoritarian States and Corporatism in
Portugal and Brazil

Founding Editor
Helder Macedo

Guest Editors
Paula Borges Santos
Luciano Aronne de Abreu

Editors
Catarina Fouto
Toby Green
Tori Holmes
Paulo de Medeiros
Paul Melo e Castro
Hilary Owen
Claire Williams

Editorial Assistant
Richard Correll

Production Editor
Graham Nelson

MODERN HUMANITIES RESEARCH ASSOCIATION

PORTUGUESE STUDIES

A peer-reviewed biannual multi-disciplinary journal devoted to research on the cultures, literatures, history and societies of the Lusophone world

International Advisory Board

DAVID BROOKSHAW   MARIA MANUEL LISBOA
JOÃO DE PINA CABRAL   KENNETH MAXWELL
IVO JOSÉ DE CASTRO   LAURA DE MELLO E SOUZA
THOMAS F. EARLE   MARIA IRENE RAMALHO
JOHN GLEDSON   SILVIANO SANTIAGO
ANNA KLOBUCKA

Portuguese Studies and other journals published by the MHRA may be ordered from JSTOR (http://about.jstor.org/csp).

The **Modern Humanities Research Association** was founded in Cambridge in 1918 and has become an international organization with members in all parts of the world. It is a registered charity number 1064670, and a company limited by guarantee, registered in England number 3446016. Its main object is to encourage advanced study and research in modern and medieval European languages, literatures, and cultures by its publication of journals, book series, and its Style Guide. Further information about the activities of the Association and individual membership may be obtained from the Membership Secretary, Dr Jessica Goodman, St Catherine's College, Oxford OX1 3UJ, UK, email membership@mhra.org.uk, or from the website at: **www.mhra.org.uk**

Disclaimer: Statements of fact and opinion in the content of *Portuguese Studies* are those of the respective authors and contributors and not of the journal editors or of the Modern Humanities Research Association (MHRA). MHRA makes no representation, express or implied, in respect of the accuracy of the material in this journal and cannot accept any legal responsibility or liability for any errors or omissions that may be made.

Parts of this work may be reproduced as permitted under legal provisions for fair dealing (or fair use) for the purposes of research, private study, criticism, or review, or when a relevant collective licensing agreement is in place. All other reproduction requires the written permission of the copyright holder who may be contacted at rights@mhra.org.uk.

ISSN 0267–5315 (print)   ISSN 2222–4270 (online)
ISBN 978-1-78188-257-3

© 2016 The Modern Humanities Research Association
Salisbury House, Station Road, Cambridge CB1 2LA, United Kingdom

Portuguese Studies vol. 32 no. 2
Authoritarian States and Corporatism in Portugal and Brazil

CONTENTS

Preface	123
Introduction: Portuguese and Brazilian Authoritarian States and Corporatism: Political Change and Institutional Practice Paula Borges Santos and Luciano Aronne de Abreu	125
The Political and Ideological Origins of the Estado Novo in Portugal Ernesto Castro Leal	128
Redefining Representation in the Dictatorship of Salazar and Marcelo Caetano: The Changing Role of Parliament (1935–1974) Paula Borges Santos	149
Memory of Resistance and the Resistance of Memory: An Analysis of the Construction of Corporatism in the First Years of the Portuguese Estado Novo Francisco Carlos Palomanes Martinho	172
Portuguese Origins and the 'True' Brazil: The Corporative Vision of Oliveira Viana Luciano Aronne de Abreu	199
Brazilian Integralism and the Corporatist Intellectual Triad Leandro Pereira Gonçalves and Odilon Caldeira Neto	225
The Technical Councils of the Brazilian Government Structure: Corporatism, Authoritarianism and Modernization (1934–1945) Cássio A. A. Albernaz	244
Reviews	262
Abstracts	270

NOTES FOR CONTRIBUTORS

Articles to be considered for publication may be on any subject within the field but must not exceed 7,500 words, and should be submitted in a form ready for publication in English, sent as an email attachment to the Editorial Assistant at portuguese@mhra.org.uk.

Contributions whose standard of English is inadequate will be returned. Any quotations in Portuguese must be accompanied by an English translation. Submissions in Portuguese may be considered, but publication will be conditional on provision of a satisfactory translation at the author's expense. The Editorial Assistant may undertake translations on request for a reasonable charge.

Text and references should conform precisely to the conventions of the *MHRA Style Guide*, 3rd edn, 2013 (978-1-78188-009-8), £9.50, $19.00, €12.00, obtainable in print or online version from www.style.mhra.org.uk. All articles are subject to independent, anonymous peer review by experts in the field; authors receive written feedback on the editors' decision and guidance on any revisions required. *Portuguese Studies* regrets it must charge contributors for the cost of corrections in proof deemed excessive.

It is a condition of publication in this journal that authors of articles and reviews assign copyright, including electronic copyright, to the MHRA. Inter alia, this allows the General Editor to deal efficiently and consistently with requests from third parties for permission to reproduce material. The journal has been published simultaneously in printed and electronic form since January 2001. Permission, without fee, for authors to use their own material in other publications, after a reasonable period of time has elapsed, is not normally withheld. Authors may make closed-access deposit of accepted manuscripts in their academic institution's digital repository upon acceptance. Full open access to the accepted manuscript is permitted no sooner than 24 months following publication of the Contribution by the MHRA. Contributions may also be republished on authors' personal websites without seeking further permission from the Association, but no earlier than 24 months after publication by the MHRA.

Books for review should be sent to: Reviews Editor, *Portuguese Studies*, Dr Paul Melo e Castro, School of Modern Languages and Cultures, University of Leeds, Leeds LS2 9JT.

Preface

It gives *Portuguese Studies* great pleasure to welcome the guest editors of the current issue entitled 'Authoritarian States and Corporatism in Portugal and Brazil', Paula Borges Santos of the Institute of Contemporary History at the New University of Lisbon and Luciano Aronne de Abreu of the Pontifical Catholic University of Rio Grande do Sul. Just as the guest editorship is a transatlantic partnership, so the articles contained herein span Portugal and Brazil, considering as a whole the history of the New States in both countries in the early to mid-twentieth century in their relation to common factors such as strong Integralist movements or the institution of Corporatist ideologies, and establishing a set of explicit and implicit dialogues between the scholars featured.

In the first article, **Ernesto Castro Leal** examines the political ideologies of the Estado Novo in Portugal, such as nationalism, authoritarianism and corporativism, and demonstrates that very many of its foundational ideas were already circulating in Portugal at the time of the First Republic (1910–26), promulgated by ideologues such as Quirino de Jesus. In the second article, **Paula Borges Santos** examines the role of the Portuguese National Assembly, which survived in a recognizable form throughout the entire time of the Estado Novo, despite the regime's alleged intention of moving towards a more Corporatist and less liberal type of popular representation, and suggests some reasons why this may have been the case. In the third article on the Portuguese authoritarian state, **Francisco Carlos Palomanes Martins** examines the dilemma facing organized labour as they were pressured to close down their independent unions and join state-sponsored labour associations. With a particular focus on bakery workers, he examines the choices and the compromises made by different ideological currents active within the labour movement.

Moving to Brazilian authoritarianism, **Luciano Abronne de Abreu** examines the role of the leader of the '1920–1940 generation', Oliveira Viana, and his analysis of the strengths and weaknesses of the 'true' Brazilian nation, and the legacy of its 'Portuguese origins', while comparing Viana's thinking with that of three other Brazilian intellectuals, namely Wanderley Guilherme dos Santos, Bolívar Lamounier and José Murilo de Carvalho. In the following article, **Leandro Pereira Gonçalves** and **Odilon Caldeira Neto** focus on Brazilian Integralism, particularly its leading intellectual, Plínio Salgado, and two other ideologues, namely Gustavo Barroso and Miguel Reale, and how they fared in the face of Getúlio Vargas's Estado Novo (1937–45). Finally, **Cássio A. A. Albernaz** looks at the way that the various Technical Councils emerged in Brazil, and became key players in the way the Corporatist state directed economic planning in Brazil in the 1930s and 1940s.

Taken as a whole, these six essays offer a valuable resource for an understanding of the ideologies and the workings of the authoritarian states in both Portugal and Brazil.

THE EDITORS

Introduction
Portuguese and Brazilian Authoritarian States and Corporatism: Political Change and Institutional Practice

Paula Borges Santos and Luciano Aronne de Abreu

At a time when studies of the historical experiences of corporativism in the inter-war period have seen new developments in the academic world, both in Portugal and in Brazil, in differing fields such as History, Sociology and Political Science, this volume of *Portuguese Studies* brings together six articles which aim to explore some of the less-visited aspects of the origins and establishment of corporative projects in the course of the dictatorships in those two countries.

Setting out from the observation that, in both cases, we witnessed the institutionalization of state corporativisms — that is, corporative projects in which the principal stimulus and initiatives were made by governmental authorities — academic analysis has been directed to two areas of discussion: on the one hand the ideological and juridical foundations of the two corporative ideologies, and on the other hand the problem of the nature, the functioning and the functionality of some of its institutions. This analytical position has in turn three aspects.

Firstly, there is a need to rethink critically the descriptions contained in the main studies of historical corporativisms in Portugal and Brazil, and of their political and institutional dynamics. In effect, while these studies benefited from being widely published and discussed, the truth is that later researches served largely to confirm the theses contained in them and to deepen certain elements. Frequently this led to the repetition of the results first presented, to the detriment of a sustained tendency towards new approaches. Hence there remain lacunae in our knowledge which deserve to be diagnosed and overcome. The choice of topics in this volume meets this concern.

Secondly, there is an interest in overcoming a certain tension that arises in studies of the historical experiences of corporativism, namely of the association popularly made between this phenomenon (either as a doctrine or in its various manifestations) and the regimes of the so-called 'fascist era'. To this end, it is necessary to avoid some of the generalizations made about the assimilation of the corporative ideal by succeeding regimes, which are common in the more ideological readings of the past, and to take care to deconstruct official and propagandistic discourses made by governments. In the same way, explanations of corporative processes made by their own doctrinal chiefs are to be rejected. We should be cautious, too, of reading historical reality through critiques of the systems, such as were made by opposition currents, or by those who, despite belonging to the establishment of these regimes, became disillusioned.

The third aspect arises from the need to question the usefulness of the customary definition of political corporatism, in so far as it dogmatically states that corporative systems were based on the exclusion of any idea of representation by way of individual suffrage. As a reading of the articles gathered here will demonstrate, historical reality in Portugal and Brazil was more complex than that. There were compromises, adaptations of organicist and liberal ideas (in turn diffused by different means and assimilated in very different forms amongst the supporters of corporative projects), and above all neither country witnessed a total rejection of traditions of civil rights.

The chronological boundaries to this volume, while not being identical for every article, cover the corporative projects in Portugal and Brazil from their first establishment up to their demise. In this way they capture both the continuities and the changes in their juridical and political foundations during the lifecycle of the institutions created and established in those countries. For Portugal this goes back to the period of the First Republic to explain how some organicist ideas from that time were spread and gained support from the political class of the time. Despite falling outside the periodization of the authoritarian state, a study of this period is fundamental to an understanding of how far criticism of the principles on which the democratic and liberal state were based had already advanced before the consolidation of the dictatorship.

While the present volume provides heuristic instruments that may contribute to the making of a comparative history of corporativism in Portugal and Brazil, the articles here do not set out to do so. Rather, they focus, for example, on certain personalities, such as intellectuals, who had a particular influence in their country, but whose thinking did not shape the victorious currents within corporative projects. They also analyse organizations that were very different both in their profile and in the functions undertaken, to highlight the degree of institutional variation in both corporative projects, whether within a particular corporatism or with regard to projects based on the same ideology. In different ways these articles call attention to particular conditions of political participation and to the autonomy of different organizations that oblige us to rethink the approaches to these two state corporativisms, particularly regarding the little that has been written about their limited political pluralism and their reduced social pluralism.

In this framework, this collection of studies aims above all to establish and inform dialogue between specialists from both countries, aiming to break with homogenous readings of the internal dynamics of those realities and to avoid the stereotypes so often seen in discussing the authoritarian regimes in Portugal and Brazil.

This collection of articles falls within the ambit of NETCOR (International Network for Studies of Corporatism and the Organized Interest), founded in Lisbon in January 2015, to which all the contributors belong. The two editors are also members of its Coordinating Committee.

The Political and Ideological Origins of the Estado Novo in Portugal

Ernesto Castro Leal

Faculdade de Letras and Centro de História,
Universidade de Lisboa

Introduction

The present article aims to reflect on aspects of the ideological and political origins of the Portuguese Estado Novo (1933–74), locating them in the times of the Portuguese First Republic (1910–26).[1] The historical and political analysis focuses on the processes of circulation and transfer of the political ideas of nationalism, organicism, corporativism and authoritarianism amongst the main political and ideological currents that were critical of the parliamentary system of government of the First Republic, with particular reference to the Christian Democracy of the Centro Católico Português,[2] the anti-liberal monarchism of the Integralismo Lusitano,[3] and the syncretic nationalism of the Cruzada Nacional D. Nuno Álvares Pereira.[4] Along with elements of Italian fascist ideology, such as the corporative *Carta del Lavoro* (1927), which would influence the Portuguese *Estatuto de Trabalho Nacional* (1933), these would all be involved in the genesis of the Portuguese dictatorial regime.

The dictatorship of the Estado Novo defined the Portuguese state in the Constitution of 1933 as a unitary and corporative Republic, and its doctrinal

---

[1] My thanks go to Paula Borges Santos and Luciano Aronne de Abreu, the editors of this special issue, to the editors of *Portuguese Studies*, to the anonymous reviewer who provided a reader's report, and to the translator, Richard Correll. This article forms part of a research programme in Atlantic Studies (Centro de História da Universidade de Lisboa) within the strategic project, and is funded by National Funds through FCT — Fundação para a Ciência e a Tecnologia under the Project UID/HIS/04311/2013. Faculdade de Letras da Universidade de Lisboa, Alameda da Universidade, 1600–214 Lisboa, Portugal.

[2] Manuel Braga da Cruz, *As origens da democracia cristã e o salazarismo* (Lisbon: Presença, 1980); Valentim Alexandre, *O roubo das almas: Salazar, a Igreja e os totalitarismos (1930–39)* (Lisbon: Dom Quixote, 2006), pp. 15–122; Centro de Estudos de História Religiosa (ed.), *António Lino Neto: intervenções parlamentares (1918–26)* (Lisbon: Assembleia da República/Texto, 2009).

[3] Manuel Braga da Cruz, 'O integralismo lusitano nas origens do salazarismo', *Análise Social*, 70 (1982), 137–82; Norberto Ferreira da Cunha, 'O tradicionalismo integralista', in *Poiética do mundo: homenagem a Joaquim Cerqueira Gonçalves* (Lisbon: Colibri, 2001), pp. 375–99; José Manuel Quintas, *Filhos de Ramires: as origens do Integralismo Lusitano* (Lisbon: Nova Ática, 2004); Ana Isabel Sardinha Desvignes, *António Sardinha (1887–1925): um intelectual no século* (Lisbon: Imprensa de Ciências Sociais, 2006).

[4] Ernesto Castro Leal, *Nação e nacionalismos: a Cruzada Nacional D. Nuno Álvares Pereira e as origens do Estado Novo (1918–38)* (Lisbon: Cosmos, 1999).

leader, António de Oliveira Salazar, in his speech *Princípios fundamentais da revolução política* (30 July 1930), delivered when he was still Finance Minister, marked out the foundations of the new political ideology: nationalism as the 'spirit of conservation' of the Portuguese nation; the consolidation of the strong state, which saw itself as 'limited by morality, by principles of the rights of peoples, by individual guarantees and liberties'; the strengthening of the power of the Executive, while respecting the separation of powers; social coordination, by way of the nation organized in the state, in order to 'construct the social and corporative state in strict correspondence with the natural constitution of society' — families, parishes, municipalities, corporations; economic progress (a directed political economy) and social peace.[5] This political culture moulded a dictatorship that was conservative, nationalist, anti-liberal and anti-democratic, integrating elements of totalitarian political regimes, such as the single party (the União Nacional), the political police (the PVDE/PIDE), political courts, political prisons (Aljube, Peniche, Caxias), a concentration camp (Tarrafal), official censorship, idolatry of the chief, state propaganda, a civil militia (the Legião Portuguesa), and official youth organizations (the Mocidade Portuguesa and the Mocidade Portuguesa Feminina).[6]

The Catholic, Quirino Avelino de Jesus[7] was an important ideologue in the initial phases of the construction of the Estado Novo, having been the author of the first version of the report and the constitutional project that was subject to internal debate, producing other versions elaborated by a small elite, headed by Oliveira Salazar, which included Domingos Fezas Vital (a constitutional expert), Mário de Figueiredo, José Alberto dos Reis, Martinho Nobre de Melo, and Manuel Rodrigues.[8] In 1932, Quirino de Jesus published his book *Nacionalismo português*, recognizing that 'nationalism is not essentially a novelty. It is, in a positive sense, anterior to an individualistic and revolutionary liberalism.' He presented a historical typology of Portuguese nationalisms: legitimist monarchical nationalism, constitutional monarchical nationalism, Catholic nationalism, republican nationalism and integralist monarchical nationalism, concluding with the Portuguese nationalism of the Dictatorship which would be an 'eclectic nationalism' and the 'most developed system that could be created at

---

[5] Oliveira Salazar, *Discursos*, 5th edn, vol. I (Coimbra: Coimbra Editora, 1961 [1935]), pp. 77–89.
[6] For interpretations of the Portuguese Estado Novo, cf. Manuel Braga da Cruz, *O partido e o Estado no salazarismo* (Lisbon: Presença, 1988); Fernando Rosas et al., *O Estado Novo (1926-74)*, in José Mattoso (ed.), *História de Portugal*, vol. VII (Lisbon: Círculo de Leitores, 1994); Luís Reis Torgal, *Estados novos, Estado Novo*, 2nd edn, 2 vols (Coimbra: Imprensa da Universidade de Coimbra, 2009); Rui Ramos, 'Idade contemporânea (séculos XIX–XXI)', in Rui Ramos (ed.), *História de Portugal* (Lisbon: A Esfera dos Livros, 2009), pp. 627–704.
[7] Ernesto Castro Leal, 'Quirino Avelino de Jesus, um católico pragmático: notas para o estudo crítico da relação entre publicismo e política (1894-1926)', *Lusitania Sacra*, 2nd series, 6 (1994), 355–89; Idem, 'A problemática da crise nacional em Quirino de Jesus: moral, política e administração', *Crises em Portugal nos séculos XIX e XX* (Lisbon: Centro de História da Universidade de Lisboa, 2002), pp. 189-99.
[8] António Araújo, *A lei de Salazar: estudos sobre a Constituição política de 1933* (Coimbra: Tenacitas, 2007).

the moment in order to guarantee to Portugal the onward march of Romano-Christian civilization, under assault from the Revolution.'[9] The three essential features of the new polity created by the dictatorship emerged, according to Quirino de Jesus, from a long historical tradition, namely an organized nation (nationalism and corporativism), the strong state (authoritarianism) and the colonial empire (colonialism).

Reflecting on Salazar, Salazarism and the Estado Novo, Eduardo Lourenço found an organic inscription and a historical lineage, rooted in a tradition of Portuguese anti-Liberalism,[10] despite the observation that 'as political and ideological mythology, "Salazarism" is History':

> Independently of other considerations, the perception of Salazar as the 'Statesman', *par excellence*, of the past century, is almost a statistical fact. Over four decades he imposed on the country his way of seeing, in practically every domain [...]. It was not Salazar who created 'Salazarism', he limited himself, and by all accounts successfully, to making politically and ideologically coherent and efficient an anti-Liberalism based on solid domestic tradition. The rest was the fashionable coloration that then existed, of a contrarian character, cheerfully and insultingly antidemocratic.[11]

Nationalism

In his speech, *As grandes certezas da revolução nacional*, given in Braga on 26 May 1936, as part of the commemorations of the tenth anniversary of the military coup of 28 May 1926, the Prime Minister, António de Oliveira Salazar, summed up the essential elements of the nationalism of the Estado Novo:

> To the souls riven by the doubt and negativity of this century we have tried to restore the comfort of great certainties. We do not dispute God and virtue; we do not dispute the Fatherland and its History; we do not dispute authority and its prestige; we do not dispute the family and its morality; we do not dispute the glory of labour and its duty [...]. In this way the great pillars of the edifice have been set in place and peace has been constructed, order, the unity of the Portuguese, the strong state, the reputable authority, the honest administration, the reinvigoration of the economy, the patriotic sentiment, the corporative organization and the colonial Empire [...].[12]

What was the origin of the three essential moral ideas — God, Fatherland, Family — that would constitute the ideological emblem of the Estado Novo? It was precisely the speech by Oliveira Salazar, *A democracia e a Igreja*, given in Porto at a meeting of the Segundo Congresso da Federação da Juventude

---

[9] Quirino Avelino de Jesus, *Nacionalismo português* (Porto: Empresa Industrial Gráfica, 1932), pp. 56–62.
[10] Ernesto Castro Leal, 'Nacionalismo e antiliberalismo em Portugal: uma visão histórico-política (1820–1940)', *História Crítica*, 56 (2015), 113–35.
[11] Eduardo Lourenço, 'O homem fatal', *Visão*, 20 January 2000, p. 114.
[12] Oliveira Salazar, *Discursos e notas políticas*, 2nd edn, vol. II (Coimbra: Coimbra Editora, 1945 [1937]), pp. 130 and 136.

Católica Portuguesa, at the headquarters of the Associação Católica (early May 1914), and repeated in Viseu, at the headquarters of the Círculo Católico de Operários, at the end of that month. In it Salazar, then still a student in the Faculty of Law at Coimbra, where he would complete his degree at the end of the year, declared:[13]

> What *is* lives almost solely from what *was*. To reconnect the broken thread of tradition is thus for a nationality a matter of life or death.
> And all national tradition can be represented in the brave sailor, burnt by eastern suns, raising before the holy altars the bride of his village. All Portuguese history is God, Fatherland, Family! It is religion, glory, love!
> This is our soul, because it is the soul of our parents living in us. So certain is it that in the world the dead are more in command than the living! [...][14]

Here we find rooted the ideological basis of the Estado Novo, indebted to the discourse of conservative Christian Democracy and social Catholicism, linked to the philosophical and theological tradition of the thinking of St Thomas Aquinas and Thomism, which the encyclicals of Pope Leo XIII would give substance for the purposes of social intervention (*Rerum Novarum*, 1891) and political activity (*Inter Sollicitudines*, 1892) on the part of Catholics. In this speech, Oliveira Salazar goes on to offer a Christian providentialist and heroic vision of history, based on the 'Miracle of Ourique', taken as the foundational myth of the nation. This myth recalls the tradition, going back to the fifteenth century, of the legendary appearance of the 'sacred image of Christ' to D. Afonso Henriques on the eve of the Battle of Ourique (1139), at which he would be victorious over the Muslims. It linked in imagination the genesis of Portuguese autonomy and destiny with the alliance between the sacred, in the Christian cross, and the profane, in the soldier's sword. In the nineteenth century Alexandre Herculano refuted the Miracle of Ourique, basing himself on a naturalistic view of history, which provoked a fierce battle with elements of the clergy,[15] but according to Vitorino Magalhães Godinho, Herculano did not know how to interpret adequately the allusion made by the chronicler Gomes Eanes de Zurara:

> The Miracle of Ourique arises out of the conquest of Ceuta [1415]. And the Miracle of Ourique does not arise by chance, it is not the simple foundation of a Peace with Castile, already secured, it is not a justification of the frontiers of which the Peace treaties do not speak, but which are

---

[13] For the biography of António de Oliveira Salazar, cf. Manuel de Lucena, 'Salazar, António de Oliveira', and António Barreto, 'Salazar, António de Oliveira. O após-guerra', in António Barreto and Maria Filomena Mónica (eds), *Dicionário de História de Portugal: suplemento* (Lisbon and Porto: Figueirinhas, 2000), vol. IX, pp. 283–390; Filipe Ribeiro de Meneses, *Salazar: uma biografia* (Lisbon: Dom Quixote, 2010).
[14] António de Oliveira Salazar, *Inéditos e dispersos (Organização e prefácio de Manuel Braga da Cruz)*, vol. I (Amadora: Bertrand, 1997), pp. 312–13.
[15] Ana Isabel Carvalhão Buescu, *O milagre de Ourique e a História de Portugal de Alexandre Herculano: uma polémica oitocentista* (Lisbon: Instituto Nacional de Investigação Científica, 1987).

marked land by land by marks of sacralization. It is that Ourique is the predestination of the imperial destiny. And in that sense Herculano did not know how to interpret the passage in Zurara, in which the sacralization of Afonso Henriques already points to that destiny of forming the empire, that myth of the crusade against the peoples of the 'base Mohammed'.[16]

According to António José Saraiva, historical myths 'are a form of phantasmagorical awareness by which a people defines its position and its will in the history of the world', and he presents the myth of the Crusade as the first great collective myth of the Portuguese. The myth of the Crusade was at that time common to the whole of the Iberian Peninsula, one that would be reinvented in the fifteenth and sixteen centuries, and it is to that 'mythical complex' that the Miracle of Ourique belongs. It is with Antero de Quental, he continues, that we see the arrival of the counter-myth to the Crusade, the myth of Decadence, claiming neither to be a myth, but rather the rational expression of reality, nor even to have the purpose of justifying and motivating collective action.[17]

In the Catholic nationalist reading of 'the Portuguese soul and history', Oliveira Salazar defined a gallery of heroes and heroines including D. Afonso Henriques, Gonçalo Mendes da Maia, D. Denis, the Queen Saint Isabel, D. Nuno Álvares Pereira, D. Filipa de Lencastre, the Prince D. Fernando (the Infante Santo), Prince D. Henrique, D. Filipa de Vilhena, the Restauration of sovereignty of 1640, and D. João IV, while highlighting the identitarian value of the Monastery of Santa Cruz de Coimbra, the Monastery of the Jerónimos in Lisbon (Belém) and the Monastery of Santa Maria da Vitória da Batalha, as well as its representative writers:

> But do I barely hear, Gentlemen, these voices impregnated with religion and Catholicism, in this little corner of the world that is my Fatherland? Perhaps... Perhaps I do not hear well... But I speak, oh! But I speak this Portuguese language. [...] I speak, we all speak the adorable language in which Bernardim Ribeiro sang his lament; João de Deus, his love; António Nobre, soft crepuscular sadnesses; Antero de Quental, profound agonies of thought; the language in which Vieira preached of God, Garrett wrote Frei Luís de Sousa and Camões left sculpted, as if in bronze — immortal verses! — the imperishable glory of Portugal![18]

The eclectic or syncretic matrix of the Estado Novo's nationalism included these identitarian points of reference within its representations of national memory, founded in divine providentialism, but also others derived from science and technology (castles, the caravel, the great ship, the armillary sphere, Manueline architecture) or from history (Viriato and Roman Lusitania, the Discoveries, Camões and *Os Lusíadas*, the symbols of the military orders, coats of arms,

---

[16] Vitorino Magalhães Godinho, 'O naufrágio da memória nacional e a Nação no horizonte do *marketing*', in *A memória da nação (Organização e nota de apresentação de Francisco Bethencourt e Diogo Ramada Curto)* (Lisbon: Sá da Costa, 1991), pp. 24–25.
[17] António José Saraiva, *A cultura em Portugal: teoria e história*, vol. I (Amadora: Bertrand, 1982), pp. 118–19, 122.
[18] António de Oliveira Salazar, *Inéditos e dispersos*, vol. I, pp. 230–31.

the national flag and the national anthem).[19] In an attempt to homogenize the various political and ideological traditions, Quirino de Jesus, who supported the adoption of a Republic in which the state was 'unitary and indivisible, liberal, social and corporative, democratic and representative',[20] warned that 'a traditionalist and progressive state, in the second quarter of the twentieth century, requires a good grasp of history, of civilization and of humanity, and a high ideal of honour, strength and justice from the Fatherland'.[21]

The cultural nationalism of the Estado Novo is indebted to various lines of thought that appeared during the First Republic,[22] in a various journals, such as the *Revista Lusitana* (1887–1943), *O Arqueólogo Português* (1890–1931), the *Arquivo Histórico Português* (1903–21), *A Águia* (1910–32), the *Revista de História* (1912–28), the *Arqueologia e História* (1922–32) and the *Lusitânia* (1924–27). Examples of the close connection between cultural activity and nationalist politics can be seen in the Catholic periodicals *Imparcial* (1912–19) and *Estudos* (1922–34) and the monarchist and integralist journal, *Nação Portuguesa* (1914–38). The critical mental attitude that informs the texts in these journals is clearly formulated in a circular from 1911, signed by Cristóvão Aires, David Lopes, José Leite de Vasconcelos and Fidelino de Figueiredo, calling for the founding of a Portuguese Society for Historical Studies:

> The idea, or better, the sentiment for senseless cosmopolitanism, which during the eighteenth century infected the people's lives, has been succeeded by the national sentiment and the recognition of the moral and social way of life characteristic of each people, thus bringing, in politics and administration, the need to build not on ideal foundations, but on real and specific national conditions. It would be a pardonable indulgence to exalt [...] the glorious part that history has played in this innovative work.[23]

[19] For interpretations of Portuguese identity, cf. Eduardo Lourenço, *O labirinto da saudade: psicanálise mítica do destino português* (Lisbon: Dom Quixote, 1978); Vitorino Magalhães Godinho, 'Reflexão sobre Portugal e os portugueses na sua história', *Revista de História Económica e Social*, 10 (1982), 1–13; Idem, 'Os portugueses em busca de si próprios', in *Ensaios e estudos* vol. I (Lisbon: Sá da Costa, 2009), pp. 91–122; Orlando Ribeiro, *Portugal, o Mediterrâneo e o Atlântico: esboço de relações geográficas*, 4th edn (Lisbon: Sá da Costa, 1986); Francisco Bethencourt, 'A sociogénese do sentimento nacional', in *A memória da nação*, pp. 473–503; José Esteves Pereira, 'Identidade nacional: do reformismo absolutista ao liberalismo', in *A memória da nação*, pp. 425–38; Ana Cristina Nogueira da Silva and António Manuel Hespanha, 'A identidade portuguesa', in *História de Portugal (Direcção de José Mattoso)*, vol. IV (Lisbon: Círculo de Leitores, 1993), pp. 19–37; José Mattoso, *A identidade nacional* (Lisbon: Gradiva/Fundação Mário Soares, 1998); Manuel Clemente, *Portugal e os portugueses* (Lisbon: Assírio & Alvim, 2008); José Manuel Sobral, *Portugal, portugueses: uma identidade nacional* (Lisbon: Fundação Francisco Manuel dos Santos, 2012).
[20] Quirino Avelino de Jesus, *Nacionalismo português*, p. 149.
[21] Jesus, p. 8.
[22] For interpretations of the Portuguese First Republic, cf. Rui Ramos, *A segunda fundação (1890–1926)*, in José Mattoso (ed.), *História de Portugal* (Lisbon: Círculo de Leitores, 1994), vol. VI, pp. 332–665; Vitorino Magalhães Godinho, *Vitorino Henriques Godinho (1878–1962): Pátria e República* (Lisbon: Assembleia da República/D. Quixote, 2005), pp. 31–456; Fernando Rosas and Maria Fernanda Rollo (eds), *História da Primeira República portuguesa* (Lisbon: Tinta-da-China, 2009); Luciano Amaral (ed.), *Outubro: a revolução republicana em Portugal (1910–26)* (Lisbon: Edições 70, 2011).
[23] *Boletim da Sociedade de Geografia de Lisboa*, 29th series, 4 (1911), 120–25 (p. 121). For a review of projects of a historical-cultural nature, cf. Luís Reis Torgal, 'Sob o signo da *reconstrução nacional*', in

The aim of this scientific society was to promote historical studies on Portugal, based on the need for a national programme for safeguarding documents and to develop national memory. As well as the four signatories mentioned, the project involved other intellectuals such as Anselmo Braamcamp Freire, António Baião, António Sérgio, António Aurélio da Costa Ferreira, António Costa Lobo, Damião Peres, Francisco da Silva Teles, Fortunato de Almeida, João Lúcio de Azevedo, José Maria Rodrigues, Pedro de Azevedo, Abade do Baçal, José Pereira de Sampaio (Bruno), Joaquim Mendes dos Remédios and Joaquim Vieira Natividade.

Despite following, in some cases, divergent philosophical and political itineraries, these intellectuals indicated an area of civic and cultural convergence. All through the 1920s, the most relevant ideological and cultural opposition was to be found between the monarchist and integralist journal *Nação Portuguesa* and the republican and socialist journal, *Seara Nova*, but there was a perception of the utility of common spaces for criticism of popular liberal and republican parliamentarianism, in particular in its Jacobin and radical guise. The journal *Homens Livres: livres da finança & dos partidos* (1923) and *Lusitânia: revista de estudos portugueses* (from 1924), were some of those spaces for plural encounters. The integralist monarchist António Sardinha showed this awareness, and in a letter to the liberal socialist, Raul Proença, declared: 'As men of intelligence and good will, we need to set an example in this society divided by ignorant and ignoble hatreds [...]'.[24] Similarly, the monarchist integralist Hipólito Raposo wrote to Proença: 'At last, the partisans of one or the other extreme seem quite upset, at least, that reality is so far from the dream, which is not a small thing [...]'.[25]

Nationalist mythology also incorporated the myth of Empire. Despite various policies adopted for the development of the colonies during the constitutional monarchy and the First Republic, it was only in the transition from the military dictatorship to the Estado Novo that, with the passing of the *Acto Colonial* (1930), 'the imperial idea takes breath and gains expression, moves from the nebulosity of myths to doctrine and public legality'.[26] It began a 'policy of "nationalization" of the empire [...], to the great displeasure of the *Foreign Office*, which saw in it a source of future complications for its interests in Africa, on account of the strong nationalism that characterized it. The action of Armindo Monteiro as Minister for the Colonies also caught their attention,

---

Luís Reis Torgal, José Maria Amado Mendes and Fernando Catroga, *História da história em Portugal (sécs. XIX–XX)* (Lisbon: Círculo de Leitores, 1996), pp. 219–39.

[24] Letter from António Sardinha to Raul Proença, 24 January 1923 (Biblioteca Nacional de Portugal/ Arquivo da Cultura Portuguesa Contemporânea — BNP/ACPC-Esp. E7).

[25] Letter from Hipólito Raposo to Raul Proença, 3 September 1929 (BNP/ACPC-Esp. E7).

[26] Fernando Piteira Santos, 'Portugal império: do mito ao conceito jurídico', *Revista da Faculdade de Letras de Lisboa*, 5th series, 2 (1984), 43–53 (p. 49). For an overview of Portuguese colonialism of the time, cf. Valentim Alexandre, *Velho Brasil, novas Áfricas: Portugal e o império (1808–1975)* (Porto: Afrontamento, 2000); Pedro Aires Oliveira, 'O ciclo africano', in João Paulo Oliveira e Costa (ed.), *História da expansão e do império português* (Lisbon: A Esfera dos Livros, 2014), pp. 341–545.

it being feared that he would persuade the Prime Minister (at the time, Salazar) to adopt an ultra-nationalistic policy in the African colonies.'[27]

The political practice of the Estado Novo shaped a centralizing colonial model within an imperial nationalism, with a view to constructing a Portuguese Colonial Empire (Constitution of 1933, article 132), which according to the *Acto Colonial* (article 2), itself incorporated into the Constitution, was justified in this way: 'It is an organic essence of the Portuguese nation to fulfil the historical function of possessing and colonizing overseas dominions and of civilizing the indigenous peoples contained in them, while also exercising the moral influence that is contracted to it by the *padroado* [religious patronage] of the East.'[28] As Valentim Alexandre explained, the doctrine was not new, seeing that it fitted into the historic imperial vision of the leading Portuguese elites; what was new was its juridical and constitutional consecration, strengthening the nationalist ideal of the Estado Novo with its project of a colonial empire.[29]

The definition of the Portuguese colonial position after the Berlin Conference (1884-85) may have been influenced by the thinking of the progressive monarchist and Catholic Henrique de Barros Gomes (Minister of Foreign Affairs, 1886-90). He took a 'Germanist' view in foreign policy, taking a negative view of the Anglo-Portuguese Alliance, which would lead to the *British Ultimatum* (11 January 1890). Quirino de Jesus, too, was once seduced by the so-called *Pink Map*, which gave the promise of a 'Brazil in Africa' by linking up Angola and Mozambique. However, once this illusion was broken, he would lose no time in affirming, in 1894:

> Today, in the face of these treaties, the foundation of an African Brazil, stretching from the Atlantic to the Indian Ocean, is an impossible dream. Ruinously, we have to stop, compelled by two iniquitous and usurping conventions, despite justice and history, before the waters of the Cassai, the mountains of Caomba and the waterfalls of Catima.[30]

With the dream of the *Pink Map* undone, Quirino de Jesus went on to be one of the main theorizers of the Third Lusitanian Empire (the designation is his own), and from then on gained the ear of the governing elite, which had its base in Angola and the Portuguese Congo:

> [...] it is principally to our East African territories, particularly the new continental backlands beyond the Zaire river, to which we should now direct and concentrate our attentions, our commitments, our efforts, our heroism, and our sacrifices eloquently demanded, as an affirmation of our

---

[27] Valentim Alexandre, *O roubo das almas: Salazar, a Igreja e os totalitarismos (1930-39)*, p. 78.
[28] *Estado Novo, União Nacional: discurso do sr. doutor Oliveira Salazar, estatutos da União Nacional, Constituição política da República Portuguesa, Acto Colonial* (Lisbon: Imprensa Nacional, 1933), p. 57.
[29] Valentim Alexandre, 'Portugal em África (1825-1974): uma perspectiva global', *Penélope*, 11 (1993), 53-66 (pp. 62-65).
[30] Quirino Avelino de Jesus, 'Angola e Congo ou o terceiro império lusitano', *Portugal em África*, 1 (1894), 3-14 (p. 12).

remaining vitality, through the highest principles of interests of religion, of politics, of administration, of morality, of law and of economics [...][31]

He advised the public authorities to redirect the flow of Portuguese emigrants then going to Brazil, with a view to the 'civilizing mission' of African colonization,[32] principally to Angola and Mozambique, to be developed by way of sending missionaries, of settling native tribes in villages, of making a systematic fusion of indigenous and metropolitan elements, the creation of colonial companies and businesses (in mining, agriculture and trade) controlled by Portuguese, along with the formation of an effective administrative network. However, he identified a fundamental problem: the path to Africa had to be prepared by the adequate technical training of leaders and middle-ranking officials in colonial schools, which, he claimed, should be based on the English model of colonial education.[33]

While Quirino de Jesus absorbed, between 1890 and 1893, some of the 'Anglophobia' that was hegemonic within the Portuguese elite in the aftermath of the *British Ultimatum*, from 1894 onwards he started to value the traditional Anglo-Portuguese Alliance, and in 1901 was defending its reinvigoration to further the Portuguese colonization of Africa:

> The Avis dynasty, by fraternizing with England, secured our independence. The Braganças, by drawing closer the same ties, certainly consolidated it for ever; and thus shielded and strengthened, we were able to create a splendid and civilized society in Brazil [...]. Their advantages were greater than ours, but even so, that of our having kept a name on the map of Europe and established a glorious offshoot of our race in South America is not a small one [...].[34]

Another of the colonial problems worth highlighting here is to do with the model of administration chosen. In the face of the centralizing tendency seen in colonial administration from 1890, within which Quirino de Jesus broadly belongs, with his idea of relative autonomy,[35] the First Republic endorsed a tendency for colonial decentralization, and with the creation in 1920 of the system of High Commissioners in Angola and Mozambique, it set out, unsuccessfully, to increase the autonomy of the colonies.[36] The atmosphere of economic and financial crisis after the First World War hindered this policy, aggravated by the 'bankruptcy of the colonial economy and finances, evident

---

[31] Jesus, 'Angola e Congo ou o terceiro império lusitano', pp. 3–14 (p. 3).
[32] Miguel Bandeira Jerónimo, *Livros brancos, corpos e almas negras: a 'missão civilizadora' do colonialismo português (c. 1870–1930)* (Lisbon: Imprensa de Ciências Sociais, 2010).
[33] Jesus, 'Educação colonial portuguesa', *Portugal em África*, 84 (1900), 593–601.
[34] Jesus, 'A aliança e a política de Portugal', *Portugal em África*, 85 (1901), 5–10 (p. 10).
[35] Jesus, 'Discurso parlamentar acerca de Inhambane e Lourenço Marques', *Portugal em África*, 26 (1896), 49–63; Idem, 'O novo regime da África Portuguesa', *O Economista Português*, 2nd series, 31 May 1919, pp. 1033–34; Quirino de Jesus e Ezequiel de Campos, *A crise portuguesa: subsídios para a política de reorganização nacional* (Porto: Empresa Industrial Gráfica, 1923), pp. 27–28.
[36] Maria Cândida Proença, 'A questão colonial', in Fernando Rosas and Maria Fernanda Rollo (eds), *História da Primeira República portuguesa*, pp. 205–28.

from the mid-1920s', which was 'one of the elements that contributed to the fall of the First Republic'.[37]

Organicism and Corporativism

The idea of a nation organized according to its natural and civic elements — family, local administrative bodies, moral, social and economic authorities — was an essential topic in the political doctrine of the Estado Novo. The Constitution of 1933 defined the Portuguese state as a unitary and corporative republic (article 5), and amongst its competencies was to 'coordinate, stimulate and direct all social activities, ensuring that a fair harmony of interests should prevail, within the legitimate subordination of private interests to the general' (article 6). However, an organicist, as opposed to an individualist, mentality had circulated in various of the ideological currents in Portuguese life since the end of the nineteenth century, to be found within republicanism, monarchism, Catholicism and fascism.

The doctrinal foundation that led to the emergence of organicist ideas was based on the perception that Enlightenment philosophers and Rousseau's theory of the social contract had contributed to the structuring of a philosophy inscribed wholly within a liberal individualist naturalism, breaking with historic communitarian doctrines and their representative organic and corporative forms, which aggregated individuals into communities that were either natural (blood, family), territorial (soil, municipality) or social (occupation, trade etc.). The need to renew the mechanisms of legitimation arose from a political and social plan, for breaking the exclusive position held by the political parties in mediating political representation and demanding the organic representation of intermediary and technical bodies.

Thomism and Positivism provided the most important philosophical justifications for those theories of political and social organization derived from organicist thinking at the time of the First Republic, which was sunk in the atmosphere of crisis that was affecting the liberal system, particularly in southern Europe, between 1890 and 1930, and aggravated after the First World War. This 'twilight of the liberal state', as Gaetano Mosca called it,[38] revealed a profound crisis in ideology, culture, economics and finance, in social legitimation and political representation, favouring the emergence of various proposals for regeneration, by the reconstruction of new systems for legitimating power and social organization, to the advantage of key concepts such as tradition, order, progress, decadence, hierarchy, unity, sovereignty, evolution, revolution, patriotism, nationalism and cosmopolitanism.

In Portugal, organicist responses to individualism divided essentially into

---

[37] Valentim Alexandre, 'Portugal em África (1825–1974): uma perspectiva global', 53–66 (p. 61).
[38] Gaetano Mosca, *Il tramonto dello Stato liberale (A cura di Antonio Lombardo e prefazione di Giovanni Spadolini)* (Catania: Bonanno, 1971), pp. 105–11.

two camps. Catholics and monarchists were drawn to a conservative organicism, occasionally traditionalist and counter-revolutionary, that looked to the encyclicals of Popes Pius IX and Leo XIII, and to the likes of Léon Ollé-Laprune, Joseph de Maistre, Edmund Burke, Jacques Maritain, Charles Maurras, Léon Daudet, Frédéric Le Play, Édouard Berth and Georges Valois. Liberals, republicans and socialists turned to a progressive and reformist organicism, based on the thinking of such figures as Immanuel Kant, Karl Krause, Heinrich Ahrens, Saint-Simon, Auguste Comte, Herbert Spencer, Émile Durkheim, Pierre-Joseph Proudhon, Benoît Malon, Charles Gide and Léon Bourgeois.

The year before the approval of the Constitution of 1933, Quirino de Jesus justified the need for corporativism as expressing the political thinking of the new governing elite:

> [...] the Constitution aims to organize the nation politically, with all its natural and civic bodies and with its citizens considered as individuals with personal and collective aims. This may be reaction to some, revolution to others, and perhaps utopia to many, who are the obscure successors to the those who puzzled at the decrees of Mouzinho [de Silveira, 1832–33] for a liberal kingdom that still did not exist. In reality it is a question of adapting now to the new necessities the ever-living genius of traditional civilization, and prudently avoiding the grave intrusions of individualism [...].[39]

The representation of organized interests was made, during the Estado Novo, within the National Assembly (as a deliberative body) and the Corporative Chamber (as a consultative body), that latter 'composed of representatives of the local authorities and of social interests, considered in their fundamental branches of an administrative, moral, cultural and economic kind' (Constitution of 1933, article 102). A previous example of such a representation was to be found in 1918, during the government of Sidónio Pais, known as the República Nova, within the Senate, which was constituted of both provincial representatives (from mainland Portugal, from the Atlantic islands, and from the overseas colonies) and of professional categories (agriculture, industry — including transport, hunting, fishing and mining — trade, public services, the liberal professions, and the arts and sciences) (Decree no. 3997, article 2, 30 March 1918). This legacy of corporative representation would form part of the 1921 *Manifesto* of the Partido Nacional Republicano Presidencialista.[40]

The idea of providing the representation of organized interests within the legislative authority, whether totally or partially, was already present, between 1911 and 1926, in various constitutional proposals and political programmes. In the republican camp, we can note the *Bases para a Constituição Política da República Portuguesa*, of 1911, by António Machado Santos, where Section

---

[39] Quirino Avelino de Jesus, *Nacionalismo português*, p. 153.
[40] *Manifestos, estatutos e programas republicanos portugueses (1873–1926): antologia* (Organização, introdução e edição crítica de Ernesto Castro Leal) (Lisbon: Imprensa Nacional–Casa da Moeda/ Biblioteca Res Publicana, 2014), pp. 56–65.

1 of the National Assembly would be composed of municipal representatives, and Section 2 of the scientific classes and institutes along with institutions for higher education.[41] In his *Projecto de Estatuto Nacional*, of 1916, Machado Santos further proposed a bicameral Congress of the Republic, with a Chamber of Deputies and a Senate, the latter being composed of senators from the municipalities and overseas provinces, and from social and religious interests (formed of clergy from all confessions), as well as professionals.[42]

In relation to the programmes of the most important republican political parties formed after the republican revolution of 1910[43] — the Partido Republicano Português (known as the 'Partido Democrático' from 1912), the Partido Republicano Evolucionista, and the União Republicana — only the 1913 *Programa* of the Evolucionistas refers to the organization of the Senate with 'representation of national groups and interests'.[44] We may also note the origins of a genealogy within moderate demo-liberal republicanism of the idea of organic and corporative representation. Examples are the 1919 *Programa* of the Partido Republicano Liberal ('advantage of including the representation of classes in the future constitution of the Senate of the Republic'),[45] the 1924 *Programa da realizações imediatas* of the Partido Republicano Nacionalista ('to introduce into the constitution of the Senate of the Republic the representation of particular classes'),[46] and the 1926 *Manifesto* of the União Liberal Republicana ('modification in the composition of the Senate of the Republic so as to make a greater appeal to the collaboration of technical elements, through the representation of classes').[47]

A different genealogy of thinking on organic and corporative representation is to be seen amongst radical demo-liberal republicans from the communitarian tradition, first expressed in the constitutional ideas outlined by Machado Santos. These were continued in the 1921 *Manifesto* of the Federação Nacional Republicana/Partido Reformista (a Senate 'constituted of representatives of the classes, as a mandatory part')[48] and the 1923 *Programa* of the Partido Republicano Radical (for a 'transformation of the Senate into a Chamber of the National Economy, with representation of regional and professional interest', though with only a consultative function).[49]

---

[41] Machado Santos, 'Bases para a Constituição Política da República Portuguesa', *O Intransigente*, 28 May 1911, p. 1.
[42] Machado Santos, *A ordem pública e o 14 de Maio* (Lisbon: Lamas & Franklin, 1916), pp. 104–16.
[43] For an overview, cf. Ernesto Castro Leal, *Partidos e programas: o campo partidário republicano português (1910–26)* (Coimbra: Imprensa da Universidade de Coimbra, 2008); Idem, 'Parties and Political Identity: The Construction of the Party System of the Portuguese Republic (1910–26)', *e-Journal of Portuguese History*, 7.1 (2009), 1–8; Manuel Baiôa, 'A Primeira República Portuguesa (1910–26): partidos e sistema político', *Arbor*, 766 (2014), a114 (1–14).
[44] *Manifestos, estatutos e programas republicanos portugueses (1873–1926)*, p. 321.
[45] *Manifestos*, p. 415.
[46] *Manifestos*, p. 527.
[47] *Manifestos*, p. 641.
[48] *Manifestos*, p. 489.
[49] *Manifestos*, p. 555.

While the republican organicist and corporative traditions envisaged a partial corporativism, by way of a representation of organized interests in one of the legislative chambers (the Senate), the monarchist and anti-liberal traditions proposed an integral corporativism in political representation. In Integralismo Lusitano's 1914 manifesto, *O que nós queremos*, the National Assembly was to be formed of 'corporative provincial, municipal and educational delegations; ecclesiastical, military, judicial delegations, etc.', assisted by a Conselho Técnico Geral in the formulation of laws;[50] in a 1924 political pamphlet, reproduced on the back covers of the journal *Acção Realista*, the official organ of the Acção Realista Portuguesa, the Cortes Geral would be composed of 'representatives of the Church, the Land, the Intelligentsia and of Production'.[51]

The fascist ideal would be partly reflected in the 1922 *Programa nacionalista*, of the Centro do Nacionalismo Lusitano, where it proposed a Dictatorship that concentrated legislative, executive and judicial powers; a Conselho Executivo/ Ministério (composed of ministerial technical bodies); a Conselho Técnico de Legislação (two members from each ministerial body and three legislative experts); a Câmara Económica, or Casa Sindical, independent of the state, bringing together representatives of organized economic groups in syndicates. National representation would belong to the Chamber, which would be 'neither a political assembly nor an economic chamber', aiming to represent the national interests (territorial representation; economic and syndical representation; representation of intellectual interests; representation inherent to position; representation of higher values, chosen by the dictatorial power; representation of the collective aspirations of the people through the national election of six members).[52]

Organic representation was also adopted in the 1926 manifesto *Orientações*, of the Cruzada Nacional D. Nuno Álvares Pereira, written by Martinho Nobre de Melo. It defended ideas such as a Head of State who really was a leader, able to choose freely his government (a presidentialism), assisted by permanent Conselhos Técnicos, or of national representation in a Chamber that would bring together members of the 'real and permanent interests of the nation', thus repudiating party representation and defending an organic, though not obligatory, syndicalism.[53]

Within the various areas of political thinking hostile to the demo-liberalism of the First Republic, there was a predominant organicist vision that gave primacy to groups over individuals, a vision derived from Positivism and Thomism. Although there were contradictory interpretations, for the most part they challenged liberalism, individualism, a contractual political philosophy, the state as arbiter and the market economy.[54]

[50] *Nação Portuguesa*, 8 April 1914, pp. 4–6 (p. 5).
[51] See, for example, *Acção Realista*, 22 May 1924.
[52] João de Castro [Osório], *A revolução nacionalista* (Lisbon: Edição do Autor, 1922), pp. 54–56.
[53] Ernesto Castro Leal, *Nação e nacionalismos*, p. 492.
[54] António Manuel Hespanha, *Cultura jurídica europeia: síntese de um milénio* (Coimbra: Almedina, 2012), pp. 460–78.

Authoritarianism

The idea of the strong state is another element of the political doctrine of the Estado Novo, nourished by the perception that the liberal state in Portugal had been a weak state, because it was too individualist and parliamentarist. This anti-liberal vision of Portuguese history between the Convention of Évora-Monte (26 May 1834) — the defeat of the absolutist D. Miguel by the liberals, led by D. Pedro — and the military coup that brought down the First Republic (28 May 1926), was systematized by Quirino de Jesus, who identified brief intervals of strong government (Costa Cabral, 1842–46; João Franco, 1907; Sidónio Pais, 1918):

> The ruin of the individualist and revolutionary system that has governed Portugal since 1834, sheltered in the first place by the throne and later by an unstable republican presidency, coincided in 1926 with the state and with the advance of a current that demanded and finally imposed, through the discipline of the Army and the Navy, its reinvigoration, allied to a national renaissance. However difficult the task was, there were for the first time the conditions to make it possible. It was the time to undertake the establishment of the *Strong State*, as a powerful factor in the nation [...].[55]

The institutional manifestation that was closest to this idea of the strong state occurred in 1918, during the government of Sidónio Pais (the República Nova). In an attempt to surpass the system of parliamentary government, Sidónio Pais argued the urgent need for a presidential system of government that would be supported by his personal charisma and by a mass populism, evolving into an authoritarian and corporative presidentialism:

> The parliamentary regime has already been put to the test over the 80 years of the constitutional monarchy and the results are negative. In this the twentieth century an absolutist regime is not possible, making it necessary to opt for a republican regime; but for this it is necessary that the country should pronounce on the form of regime that should be adopted: whether parliamentary or presidentialist.
> The first has failed; the second is the New Idea! [...].[56]

The justification for an authoritarian government was current amongst right-wing republican, monarchist and Catholic circles as a response to their diagnosis of the national crisis, in which the problem of public order was foremost. The conservative and positivist republican, Alfredo Pimenta, who from 1915 would become an anti-liberal monarchist, reflected on this question in this 1913 proposal for the programme of the new Partido Republicano Evolucionista, led by António José de Almeida, giving the general view of the conservative

---

[55] Quirino Avelino de Jesus, *Nacionalismo português*, p. 175.
[56] Sidónio Pais, 'Discurso nos Paços do Concelho de Beja (17 February 1918)', in Feliciano de Carvalho (ed.), *Um ano de ditadura: discursos e alocuções de Sidónio Pais (Estudo político de João de Castro [Osório])* (Lisbon: Lusitânia, 1924), p. 50.

political culture towards authoritarianism:

> It is clear that the fundamental problem in the present historical moment of the nation is the problem of order. Without that there are neither financial measures nor developmental measures that can give viable results. But the problem of order, in its three essential points, discipline, tolerance and competence, must be resolved more by the decision of the citizens than by the action of governments themselves. The philosophers who begat the Revolution of 1789 believed that the moral question was a social question. The experience of a century clearly demonstrates, on the contrary, that the social question is a moral question. Rousseau is the representative of the first opinion, just as Auguste Comte is the representative of the second. The political and economic transformation of the peoples is nothing unless there is a prior transformation of their ideas and their habits [...].[57]

Amongst radical nationalist and anti-liberal currents, theories of order were central to the discourses of Integralismo Lusitano,[58] Acção Realista Portuguesa,[59] and the Centro do Nacionalismo Lusitano.[60] They also appear in the ideological discourses of moderate nationalists or conservative republicans, as in the following examples: 1) the position already mentioned of Alfredo Pimenta, who in 1911 affirmed: 'Desiring order in the streets and in consciences is not revolutionary';[61] 2) the declaration in the *Manifesto* of the Partido Republicano Conservador, written by Basílio Teles ('to conciliate tradition with evolution, excluding equally immobility and adventure');[62] 3) the allusion in the 1921 *Manifesto* of the Cruzada Nacional D. Nuno Álvares Pereira, written by Henrique Trindade Coelho ('Order in the streets. Order in minds. And order in the home, then. Without order, the state cannot live');[63] 4) the reference in the 1923 *Manifesto* of Partido Republicano Nacionalista, written by António Ginestal Machado ('to re-establish definitively in Portugal social discipline and the indispensable order — order in the streets, order in minds, order at work').[64] This concern for order was reflected in the political ideology of the Estado Novo, as systematized by Oliveira Salazar in his speech *Ditadura administrativa e revolução política* (28 May 1930), where he analysed the 'Battle for order' in financial, economic, social and political life.[65]

---

[57] *Manifestos, estatutos e programas republicanos portugueses (1873–1926)*, pp. 331–32.
[58] Manuel Braga da Cruz, 'O integralismo lusitano nas origens do salazarismo', *Análise Social*, 70 (1982), 137–82.
[59] Ernesto Castro Leal, 'Acção Realista Portuguesa: An Organization of the Anti-liberal Right, 1923-26', *Portuguese Studies*, 30.1 (2014), 47–66.
[60] António Costa Pinto, 'O fascismo e a crise da Primeira República: os nacionalistas lusitanos, 1923–25', *Penélope*, 3 (1989), 43–62; Ernesto Castro Leal, *António Ferro: espaço político e imaginário social (1918-32)* (Lisbon: Cosmos, 1994), pp. 113–20.
[61] Alfredo Pimenta, *Aos conservadores portugueses* (Lisbon: Cernadas, 1911), p. 57.
[62] *Manifestos, estatutos e programas republicanos portugueses (1873–1926)*, p. 378.
[63] Ernesto Castro Leal, *Nação e nacionalismos*, p. 462.
[64] *Manifestos, estatutos e programas republicanos portugueses (1873–1926)*, p. 525.
[65] Oliveira Salazar, *Discursos*, vol. I, pp. 51–65.

Between 1919 and 1926, the problem of the state's lack of authority was the subject of various public discourses, and support was gained for blaming the parliamentary system of government (with the strong dominance of the legislative body, from within which the President of the Republic was elected), which led to the formulation of different types of proposal for strengthening the state. On the republican side, the most important was for the creation of a presidential republic, reconciling the element of elective suffrage with the element of organic and corporative representation (i.e. a harmonization of the legislative and executive powers). On the monarchist side, the most important proposal was for a traditionalist and organic monarchy, based exclusively on the element of organic hierarchical power (the supremacy of the executive power).

Following the line of reflections by João Tello de Magalhães Colaço on the transformative 'illusions' in Portuguese political life during the First Republic, one can say that in the face of the 'illusion about the power of laws' (1910–17, 1919–20) there appeared the 'illusion about technical governments' (1921–24) and the 'illusion about dictatorships' (1918, 1925–26).[66] The point of arrival in the discourses on the strong state was the government of the Estado Novo, which evolved, according to Manuel Braga da Cruz, from a 'bicephalous or dyarchical presidentialism' to 'dictatorship of the executive, or of the government', and from there to a 'personal dictatorship of its head',[67] while Marcello Caetano concluded that there had existed in practice a 'presidentialism of the Prime Minister'.[68]

The republican intellectual Raul Proença participated in public polemics between 1907 and 1940,[69] and in the 1920s formulated the most relevant criticisms of the conservative theories of social order and political authority that had been published by the Cruzada Nacional D. Nuno Álvares Pereira and Integralismo Lusitano.[70] His case was rooted in a liberal and democratic vision of political philosophy:

> Order — the Order that cannot conceive of itself except as an equilibrium of divergent wills and thoughts — as an affirmation of spiritual Unity within the diversity of what is Multiple — that cannot be violently imposed on minds without denying itself [...]. Liberty is a decisive triumph for Man. No more could you conceive of a modern world without liberty than one without electricity — which is only a little more recent. If you wish to abjure the 'stupid nineteenth century',[71] why not also snuff out the electric lights?

[66] João Tello de Magalhães Colaço, *Da vida pública portuguesa*, vol. I (Lisbon: Edição do Autor, 1925), pp. 16–35.
[67] Manuel Braga da Cruz, *O partido e o Estado no salazarismo*, pp. 96–105.
[68] Marcello Caetano, *Constituições portuguesas*, 4th edn (Lisbon/São Paulo: Verbo, 1978), p. 116.
[69] Raul Proença, *Polémicas (Organização, prefácio e cronologia de Daniel Pires)* (Lisbon: Dom Quixote, 1988).
[70] António Reis, *Raul Proença: biografia de um intelectual político republicano*, vol. I (Lisbon: Imprensa Nacional-Casa da Moeda, 2003), pp. 378–91.
[71] Raul Proença is alluding to a book that became a point of reference in conservative and counter-revolutionary thinking in the twentieth century: Léon Daudet, *Le Stupide XIXe Siècle: exposé des insanités meurtrières qui se sont abattues sur la France depuis cent trente ans, 1789–1919* (Paris: Nouvelle

[...] We too wish for Authority, but so that Liberty and Democracy can become a fact.[72]

In this article, published just two months and twenty-two days before the military coup of 28 May 1926, he warns of the conspicuous 'danger of fascism' in Portugal, at a time of heightened civil and military plotting amongst the nationalist, authoritarian and anti-liberal right, including the Cruzada Nuno Álvares, which had advocated since the beginning of January 1926 'a movement analogous to Italian fascism', although it feared, ironically, that it would be 'a fascism without the fascist masses and without Mussolini'.[73] Proença praised Democracy's spirit of liberty, of pluralism and of tolerance in opposition to the violent principles of fascism, which he classified as 'a sheaf of ears of corn all equal — where a stalk that dares to sway higher [...] is at once cut down by the flag [...]', and he appealed for a rejection of an 'aggressive return to the Past', for which 'action was necessary'.[74]

Raul Proença's ideological combat against the conservatism of anti-liberal traditions, whether of a counter-revolutionary monarchical or an authoritarian republican mould, acquired more visibility with the appearance of the group *Seara Nova*, and the journal of the same name, in which he took part. His first texts about the political ideas of the Cruzada Nuno Álvares were published in issue no. 1 (15 October 1921) and no. 4 (5 November 1921) of the journal. The political manifesto of the Cruzada had appeared on 20 March 1921, signed, amongst others, by conservative republicans (Anselmo Braamcamp Freire, Pedro José da Cunha, António Egas Moniz, Henrique Trindade Coelho), conservative monarchists (D. Tomás de Melo Breyner, José Lobo de Ávila Lima, António Centeno, Anselmo de Andrade), radical monarchists (José Pequito Rebelo, António Sarmento Pereira Brandão), Catholic clergymen (José Dias de Andrade, Carlos Martins do Rego) and military men (General Manuel Gomes da Costa, Colonel Alfredo Freire de Andrade, Admiral D. Bernardo da Costa Mesquitela, Vice-Admiral Vicente de Almeida de Eça). In response Proença stated that he considered the manifesto very conservative, and an 'insult to the whole Portuguese intelligentsia'.[75]

In his analysis of this political manifesto, Proença criticizes the attachment to old forms of retrospective patriotism, the appeal to an essentialism of Portuguese identity through a cult of national heroes, most notably Nuno Álvares Pereira, the notion of the fatherland as a simple aggregation of families, the indissolubility of marriage in the reconstruction of the traditional family, the nationalization of scientific enterprise, social discipline and public order imposed by force, and colonial imperialism, ideological topics that referred, he

Librairie National, 1922).
[72] Raul Proença, 'O fascismo e as suas repercussões em Portugal' (*Seara Nova*, 6 March 1926), in Proença, *Polémicas*, pp. 561 and 566.
[73] Proença, *Polémicas*, p. 567.
[74] Proença, *Polémicas*, pp. 560 and 568.
[75] Proença, *Polémicas*, pp. 383–84.

believed, to a political culture 'of *Order* and *Tradition* around which the whole thinking of the Cruzada gravitates'. He concluded that their political manifesto was not an isolated instance in Portuguese culture: 'The same mental vices affect all the Orfeístas, futurists, integralists, nationalists, saudosistas, who is in this land have raised the barbarous banner of the vacuous phrase and of confusion of the spirit. The damage is profound.'[76]

Raul Proença's first text on Integralismo Lusitano would be published in issue no. 5 of *Seara Nova* (24 December 1921). He attributed this ideological and political movement in Portugal to European reactionary and monarchist thinking, inspired essentially by the French traditionalism of Charles Maurras, Maurice Barrès, René de la Tour du Pin, Henri Vaugeois and Georges Valois, while ignoring important contributions to Portuguese traditionalism by José da Gama e Castro, Marquês de Penalva, José Agostinho de Macedo, José Acúrcio das Neves and António Ribeiro Saraiva:

> We are dealing, then, with a movement broader than a simple national movement: it is against all the hosts of Reaction, against the *politique du fait*, that we have to fight. To pass in silence over a whole philosophy of political action, with groups in the most varied nations of the earth, might be convenient, but it would not be honest, or helpful for the future of democracy.[77]

Basing himself on texts by intellectuals of the Integralismo Lusitano, he identified in integralist doctrine an essential opposition, at the level of political philosophy, between the method of a 'politics of ideas', characteristic of democracy (cosmopolitanism, reason, liberty, freedom of conscience, progress, change, individual suffrage) and the method of a 'politics of fact', characteristic of integralist monarchism (nationalism, history, authority, dogma, tradition, vital force, organic suffrage). This was reflected at the political level in the clash between the Republic (democratic, liberal and individualist) and the Monarchy (traditional, anti-parliamentarist and organic).[78] In refuting Proença's analysis, the integralist monarchist Alberto Monsaraz insisted on an essential difference between the European cultural heritages of Integralismo Lusitano and *Action Française*, not previously mentioned: the first was neo-medieval, seeking the 'foundational institutions of the fatherland', while the second was neo-classical, pointing to the 'highest expression of its national equilibrium'.[79]

In later texts published in *Seara Nova* (14 January, 1 February, 1 March, 1 April and 1 July 1922), Raul Proença analysed the 'internal contradictions' of integralist monarchist doctrine, highlighting some essential points: Portuguese nationalism practically reproduced the nationalism of *Action Française*; traditionalism was selective, to the convenience of its political ideas; nationalism

[76] Proença, *Polémicas*, pp. 384–90.
[77] Proença, *Polémicas*, p. 399.
[78] Proença, *Polémicas*, pp. 400–05.
[79] Proença, *Polémicas*, pp. 408–09.

and traditionalism were at the service of an anti-parliamentary monarchism; the distinction between a politics of ideas (reason) and a politics of facts (history) was false, since it was in human nature to reason, making value judgements and modifying social reality; the opposition between anti-liberal egalitarianism and anti-egalitarian liberty was also false, since it was impossible to detach them and consider them absolute metaphysical concepts; the critique of progress as an illusion was contradicted by the advance in civilization throughout human history; the opposition between nationalism and internationalism was contradicted by an analysis of the history of Portugal, which showed a universalist tradition, supporting a considered articulation between the two.[80]

In the face of the supposed antimony between liberty and authority, as expressed in conservative theories of order, Proença stated that, rather than the play of purely abstract concepts, one should try to satisfy all the needs of the human soul, defining those concepts concretely in society. In this way, 'Liberty and Authority not only are not mutually exclusive, but they are the essential condition of one another.'[81]

Conclusion

Despite their differences around the myth of the nation and the myth of the state, the various nationalisms existing at the time of the First Republic had a common political imaginary of the historical and imperial nation, and a recognition of the institutional symbolism of the coat of arms of the King, present in both the monarchist flag and the republican flag. The ideological consensus between elements of the nationalist elites (including moderate republicans) turned on certain essential ideas: Christian morality, patriotism, a unitary state, empire, a presidential republican regime, a government with a strong technical component, separation of Church and State (with increasing support for a concordat enacting judicial separation from the Catholic Church), corporativism (representation of mediating social bodies) and the formulation of a project for economic and social development, with state intervention.

Some nationalisms aimed at political activity put forward providentialist rhetorics, with sometimes surprising narratives around the model for a leader, be it Henrique de Paiva Couceiro, Afonso Costa, Sidónio Pais, Francisco da Cunha Leal, Filomeno da Câmara, Manuel Gomes da Costa or António de Oliveira Salazar. They evoked a new D. Nuno Álvares de Pereira or a new D. Sebastião, thus looking to the myth of the saviour (chief as the state), linked to the myth of unity (society as the nation), particularly between 1918 and 1926, the period of greatest disturbance to the political system and of social, economic and financial crisis in the First Republic.[82]

---

[80] António Reis, *Raul Proença: biografia de um intelectual político republicano*, vol. I, pp. 384–89.
[81] Proença, *Polémicas*, p. 586.
[82] Hermínio Martins, 'O colapso da I República', in *Classe, status e poder e outros ensaios sobre o*

Political and Ideological Origins of the Estado Novo 147

João Ameal, an integralist and anti-liberal monarchist, felt the need in 1926 to distinguish two types of messianism, in order to justify one of them. On the one hand there was a pessimistic messianism, reflected by Oliveira Martins in his *História de Portugal*, or by Ramalho Ortigão in his *Últimas farpas*, two 'lucid nationalist teachers', but whose bleak and passive vision of the past 'was at odds with its modern reflowering'. On the other hand there was an optimistic messianism, publicized by António Sardinha in his *Aliança peninsular*, by Carlos Malheiro Dias in his *Exortação à mocidade*, by Antero de Figueiredo in his *D. Sebastião*, or by Martinho Nobre de Melo in his *Para além da revolução*.[83]

During the ceremonies (7 April 1921) to honour the two Unknown Soldiers of the First World War, the President of the Republic, António José de Almeida, after declaring that he had been 'always against political messianism' and paid 'little attention to the supernatural faculties of the great leaders of men', nevertheless argued the need for a social messianism as a guide, 'a triumphal and healthy messianism, derived from the soul of the nation, intrinsically and physiologically popular, instilling faith, giving hope, [...] full of indulgence and valour, of heroism and forgiveness [...].[84] This attitude was reflected in the messianism of the myth of Prometheus, which was used as an identitarian argument in republican humanism, incorporating the Positivist ritualization of Great Men.[85]

On the floor of the Chamber of Deputies (9 January 1924), António Lino Neto, parliamentary leader of the Centro Católico Português, expressed the critical view that the Catholic Church had of political messianism — allowing only for a divine messianism — and denounced revolutions, dictatorships and the hope for a Messiah, since 'the Messiah, the Hidden One, the Saviour, are within each one of us [...].[86] In 1925, the Catholic journal *Novidades*, in an editorial, continued to warn of the danger of messianism, whether civil or military:

> while everyone at the moment puts their trust in the *hidden one*, we have ever less hope of a *Messiah*. The salvation of the country will either be made through unity, organization and cooperation of moral values (we do not say conservative ones) that still exist in every field, or there will be no remedy except on the pathways that Providence knows and which at times lead peoples through catastrophes to resurrection. Those, however, belong to God alone.[87]

Portugal contemporâneo (Lisbon: Imprensa de Ciências Sociais, 1998), pp. 69–98.
[83] João Ameal, 'Os dois messianismos', *A Reconquista*, 15 January 1926, pp. 10–11.
[84] *Em honra dos Soldados Desconhecidos: discursos proferidos pelo Presidente da República Portuguesa Dr. António José de Almeida na sala e no átrio do palácio do Congresso, em 7 Abril 1921* (Lisbon: Imprensa Nacional, 1921), pp. 20–21.
[85] Amadeu Carvalho Homem, *A ideia republicana em Portugal: o contributo de Teófilo Braga* (Coimbra: Minerva, 1989), pp. 171–206; Fernando Catroga, *O republicanismo em Portugal: da formação ao 5 de Outubro de 1910* (Coimbra: Faculdade de Letras da Universidade de Coimbra, 1991), pp. 441–64; Ernesto Castro Leal, 'A ética positivista de Teófilo Braga: virtude moral e dever cívico dos centenários', *Estudos Filosóficos*, 11 (2013), 33–44.
[86] *Diário da Câmara dos Deputados*, session no. 17, 9 January 1924, p. 19.
[87] 'Desorientação', *Novidades*, 12 March 1925, p. 1.

The political response to the so-called 'crisis of the modern state'[88] (the liberal state), of which Oliveira Salazar spoke in his speech *Princípios fundamentais da revolução política* (30 July 1930), would summarize the most important elements of conservative, anti-liberal and authoritarian nationalist thinking. It was created fundamentally from concepts of three kinds: one that was socially corporative and Catholic, one that was reformist, authoritarian and organicist (whether liberal or republican), and one that was corporative, monarchist and traditionalist. It constituted a model that was nationalist, authoritarian, corporative and colonial, that included political violence as an instrument of domination and articulated elements of these three types of nationalist ideology in an eclectic or syncretic ideological framework.

Translated from Portuguese by Richard Correll

---

[88] Oliveira Salazar, *Discursos*, vol. I, p. 72.

Redefining Representation in the Dictatorship of Salazar and Marcelo Caetano: The Changing Role of Parliament (1935–1974)

PAULA BORGES SANTOS

Instituto de História Contemporânea — Universidade Nova de Lisboa

The Construction of the National Assembly in a Climate of 'Institutional Reform'

The Portuguese authoritarian regime projected itself as an alternative to the crisis in the process of consolidation of a liberal democracy, attempted by the various republican governments that had been formed since the overthrow of the constitutional monarchy on 5 October 1910. It promoted a change in the governing order and defined new goals for the state, in a move that allowed political decision-makers and some jurists supportive of the regime to assert that a new constitutional settlement was being made in Portugal. In a way this discourse signalled a revolutionary impulse, encapsulated in the proposal for 'a unitary and corporative republic', and which presupposed a reform of institutions, based on differing political and juridical options.

The corporative formulation looked back to an essentialist or organic conception of society and political life that was accepted by many different currents, both within Portugal and abroad, which had in common a repudiation of individualism and parliamentarianism.[1] The fact that the corporative ideal neither expressed nor looked back to any homogenous position explains why, especially during its constitutive period, both legislators and the political class as a whole supported the idea that the construction, or development, of the corporative model should take place after the event. Hence the corporative dimension of the nationalist project underlying the Constitution of 1933 was to have an 'animating' and not a 'stabilizing' character, intended to stimulate dynamics that did not yet exist and whose endorsement would come only later.[2]

---

[1] For an elaboration of this idea see Ernesto Castro Leal, 'Tradições organicistas: ideias políticas e práticas de representação na República Portuguesa (1910-1926)', *Espacio, Tiempo y Forma*, 27 (2015), 39-58; Paula Borges Santos, 'O modelo político do Estado autoritário português: a ideia corporativa na constitucionalização do regime (1931-1933)', *Espacio, Tiempo y Forma*, 27 (2015), 68-76.

[2] In fact the idea that the full aims of the corporative project were yet to be achieved persisted throughout its lifespan. The relationship between the state and corporative organization also remained strained. In the final years of the Second World War, a time of harsh criticisms of the evolution of the system from various theorists and leaders, Salazar blamed the failure to keep faithfully to corporative doctrine and the hindrances to the 'realization of corporative objectives' on two factors: firstly, he

In the face of a state that was perceived as being atrophied and dysfunctional, the project was destined, primarily, to satisfying an organizational need, in search of an ideal of efficiency. Hence to govern was to organize the nation, to combat the dispersion of a society based on individuals, acting autonomously. Social and economic roles were to be attributed to 'natural groupings' or 'intermediary bodies'. The system was to be impregnated with an economistic leaning, in the belief that its solidity and stability resided there. It was to promote social order (coordinating and orientating all social activities for the 'common good'), identifying itself with order within the state. It was to recognize the primacy of the state, belittling all forms of law disconnected from state institutions. It was to put executive power at the heart of government, giving it control over parliament, limiting its legislative power.[3]

With this in view, the political system underwent reformulations, consolidated in the Constitution of 1933. However, despite the claims to novelty made by the government it conserved many elements typical of liberal political representation, and did not demand an exclusively organic representation of organized interests within the state, as would be presupposed by the corporative ideal. Thus the authoritarian state retained a parliamentary chamber, the National Assembly, with both legislative functions and oversight of the activities of the Government and the Administration, elected by direct (but not universal) suffrage, in a single list until 1945 and in multiple lists thereafter, but always with a single party. As early as the constituent period, the possibility of a corporative parliament was rejected.[4] A Corporative Chamber was instituted, composed of representatives of local authorities and social interest groups (administrative, moral, cultural and economic), but it was not given powers of deliberation and was not considered an organ of sovereignty, as was the National Assembly. Its place in the political structure was secondary, having only consultative powers and was in a dependent relationship to the chamber of political representation, and, after the constitutional revision of 1935, to the government. The legislative preference for solutions of a liberal rather than organicist kind was also evident in the formal separation between the executive, legislative and judicial power, and in the preservation of direct suffrage in elections for President of the Republic (up to 1959).[5]

---

said that 'we live in a moment when the mental revolution, instead of preceding, must follow the legal revolution, which for that reason meets, by force of inertia, many tired spirits of opposing principles (many of our people argue like liberals or socialists, even when they aim to be corporativists); secondly owing to a lack of educational propaganda for the masses and appropriate culture for the leading elements.' Speech by António Oliveira Salazar, delivered on 23 July 1942, transcribed in *O pensamento de Salazar. 32 anos ao serviço de Portugal. Revolução corporativa* (n.p.: Ed. Lit. António Cruz, 1960), p. 41.

[3] This idea is to be found in many of Salazar's public pronouncements, such as the speech he gave at the Teatro S. Carlos, in Lisbon, on the evening of 5 June 1933. See Pedro Teotónio Pereira, *As ideias do Estado Novo: corporações e previdência social* (Lisbon: Edições do Subsecretariado de Estado das Corporações e Previdência Social, 1933), pp. 6–7.

[4] On this point, see António de Araújo, *A lei de Salazar* (Coimbra: Edições Tenacitas, 2007), pp. 45–49, 55.

[5] It should be emphasized that even the Corporative Chamber was not based exclusively on the

In fact, throughout the dictatorship the corporative project never had a strong political dimension and organic representation was never demanded by the leading political class, except after the end of the Second World War; and even then, as we shall see, it operated primarily as a political means to restrain the activities of the opposition. The fact that organic suffrage was never used as a method of election for the National Assembly demonstrates that the liberal principle of sovereignty was never challenged. This point is better understood if we consider that it was never necessary for the constructors of the authoritarian state to combat the republican ideal of political representation as a delegation of power. The explanation is to be found, as Gomes Canotilho has recently demonstrated, in the fact that during the course of the First Republic the republican concept of representation had already undergone a political neutralization and an emptying of its theoretic content.[6] This was due to the hostility, widespread from the late nineteenth century in political and intellectual circles (particularly in the Faculties of Law in Coimbra and Lisbon), to models of representation based on individual suffrage. Consequently, at the time of the Constitution of the Estado Novo, that space had been occupied by juridical and political sensibility, gradually formed over the previous decades, based on the sociology of Auguste Comte, the philosophies of Kant and Hegel, and the theses of the German School of History, which contributed, in different ways, to value representation as 'selection by capacity', and to reject either the atomization of society as individuals or the reduction of state power to a continual negotiation between individuals and parties.[7] In this optic, the corporative framework, taken as a defining element of the authoritarian nationalist project in Portugal, did not need to be invoked to redefine the principle of sovereignty and its representative form, contributing rather to reinforce the idea of the unity and coherence of the state, as a single agent, integrating all its parts, able to take on the role of defending the 'common good' (or the 'national interest'), and the authority of the government, not only as an economic regulator but also as the defender of the political system capable of containing the decline of institutions seen under successive liberal governments.[8]

---

organic model of representation, given that a part of its membership was appointed by the Government, through its Corporative Council.

[6] J. J. Gomes Canotilho, 'Representação: entre a forma de governar representativa e a representação de nada no direito constitucional português', in *Res Publica: cidadania e representação política em Portugal, 1820-1926*, ed. by Fernando Catroga and Pedro Tavares de Almeida (Lisbon: Assembleia da República, 2010), pp. 143-46.

[7] António Manuel Hespanha, 'A representação orgânica', in *Res Publica: cidadania e representação política em Portugal, 1820-1926*, ed. by Fernando Catroga and Pedro Tavares de Almeida (Lisbon: Assembleia da República, 2010), pp. 123-36; Paula Borges Santos, 'Nas origens do nacionalismo político da I República Portuguesa: o projeto da "nacionalização do Estado" e o debate jurídico e político em torno da conceção da soberania e do modelo de representação política', in *Dimensões do poder: história, política e relações internacionais*, ed. by Marçal de Menezes Paredes, Leandro Pereira Gonçalves, Luciano Aronne de Abreu and Helder Gordim Silveira (Porto Alegre: EDIPUCRS, 2015), pp. 69-78.

[8] Note the following remark by Salazar, from 1953: '[...] I remain convinced that it is only through

All these elements help to explain the long existence of the National Assembly, inaugurated in January 1935 and only suspended after the coup of 25 April 1974, not a small matter since, as we shall see, its *raison d'être* was disputed at various points. They also explain the visibility, in comparison to the Corporative Chamber, of its functioning and of the work it carried out. Despite the fact that the National Assembly only met for three months a year (four and a half after the constitutional revision of 1971), it opted to keep its plenary sessions public and to continue the publication of an official record of parliamentary debates, following the model of the Monarchy and the Republic. Despite the constraints of the censorship, these features allowed for public scrutiny of the work of the deputies, essentially by means of the press. It was also by way of the Assembly that the work done in the Corporative Chamber received publicity. In effect, the proposals of this chamber, expressed in the form of opinions produced by an attorney acting as a rapporteur, became public through discussion in the Assembly, since the meetings of the sections and subsections of the Corporative Chamber were closed. The publication of their opinions was through the *Diário das Sessões*, as supplements to the record of the debates in the Assembly. The publication of the decisions of the Corporative Chamber from 1953, when it was presided over by Marcelo Caetano, did not serve to improve communication with the extra-parliamentary world, as they only covered the complete reports of public sessions and the results of elections to the *Mesa* [Board], summaries of the work of preparatory committees, verification of the powers of the attorneys, the composition of the sections, the *Regimento* [standing orders] and alterations to it, and the opinions themselves. While it did not excel in either its powers or its functioning, the Corporative Chamber was especially associated with the circumstances in which its opinions, particularly those that were produced by its most prestigious sections (such as those of Political and General Administration, and of Finances and General Economy) or those that were highly technical, served to justify or contradict the legislative direction of bills put forward by the Executive, by deputies, and by the permanent and ad hoc commissions of the Assembly, creating, for these same reasons, occasions for vigorous political debate.[9]

---

corporativism that we can avoid the clashes of class struggles in the social field and the tendency to partisanship in the political terrain'. Speech by António Oliveira Salazar, delivered on 10 July 1953, transcribed in *O pensamento de Salazar. 32 anos ao serviço de Portugal. Revolução corporativa* (n.p.: Ed. Lit. António Cruz, 1960), p. 49.

[9] On the role of the Corporative chamber in defining public policy in Portugal see Philippe C. Schmitter, *Portugal: do Autoritarismo à Democracia* (Lisbon: Imprensa de Ciências Sociais, 1999), pp. 133, 140–42; José Luís Cardoso and Nuno Estevão Ferreira, 'A Câmara Corporativa (1935-1974) e as políticas públicas no Estado Novo', *Ler História*, 64 (2013), 31–54.

A 'Legislative Assembly' that Never Had the Traditional Role of a Parliament

In the light of what has been said above it will be seen that throughout the dictatorship the National Assembly, although it was a chamber of political representation, never fulfilled the traditional role of a parliament, in the sense of an effective participation of the citizens in government. Nor was it presented as such by politicians, especially Salazar, who was always the person to explain the system of representation and its instruments. Defining the state as 'representative but anti-democratic', he created a line of argument that opposed 'organized interests' to 'national interests'. The former were embodied in the corporations, the latter were 'interests properly of the state', expressed by 'independent men, not linked to political organizations and working loyally, agreeing or disagreeing with this or that point', and who did not question the 'principle of national unity'. These latter interests were united in the National Assembly, rejecting both 'separate representations of interests, disputes, regions or doctrinal currents' and 'oppositions even if combined, even if sympathetic, even if friendly, speaking and voting systematically against'. The Corporative Chamber accommodated the corporations and 'technicians', charged with preparing 'studies that would serve as a basis for votes in the National Assembly'. The originality of the system lay, according to Salazar, in the complementary relationship between the two types of interests, even though they were placed in separate chambers. Hence he did not believe in the 'benevolence of the solution' outlined by Mussolini, of closing the *Camera dei Deputati*, and moving legislative competence to the *Camera dei Fasci e delle Corporazioni*, because, he said, 'whatever the extension of the organized interests in the corporations, there will always be lacking there the representation of the national interests, [...] because it would be very dangerous, without preparation through long experience, to hand over the definition or the defence of a particular interest to the possible understandings of other organized interests'.[10]

In a calculated ambiguity, Salazar did not distinguish between the functions of the National Assembly and the Corporative Chamber, and emphasized that the chambers should be recognized as holding 'the exclusive prerogative of controlling government, of giving a general orientation to the political advancement of the state, and of making laws'. Such laws were limited to the 'fundamental bases of the juridical regimes', because only in that way could there be a guarantee of agility in the discussion of bills. The government naturally occupied a privileged position in the legislative function, whether legislating by decree-laws (*decretos-lei*) or by being able 'to modify laws in certain cases by simple decrees, in order to overcome the deficiencies of the

---

[10] António Oliveira Salazar, 'A constituição das Câmaras na evolução da política portuguesa', speech delivered on 9 December 1934 and broadcast by radio, for propaganda sessions taking place in União Nacional centres all over the country, in *Discursos, 1928–1934* (Coimbra: Coimbra Editora, 1935), pp. 379, 383–85.

short legislative sessions, to attend to very urgent matters, to unblock the administration'.[11] To this end it was necessary that the Executive should 'be as independent and as legitimate a representative of the Nation as the Legislative Power', and put an end to the submission of the former to the latter, 'exercised by variable and unpredictable majorities, and at the mercy of the votes of parties alien to the responsibilities of power'.[12]

Salazar insisted on these features until the mid-1940s, leaving open the question of changing the composition, the method of formation or the working of the chambers. He explained that he foresaw that 'parliaments, even if they do not come to be converted, in the future, into purely political organs and alien to the legislative function, will be forced to approve only the bases of the main laws, leaving it to the Executive Power, being responsible for administration, wider prerogatives than the simple regulatory function that it exercises today'.[13] He considered that only that step could regenerate the political system, and not 'ridiculous measures' such as 'slight alterations to the internal running of the chambers, limits on the length of speeches, restrictions on the right to speak, etc.'[14] In December 1934, at the height of the campaign for the first elections to the National Assembly, discussing the list of candidates sponsored by the União Nacional, he did not hesitate to say that it would have been 'different, [...] if unhappily we had not found, from the first soundings [...] old prejudices and ideas inapplicable to our political practice'. He declared he was 'convinced that within twenty years, if there is no reverse in political evolution, there will be no legislative assemblies in Europe', and all because it was facing 'new needs, of an urgent nature, requiring the legislative assembly to work very fast, and the inability of a large collective body to produce work of a high standard'.[15]

The same could not be said of the future of the 'purely political assemblies'.[16] Asked, in 1938, if it would not be preferable to close the National Assembly, passing some of the functions to the Corporative Chamber, Salazar insisted that the Assembly should 'in any case continue to exist as a political assembly', so that it could continue to transmit 'to the Government the great national aspirations and supervise the public administration'. The legislative function might fall to the Government, 'with the consultative collaboration of a Corporative Chamber, possibly complemented by a Technical Council on laws'.[17] In 1942, during the preparation for the legislative elections for that year, Salazar continued to advocate the need for a parliament, formed of 'selected competencies across the whole nation', taken particularly from the civil service, which should act as

[11] Ibid., p. 383.
[12] António Oliveira Salazar, *Como se levanta um Estado* (Lisbon: Golden Books, 1977), p. 72 [Portuguese translation of the French edition of 1937].
[13] Ibid., p. 71.
[14] António Ferro, *Salazar, o homem e a sua obra*, 3rd edn (Lisbon: Empresa Nacional de Publicidade, 1938), p. 108.
[15] António Oliveira Salazar, 'A constituição das Câmaras na evolução da política portuguesa', p. 385.
[16] Ibid., pp. 381–82.
[17] Ferro, *Salazar*, pp. 274–75.

'assistant to the Government', with the latter being the true 'guiding star' in the life of the state. He understood that it was appropriate for parliament to have 'a certain power of criticism', so as to 'substitute for freedom of the press and of association'. Its functions were 'to represent and supervise [...], in the first place, it represents, studies and evaluates the movements in public opinion; in the second place, it supervises the acts of the Government, approving and debating the General State Budget and the respective Accounts'. He repeated that the future would attribute 'legitimate national representation' to the Government, having as 'collaborator, in the shaping of laws, the Corporative Chamber'.[18] In 1956, Salazar would concede only the possibility that in the future there might be a development of its 'functioning by way of specialized groups for the study of various problems'. He highlighted, though, that there had been the 'experience gained through the functioning of the Corporative Chamber' that had enabled the securing of 'in many cases, some first aggregations of functions and associated interests', that corresponded to the 'image of representation' of the first corporations created in that year.[19]

Up until the Second World War, what Salazar called 'legislative duality' — i.e. the distribution of legislative power between the National Assembly and the Government, with the former acting independently of the latter — was the element most directly marked out for a possible, and necessary, transformation, because it was considered merely an 'intermediary form'.[20] And in fact, by way of the laws on constitutional revision published during the constituent periods of 1935–38 and 1945, there was some progress towards making the Government more independent of the National Assembly and reinforcing its legislative powers. For example, severe restrictions were placed on the deputies' legislative initiative, and only decree-laws published when the Assembly was sitting were subject to its ratification (1935–38 revision). A little later, a formal parity in legislative power between the National Assembly and Government was established, with the latter now able to make decree-laws in normal circumstances, and not just in cases of emergency or public necessity (1945 revision).[21]

In the post-war period the trend was inverted: the constitutional revisions of 1951 and 1959 saw a formal reinforcement of the legislative competence of the Assembly and a strengthening of the mechanisms for the political chambers to intervene in the workings of Government. The Assembly gained the power

---

[18] 'Lição de Salazar para reunião dos Governadores Civis', transcribed in Rita Almeida de Carvalho, *A Assembleia Nacional no Pós-Guerra, 1945–1949* (Porto and Lisbon: Edições Afrontamento/Assembleia da República, 2002), pp. 284–86.
[19] Speech by António Oliveira Salazar, delivered on 13 March 1956, transcribed in *O pensamento de Salazar. 32 anos ao serviço de Portugal. Revolução Corporativa* (n.p.: Ed. Lit. António Cruz, 1960), p. 62. He was discussing the following corporations: Farming, Industry, Commerce, Transport and Tourism, Credit and Securities, and Fish and Conserves.
[20] Ibid., p. 274.
[21] Jorge Miranda, 'Constituição de 1933, Revisões da', in *Dicionário de História de Portugal*, ed. by A. Barreto and M. F. Mónica, vol. VII (Porto: Livraria Figueirinhas, 1999), p. 411.

to evaluate the acts of the Government and the Administration, and deputies were able to put questions to the Government. The Corporative Chamber was given the ability to formulate suggestions for future measures. As has been emphasized by other writers, the Government was interested in projecting to the outside world the idea that it was following the democratic trend in Western Europe, leading to constitutional revisions, even if mainly semantic, in favour of parliamentary institutions.[22] It is believed, though, that such changes led to previously unseen cases of the Executive giving way, if not totally or immediately, to pressure from the deputies. This type of event became more common in the post-war political scene, leading to a demand for a correction in the imbalance between the various organs of sovereignty.

In fact, in the constituent periods of 1951 and 1971, various bills were presented advocating the reinforcement of the legislative and supervisory capacities of the National Assembly, and also a respect for the process of ratification, practically a dead letter. Although they had different aims, these initiatives demonstrated an increasing belief amongst deputies that the legislative function was for parliament and not the Executive, rejecting also the Government's argument that the Assembly as a body was clumsy in its composition and actions, and so insufficient to respond to modern legislative needs.[23]

Between 1959 and the end of his time as *Presidente do Conselho* [Prime Minister], Salazar continued to show confidence in the established political system and to reject changes. In the 1960s, confronted by demands for political pluralism from some sectors of society, notably by some Catholics,[24] Salazar maintained the principle that any political intervention should be circumscribed within the ambit of the União Nacional. He downplayed the importance of political parties, declaring that 'within the National Assembly there are represented many, if not all, sectors of opinion'. Making a point of using a 'term that is in fashion', Salazar described these 'sectors of opinion' as 'pressure groups, in the sense that their political and philosophical thinking intervenes in government activity as legitimate elements in defining anxieties and objectives, thus taking on the character of a real, although not organic, representation'. He understood that a different role fell to the cultural groups and syndicates, which, as he pointed out, could be deduced from reading the

---

[22] Nuno Piçarra, *O inquérito parlamentar e os seus modelos constitucionais: o caso português* (Coimbra: Edições Almedina, 2004), pp. 455–56.

[23] A. Carlos Lima, *Órgãos da soberania: a Assembleia Nacional: um debate* (Lisbon: Moraes, 1971), pp. 15–22.

[24] One of the most famous cases was that of the Bishop of Porto, in 1958–59, when the said bishop, D. António Ferreira Gomes, in a memorandum addressed to Salazar which became public, made wide-ranging criticisms of the corporative project in Portugal and demanded political autonomy for Catholics. This was interpreted by Salazar and large sections of society as implying the formation of a Catholic political force as an alternative to the model in place. Salazar considered this intervention unacceptable and started a move against D. António that forced him into exile. On this topic see José Barreto, *Religião e Sociedade: dois ensaios* (Lisbon: Imprensa de Ciências Sociais, 2002), pp. 150–51 and Paula Borges Santos, 'The Question of the Political Organization of Catholics under the Portuguese Authoritarian Regime: The "Bishop of Porto Case" (1958)', in *Portuguese Studies*, 30.1 (2014), 94–111.

opinions of the Corporative Chamber.[25] Without showing enthusiasm for organic representation, he accepted that 'if the corporative experience had been more advanced', the elections could have been organized in a different way, but he did not regret it. He only resorted to this argument in an instrumental way, during electoral campaigns, which allowed, so he believed, the reappearance of 'a known evil — our political dissensions'. In this way he asserted that the way forward was by 'not giving importance to unexpected divergences', but by gathering 'the greatest share of wills and intellects' by way of the 'national interest'.[26]

Salazar's successor as head of the Government, Marcelo Caetano, showed the same unwillingness to reformulate the political institutions on which the state depended or to recognize the right to exercise fundamental freedoms, in particular the right of individuals to contest the leadership and authority in society, in conditions of open political contention. Under his government the creation of political parties remained illegal, and non-competitive elections continued: ballots remained a mere formality, with limits on the presentation of opposition candidates, restrictions on the freedom of assembly, association and expression, while the preparation of electoral rolls remained under the exclusive control of the leaders of the União Nacional and government agents, with predictable results.[27] In 1969 he allowed the formation of electoral commissions, but they were ordered to dissolve as soon as the elections were over.

Under the constitutional revision of 1971, the Government proposed only the reorganization of the sections of the Corporative Chamber corresponding to the various interests of an administrative, moral, cultural or economic kind. As for the National Assembly, in the wake of the revisions of 1951 and 1959 its legislative and supervisory roles were reinforced, and the scope of its influence was increased. The chamber acquired a broader role in the ratification of decree-laws. A legislative process was created for urgent questions, and the duration of legislative sessions was increased, from three months to four.

What Was the Significance of the Evolution of the National Assembly over the Life of the Regime?

As has been shown, it is undeniable that, in terms of its competencies and its prerogatives, the Assembly saw its constitutional position reinforced from the 1950s onwards. However, we should ask to what extent these changes affected the powers of the deputies, and whether in fact they strengthened the position

---

[25] António de Oliveira Salazar, *Entrevistas, 1960–1966* (Coimbra: Coimbra Editora, 1967), pp. 166–68.
[26] António de Oliveira Salazar, *Discursos e notas políticas*, vol. V (1951–1958) (Coimbra: Coimbra Editora, 1959), pp. 488–93, 514–17.
[27] For more detailed discussion of the conditions imposed on the regime's elections, see the following case study: José Reis Santos, *Salazar e as Eleições: um estudo sobre as eleições gerais de 1942* (Lisbon: Assembleia da República, 2011), pp. 69–79.

of the Assembly. On the first point it is clear that the constitutional powers of the deputies increased in line with the evolution of constitutional norms for the Assembly.[28] By way of example, after the 1959 revision deputies had the power to submit written questions on any action by the Government or the Administration. After the 1971 revisions, parliamentarians gained the right to official precedents — i.e. a recognized place in the protocol of public processions and the like — in a move that sought to contribute towards the rehabilitation of their image amongst the functionaries of the state.

However, while these powers were reinforced, the same cannot be said of the powers of participation of deputies,[29] which were reduced by the two main alterations to the Assembly's *Regimento* [Regulations].[30] The first, passed in 1935, was marked by a determination to 'remove everything that might have a political character'.[31] To mention only the most relevant, the powers of the President of the Assembly were increased to the detriment of the deputies, being given the right to give official acknowledgment to the *Presidente do Conselho* [i.e. Salazar] of prior notices (*avisos prévios*), and to deny requests from deputies for closed sessions, or to consult the minutes of such meetings.[32] The right to propose legislation was further limited when it involved an increase in spending or a reduction in state receipts, by demanding the support of a special evaluation commission.[33] Between 1946 and 1960 the time limit on

---

[28] These powers were governed by constitutional norms: to propose a bill, scrutiny of government, obtaining information or explanations from Government and the Administration. These powers are indicative of the autonomy of the Assembly compared to other organs of sovereignty, particularly in relation to the Government. See Jorge Miranda, 'Deputado', in *Dicionário Jurídico da Administração Pública* (Coimbra: Atlântida, 1974), pp. 29.

[29] These powers, which related to the strengthening of competencies and were subject to regulatory norms, defined the freedoms and capacities of the deputies. Examples include the right to address the Assembly before and during the order of the day and of parliamentary commissions, the power to perform specific functions in the Assembly, and the power to influence the functioning of the Chamber, through alterations in the Regulations.

[30] Coming into force in January 1935, the National Assembly resorted to a provisional *Regimento* that had been completely overhauled by Salazar (Cf. PT/TT/AOS/CO/PC — 17, fols 107-24). Discussed at the parliamentary sessions of 17 and 22 January 1935, the final draft of the text was published in the *Diário das Sessões*, no. 8, on 4 February 1935. As a result of modifications to the Constitution by Laws nos. 1885 and 1910, the *Regimento* underwent further alterations, and it was published once again in the *Diário das Sessões*, 1st supplement to no. 192, on 2 May 1938. New provisions introduced into the *Regimento* required further publication in the *Diário das Sessões*, 1st supplement to no. 104, on 3 March 1941; no. 16, on 18 January 1946; 2nd supplement to no. 177, on 12 May 1960. Finally, because Law no. 3/71 had introduced various alterations to the text of the Constitution, the *Regimento* underwent further amendments, and the new text was published in the *Diário das Sessões*, 1st supplement to n.º 252, on 16 Abril 1973.

[31] *Diário das Sessões*, no. 6, 19 January 1935, p. 49.

[32] These aspects were strongly criticized by deputies Manuel Fratel and Querubim Guimarães. See *Diário das Sessões*, no. 7, 21 January 1935, pp. 57-60.

[33] The debate on this version of the *Regimento* was dominated by discussion of the following problems: inclusion or not of elements of a constitutional character in the *Regimento*; the dissolution of the Assembly; parliamentary immunities; the powers of the President of the Assembly; the existence or not of the period prior to the order of the day. *Diário das Sessões*, nos. 5, 6, 7 and 8, respectively of 18, 19, 21 and 23 January 1935, pp. 25-36; pp. 39-49; pp. 60-64; pp. 103-06.

interventions made before the order of the day, initially limited to ten minutes, was increased to thirty minutes, until limits were lifted entirely.[34]

A second important alteration to the *Regimento*, made in 1973, shortly before the fall of the regime, strengthened the powers of the parliamentary commissions,[35] which led to greater restrictions on legislative initiatives for deputies. It stated that voting on proposed legislation should give preference to the text provided by the relevant parliamentary commission, and it allowed commissions to propose amendments to bills, or even to submit complete new texts instead.[36] Furthermore, commissions no longer had to decide within three days which bills could be presented, leading to the possibility of an indefinite delay.[37] The handling of prior notices also restricted deputies' right to speak. The subject of the prior notice came to be submitted to the commission or commissions that the President of the Assembly considered most appropriate, with the participation of a member of the government, also chosen by him.[38] The commission would produce a report on the subject, which was then added to the order of the day. The deputy giving notice could speak, and if he asked for debate it was for the President of the Assembly to decide. The extensive powers of the President allowed him, even, in the final legislative session of the Assembly to prevent the publication, in the *Diário das Sessões*, of declarations by deputies renouncing their mandates.[39] And, for the first time, the *Regimento* recognized the position of the deputy designated by the Government charged with maintaining links with the Assembly.[40]

The evolution of the Assembly between 1935 and 1974 has arguably been misunderstood. Slowly, and in a formal sense, its position was strengthened, but since this was effected mainly through the increased powers of the parliamentary commissions, particularly from 1971, this in itself became

---

[34] *Diário das Sessões*, no. 211, 16 January 1973, p. 4200.

[35] According to the deputy Veiga de Macedo, Salazar always tried to avoid what he called the 'dictatorship of the commissions', not because he considered them parliamentary instruments, but because he believed that a political chamber was best run by means of plenary sessions. *Diário das Sessões*, no. 215, 25 January 1973, pp. 4288–89.

[36] At the time, some commentators denounced this measure as unconstitutional, since only the Government and deputies had the formal right to table such amendments. Jorge Miranda, 'Deputado', p. 39.

[37] This rule was criticized in plenary session by the deputy João Bosco Mota Amaral, who conceded only that the President of the Assembly had the right to rule on the constitutionality of a bill. *Diário das Sessões* no. 213, 18 January 1973, p. 4245.

[38] This move was opposed by the deputies Oliveira Ramos and Pinto Machado. *Diário das Sessões*, no. 217, 26 January 1973, pp. 4445–47.

[39] The most famous case was of the lawyer, Francisco Sá Carneiro, in 1973, who cited the 'systematic declaration of inconvenience' made against six of his bills, the last of which dealt with 'Amnesty for political crimes and disciplinary failings'. *Ser ou não ser deputado*, ed. by José Silva Pinto (n.p.: Editora Arcádia, 1973), pp. 153–57).

[40] The figure of the *leader*, as such a deputy was known, had existed informally since the 1st Legislature. However, the statuary provision for such a representative of the Government was strongly contested in 1973 by Pinto Machado, who defended the need to keep the 'organs of sovereignty completely independent'. *Diário das Sessões*, no. 216, 26 January 1973, p. 4316.

an obstacle to the individual actions of the deputies.[41] The debate on the alterations to the *Regimento* in 1973 showed that there were two main views as to the political functions of the Assembly. One view was reconciled to the idea that the legislative role of political chambers was in general decline, and aspired to perfecting the instruments for effective oversight of Government activities.[42] The other view, seeking political pluralism and greater freedoms for deputies, sought a reform of the Assembly to transform it from an organ of sovereignty to a legislative organ.[43] In the extra-parliamentary sphere, the discussion was followed in the press. It recognized that, since the first session under the Government of Marcelo Caetano, the chamber was now working harder, scrutinizing important decisions.[44] Attention to the Assembly was heightened by the existence within it of the so-called 'liberal wing', a heterogeneous group of deputies, elected during the Tenth and Eleventh Legislatures, who had been exerting a certain political pressure in the course of their duties. They sought a different direction for the state, particularly in the sense of restoring basic freedoms, of finding a solution to the armed conflicts in the Portuguese territories in Africa, and of a transition to a western-style pluralist democracy.[45]

---

[41] *Diário das Sessões*, no. 217, 26 January 1973, p. 4447.

[42] This argument, based largely on the increasingly technical nature of legislation and the need for speed, was taken up by different speakers, from traditionalist deputies such as Veiga de Macedo, former Minister of Corporations between 1955 and 1961, to others with a more modernizing agenda, such as Victor Aguiar e Silva, a university professor, and Joaquim Magalhães Mota, a lawyer. Curiously, some of the latter group put forward this opinion with a view to making the regime more democratic. More equivocal were the ideas of these deputies as to how far the assembly's legislative powers should reach. The majority view was that the Government would always hold the monopoly on proposing legislation. By means of decree-law no. 226/72 of 5 July 1972, the Government tried to meet the complaints about the Assembly's lack of resources by creating two First Class technical places to give direct support to the parliamentary commissions. *Diário das Sessões*, no. 213, 18 January 1973, p. 4251; testimony of Victor Aguiar e Silva and Joaquim Magalhães Mota, in *Ser ou não ser deputado...*, respectively pp. 72–73 and p. 126.

[43] This idea was proposed particularly by João Bosco Mota Amaral and Francisco Sá Carneiro. The former proposed an immediate removal of the restriction on increasing expenditure or reducing revenue; an end to being allowed only to formulate the general legal basis of the juridical regime; and an end to the ban on challenging the constitutional validity of bills. Sá Carneiro, for his part, defended a return to political parties and the option of a presidential regime in which the Assembly would be the sovereign legislative body. *Diário das Sessões* nos. 213 and 215, respectively of 18 and 25 January 1973, pp. 4246 and 4290; interview with Francisco Sá Carneiro, in *Ser ou não ser deputado...*, p. 28.

[44] See, for example, the column 'Os trabalhos de S. Bento', in *Seara Nova*, June 1970, p. 188.

[45] The study of the 'liberal wing' has been premised on the idea that, within Caetano's political *establishment*, they formed an 'exception': they contested power, in the name of liberalization, and divided the Catholic camp. Their activity in the National Assembly has thus been categorized as an opposition, with little attention to the contradictions facing the liberals from the outset: the absence of leadership (often imputed to Sá Carneiro, without demonstrating this), and their support for many political positions, whether taken by the Assembly or by the Government. Mentioned by many researchers, the liberal wing has been the object of one detailed study: see Tiago Fernandes, *Nem Ditadura, nem Revolução: a Ala Liberal e o marcelismo (1968–1974)* (Lisbon: Assembleia da República/ D. Quixote, 2006).

Criticism of Parties and Parliamentarianism and Defence of Other Models of Representation

The idea of the decline of legislative assemblies and their subordination to Executives, even in democratic regimes created post-1945, to meet the needs for greater technical skill and speed in formulating legislation, was most evident after 1950. It followed on, so anti-parliamentary elements of the political class argued, from the idea of a crisis in the system of parties and parliamentarianism seen with the advent of the authoritarian state. These two aspects were inseparable from the view that that the political crisis had much to do with the problem of the division of powers between the Executive and the Legislature.

Hostility to the democratic republican experiment, between 1910 and 1926, was largely based on these premises. This discourse was already present in the constituent discussions of 1932–33, and repeated with greater force at the time of the first elections to the National Assembly, in 1934.[46] Later, Salazar too stated that it was necessary to stop the chambers from retaining 'the right to nominate and dismiss ministers and to cause obstructions in public life'.[47] They had to eliminate 'struggles for the possession of power in the National Assembly', which were incompatible with the principle of national unity,[48] and create institutional spaces for expressing the cases and interests of the different professional elements, while simultaneously guaranteeing that 'professional egotisms did not put into question the general interest'.[49] In a careful manner, Salazar did not underline the advantages of the chosen system of representation in associating the so-called 'living forces' with the management of public affairs, but merely mentioned their direct intervention 'in the constitution of the highest bodies of the state', reducing the political rights of families, municipalities and corporations 'to their influence in the organization of the state'.[50]

Hostility to parliamentarianism led some supporters of the dictatorship to contest the system instituted by the Estado Novo, showing signs of aspiring to a wholly organic system of representation and a total detachment from the principles of political representation. For example, only two months after the National Assembly had started functioning, some deputies were already criticizing parliamentary proceedings, seeing for example the amendment of a decree-law as a sign of the diminished authority of the government, 'weakened because it is not only it that governs'. They suggested to Salazar that he should

---

[46] See, for example, Luís da Cunha Gonçalves, *O Estado Novo e a Assembleia Nacional: discursos proferidos na propaganda eleitoral* (Lisbon: n.pub., 1934), pp. 11–12.
[47] António Oliveira Salazar, *Como se levanta um Estado...*, pp. 70–71.
[48] Ibid., p. 78; *I Congresso da União Nacional: discursos, teses e comunicações*, vol. I (Lisbon: Edição da União Nacional, 1935), p. 73 [speech by Oliveira Salazar]; Luís da Cunha Gonçalves, *O Estado Novo e a Assembleia Nacional*, pp. 17–18.
[49] F. I. Pereira dos Santos, *Un état corporative: la constitution sociale et politique portugaise* (Paris: Librairie du Recueil Sirey, 1935), pp. 181–82.
[50] António Oliveira Salazar, *Como se levanta um Estado...*, pp. 73–74.

move towards a 'reduction of the legislative organs to the Corporative Chamber', dissolving the political chamber, stating that 'when the National Assembly does not meet, the situation gets better'.[51]

A little later, in 1944, at the Second Congress of the União Nacional, several speakers seemed convinced that the Corporative Chamber was the institution that could best represent the nation. They urged that this be organized as quickly as possible 'within the corporative system', to turn it into an 'organ of opinion, to fulfil a supervisory role over administrative activity, [...] [and a] consultative organ in the preparation of laws'.[52] However, in defence of the existing arrangement a prominent jurist and supporter of the regime, Afonso Rodrigues Queiró, argued in a speech, also to the União Nacional, in 1949, that 'there is nothing to recommend a substantial modification of the structure and functions of the Corporative Chamber'. He insisted on the importance of maintaining political representation and he thought it 'unviable' to turn the second chamber into a political assembly. In his view, the Corporative Chamber could never 'function as a homogenous corporation, since politics [...] has no place in it', and 'each representative only needs to be familiar with the interests he defends', being 'as expert in those interests'. He also rejected the possibility that the chamber could come 'to function as a legislative organ, concurrently with the National Assembly', pointing to the difficulties, underlined by the lessons from classic bicameral systems, in instituting a bicephalous legislative power. He allowed only, and with little enthusiasm, that the procurators or the sections of the Corporative Chamber might be allowed to propose legislation, 'while retaining for the National Assembly, in these cases, the exclusive right to the final political decision'.[53]

Disquiet with the consultative nature of the corporative structure, not representative of the whole Nation and deviating from the ideal of a self-governing economy and dominated by social action, persisted within the political class, including supporters of the regime, and reappeared sporadically. At one point it found expression in a commission (of unknown composition) formed by Salazar between the elections of 1949 and the middle of 1950, charged with studying 'political problems impacting on constitutional texts', in the framework of preparations for the constitutional revision of 1951. Charged with drafting proposals for changes to the constitution, the commission selected four principal matters: the method of election for the President of the Republic; the designation of deputies to the National Assembly by indirect election, by

[51] PT/ANTT/AOS/CP-36: letters from the deputy Vasco Borges to Salazar, dated 9 and 18 February 1935.
[52] Carlos Alberto Lopes Moreira, 'O Governo e a Função Legislativa e Fiscalizadora da Ação Governativa', in *II Congresso da União Nacional: Resumos das Teses da 1.ª subsecção. Organização Política: O Estado segundo a Constituição: orientação de possíveis reformas constitucionais* (Lisbon: Casa Portuguesa, 1967[?]), p. 9; Alberto de Araújo, 'Órgãos de representação — Assembleia Nacional e Câmara Corporativa', in *A Lei de Salazar*, pp. 12–13.
[53] Afonso Rodrigues Queiró, *A evolução da Câmara Corporativa*, 2.ª Conferência da União Nacional (Porto: Emp. Nacional Editora, 1949), pp. 5–13.

way of the local municipalities; the mode of functioning of the Corporative Chamber; and the relationship between ministers and the National Assembly, specifically a requirement that they be present at certain debates. The proposed amendment concerning the functioning of the Corporative Chamber, aiming to involve it 'more intensively and more widely in the study of bills and proposed decree-laws' drew no objections from the Government. However, the remaining points were not approved by the Executive. Regarding the relations between the Government and the Assembly, it was thought that the proposal had gone too far, supporting only the 'appearance of members of the Government (ministers or sub-secretaries of state) at working sessions of the Corporative Chamber and even, though less certainly, at the sessions of the permanent specialized commissions of the National Assembly, when they were studying proposals or bills to be discussed in public session'. Finally, Salazar feared that 'the adoption of practices so characteristically parliamentary risks our slipping unwittingly into a situation that no one wishes to see recur.' On the election of the President of the Republic, the proposal that it should be handed to the two chambers was rejected by Salazar, because it seemed a mechanism 'inferior to that of the Constitution of 1911', and because it excluded 'the direct intervention by the Nation', something that could not happen as long as they had not extended 'sufficiently the corporative system'. He also rejected the indirect election of deputies, because it conferred 'a lesser degree of representative legitimacy than the current direct election', as well as having the disadvantage of bringing into the National Assembly 'the business of local elections and the greater intensity of political strife, which everything advises us should be kept to the minimum'.[54]

During the constitutional revision of 1959, the question of the method of election of the President of the Republic and the deputies re-emerged. In a change to what had been said in 1951, and mainly as a response to the results achieved in 1958 by the opposition candidate, Humberto Delgado, the Government presented a proposal for ending the election of the President by direct suffrage of the citizens. The political circumstances led to a parliamentarian proposing, for the first time in the entire lifecycle of the National Assembly, the eradication of representation by universal suffrage and the substitution of a system of organic democracy. The initiative, which fell to the monarchist physician Augusto Cerqueira Gomes, was related to a proposal from the Government, but exceeded it in its scope and was indicative of a different kind of thinking. From the outset, it would deepen the dynamic of organic suffrage involved in the election of the head of state. The Executive was proposing that the election should pass (as indeed it did) to a restricted electoral

[54] This information was transmitted, on 13 November 1950, to the Comissão de Legislação e Redação da Assembleia Nacional, and to Mário de Figueiredo, whom Salazar had charged with making 'in a merely personal capacity and to assist the Government, the textual revision of the Constitution', following the 'dissolution of the earlier commission'. See PT/TT/AMC, Cx. 3, n.º 1: Minute by Salazar sent to the Comissão de Legislação e Redação da Assembleia Nacional, dated 13 November 1950.

college, formed of members of the Assembly and the Corporative Chamber, of municipal representatives of each district and of each overseas province not divided into districts, and of representatives of the legislative councils and provincial governing councils. Cerqueira Gomes, however, proposed that the electoral college should be constituted of deputies and procurators not chosen by the Government, by members of the ecclesiastical hierarchy, representatives of the magistrates, of the senior officers of the armed forces, of higher education and of important cultural institutes. His suggestion for the elections to the National Assembly were even more novel and daring, proposing election for five-year terms, by district constituencies and electoral colleges composed of municipal representatives from metropolitan Portugal and the overseas provinces, members of district committees, representatives of moral, cultural and economic organizations and institutions defined by law. The method of election of the President of the Republic was duly altered, in line with the Government's bill. However, Cerqueira Gomes's proposal did not even secure a parliamentary debate, falling simply because it did not meet with the approval of either the Corporative Chamber or the National Assembly.

The Weakness of the Debate

From what has been said above, it can be seen the question of representation was more divisive within the regime than is suggested by the discussion in the parliament, where, perhaps for this very reason, debate was avoided. On the other hand it was easier to discuss the competencies and prerogatives of the Assembly, and its relationship to the Government, and there were some opportunities to express positions favouring an evolution towards a more classically parliamentary chamber.

If the authoritarian conditions that configured the deputies' mandates[55] help to explain the limitations on parliamentary discussion, it is less obvious why, in other forums too, the topics of representation and the relationship between the executive and legislative powers were little discussed. In fact, without prejudicing the necessary future research, the information presently available suggests that legal publications rarely touched on these subjects, despite their importance to jurisprudence. In the press there was practically no discussion of the questions, except in the coverage of the work of the constituent bodies, although it remains to be ascertained if that was due to censorship. Even so, it seems that the existence of mechanisms for the repression of freedom of expression and the limitations on political pluralism in Portuguese society are insufficient to explain the near total absence of philosophical or political discussions on such subjects. Other features, such as the lack of motions presented to the congresses of the União Nacional or the preference of various

---

[55] Compared to the breadth and the characteristics of the elections by which they were selected.

individuals to express their thoughts on the functioning of the chambers and parliamentary business directly to Salazar, in private correspondence, suggest a political atmosphere of great intellectual and ideological weakness. Compared to the very lively debate on parliamentarianism and its functioning throughout the liberal period, particularly the final years of the constitutional monarchy and the First Republic,[56] it is fair to say that such discussions practically disappear from the internal life of the authoritarian regime.

It is notable, too, that even the opposition to the regime gave little attention to these questions, in sharp contrast to opposition currents in other countries such as France, Belgium and Italy.[57] A first investigation, which deserves to be continued, reveals that the most trenchant criticisms of the political system, as well as the presentation of alternatives to the configuration of the powers of the state, the prerogatives of Parliament and methods of election appear very late, in the course of the 1969 elections, in the manifestos and programmes of the Comissão Democrática Eleitoral (CDE), the Comissão Eleitoral de Unidade Democrática (CEUD) and the Ação Democrato-Social. The Comissão Eleitoral Monárquica (CEM), in turn, did not touch on such matters. Even though they had concerned themselves with problems that were fundamental to the creation of democracy — political liberties, organization of political parties, social rights, reform of the justice system — these bodies did not emphasize the construction of a systematic political and constitutional philosophy that could offer solutions to the problems of political organization that would be brought about by the fall of the authoritarian regime. Hence, the ideas that they put into circulation, as well as avoiding a confrontation of the doctrinal positions underlying the ideological motivations of the various opposition forces (whether between groups, essentially divided between a communist and a socialist ideology, or internally), fell broadly into two directions: one, an opening up of the existing political system; the other, a complete transformation, with the substitution of a new model. Regarding the latter view, a proposal put forward by the CDE, in 1969, proposed a separation of the three powers of the state,

---

[56] A number of studies analyse the debates of these times: Fernanda Paula Sousa Maia, *O discurso parlamentar português e as relações Portugal-Brasil: a Câmara dos Deputados (1826–1852)* (Braga: Fundação Calouste Gulbenkian, 2002), pp. 80–81; Ernesto Castro Leal, *Partidos e programas: o campo partidário republicano português, 1910–1926* (Coimbra: Imprensa da Universidade de Coimbra, 2008), pp. 15–108; Paulo Jorge Fernandes, 'O papel político e o funcionamento do parlamento em Portugal', in *Das urnas ao hemiciclo: eleições e parlamento em Portugal (1878–1926) e Espanha (1875–1923)*, ed. by Pedro Tavares de Almeida and Javier Moreno Luzón (Lisbon: Assembleia da República, 2012), pp. 165–219; Luís Bigotte Chorão, *A crise da República e a Ditadura Militar* (Lisbon: Sextante Editora, 2009), pp. 198–99, 234–88.

[57] The French resistance was particularly active in this respect, with the creation of various working committees, commissions for a reform of the state, constitutional plans, and an abundance of books, articles, pamphlets and reports, produced in London, New York and Algiers. In the majority of cases, following the discrediting of the parliamentary regime in 1940, they supported the idea of a government that could be strong and stable, but still answerable politically to the National Assembly. See Henri Michel and Boris Mirkine-Guetzévitch, *Les Idées politiques et sociales de la Résistance (documents clandestins, 1940–1944)* (Paris: Presses Universitaires de France, 1954), pp. 39–65.

with the National Assembly retaining legislative power, though shared with the President of the Republic.[58] Later, in 1973, the Third Congress of the Oposição Democrática voted to place exclusive legislative authority in a 'future National Democratic Assembly that will be able to delegate to the Government, but which will, however, always be at all times answerable to it'. It also envisaged the establishment of a National Constituent Assembly, whose method of elections and electoral law would be 'decreed by the Democratic Government that will follow fascism', and future National Democratic Assemblies, set up later in accordance with the new constitutional settlement. The Executive would remain under the control of the legislature.[59]

The CDE's most frequent demands were for the legalization of political parties, on an equal footing with the União Nacional; for elections of the President of the Republic to be returned to direct suffrage; for the promotion 'outside the National Assembly, [of] complete information on the proceedings of the Chamber of Deputies whenever the daily press does not do it'; for the 'effective supervision of the actions of the Government, restoring to its true dignity the function of deputies, who should not be mere participants in an obedient choir'.[60] It also aimed to see Opposition candidates elected to the National Assembly, in the belief that they would be constitute a 'powerful factor in energizing' the chamber, while denouncing 'all the frauds and shady deals that have been perpetrated in this country'.[61] Related to this aspiration, visible in the discussion of the composition of the Assembly, we can identify two principal criticisms of the system then in force: the absence of many citizens from the electoral rolls, and the lack of safeguards in electoral legislation. These criticisms, widespread amongst oppositionists, had been expressed early on, since 1945.

These questions were posed, debated and systematically publicized by the Lisbon lawyer, José Magalhães Godinho, born into a middle-class republican family that was well known for its opposition to the Military Dictatorship and to the Salazar regime. Godinho rejected the adequacy of decree no. 34938, of 22 September 1945, which abandoned the system of election of deputies in a single constituency and created both electoral divisions and administrative districts. In defence of an electoral system that would assure the representation of minorities, he opposed bicameralism (even when it involved chambers with a merely consultative function) and insisted that the right to be included on the electoral register should be written into the Constitution. He defended the supervision of the election (by way of electoral delegates freely chosen by

---

[58] 'Manifesto da CDE de Castelo Branco [1969]'. in *Para um dossier da Oposição Democrática*, ed. by Serafim Ferreira and Arsénio Mota, 2.ª série (Porto: Tipografia do Carvalhido, 1969), p. 153.
[59] 3º Congresso da Oposição Democrática. Aveiro 4 a 8 de Abril de 1973. Conclusões (Lisbon: Seara Nova, 1973), pp. 117 and 148.
[60] 'Proclamação da CDE [Aveiro, 2 October 1969]', in *Para um dossier da Oposição Democrática...*, pp. 38–39, 42.
[61] 'Manifesto da CDE [August 1969]', in ibid., pp. 45–46.

those participating in any list), the publication of legal provisions to assure equal conditions for all candidates (including access to radio and television and the availability of meeting places for election rallies), and the absence of government interference in the electoral process. In line with these principles he proposed, in 1969, that the National Assembly, elected in that year, should pass a law against press censorship, ensure the right to meet and associate, allow for the creation and lawful functioning of political parties, guarantee the freedom and physical safety of citizens by allowing a lawyer to witness all interrogations, guarantee that they could not be sent to prison without due process, and guarantee the legality of all arrests by presenting the prisoner within 24 hours before a judicial magistrate (and not a government official acting as a magistrate for that purpose).[62]

Given his extensive civic and political campaigning against the regime, Magalhães Godinho quickly turned himself into an essential point of reference on the problems of electoral registration and electoral law, one whose arguments and proposals were adopted by all sectors of the opposition, without exception. It is not surprising, therefore, that the Third Congress of the Oposição Democrática, previously mentioned, formulated similar ideas, such as the right to vote for those over 18 years, regardless of other qualifications, and without ideological discrimination', or the proposal for a new kind of electoral registration, involving the creation of an elector's card that that could be used in any constituency, regardless of the holder's place of residence.[63]

Finally, it is worth noting that opposition currents did not address the questions of organic representation or the existing parliamentary architecture. They had no plans to develop the political system on that basis, nor did they concern themselves with the Corporative Chamber, even when they dealt with the subject of 'corporative reconversion'.[64]

From what has been said it can be seen that what happened in Portugal was very different to the other European dictatorships of the inter-war period. From the First World War onwards, denunciations of the defects of the parliamentary system become frequent in Spain, France, Italy, Germany, Austria, Belgium, Poland, and in the Kingdom of Yugoslavia and the Baltic republics. In each country specific discourses were developed on national sovereignty and

[62] Amongst the various writings that Godinho devoted to these topics, see particularly José Magalhães Godinho, *A legislação eleitoral e a sua crítica* (Lisbon: Prelo, 1969); Idem, *Ano de Eleições* (Lisbon: República, 1973).
[63] Idem, ibidem, p. 157; "Manifesto da Ação Democrato-Social [Lisboa, 1969]" in ibidem, pp. 398–99; "Proclamação da CEUD [Lisboa, 1969]" in ibidem, pp. 351–52; *3º Congresso da Oposição Democrática...*, p. 125. After the coup of 25 April 1974, in recognition of the fact that he had made this one of the principal questions under the dictatorship, he was invited to chair a commission charged with drawing up legislation for elections to the Constituent Assembly. Nominated by the Socialist Party, of which he was member, he later sat on commissions to deal with elections to the Presidency of the Republic and the Assembly of the Republic. From 1976 he participated in the National Electoral Commission.
[64] 'Proclamação da CEUD [Lisboa, 1969]', in *Para um dossier da Oposição Democrática...*, p. 359. The only mention is a criticism of the lack of 'any representative character in the selection' of the Corporative Chamber, in the 'Programa Político da CDE [Lisboa, 1969]', in ibidem, p. 235.

forms of representation, on the crisis of liberal democracy, on parties and political chambers. The leading politicians and supporters of the different national governments presented differing proposals either for alterations in the parliamentary process or for changes in the political system, such as rejecting the principle of separation of powers with the aim of reinforcing Executive power, or for a reform of the state itself.[65]

A confrontation between doctrines and juridical systems was evident in the case of Italy, for example. Between 1922, the year in which Mussolini took the post of Prime Minister, and 1939, the year in which the *Camera dei Fasci e delle Corporazioni* was formed, there were extensive discussions in intellectual and juridical circles, as well as amongst political operators, over the representation of interests and even electoral and constitutional reform. In 1923, Mussolini had advocated not the abolition of parliament, but rather its reform, saying that its functioning had been damaged by syndicalism and journalism. Ten years later, however, following the approval of laws on electoral reform (1925), changes in political representation and the constitutional acceptance of the *Gran Consiglio* (1928), and various studies, such as that of the Fascist party secretary, Giovanni Giuriati, in 1931, proposing institutional reform and the abolition of the Senate, he already regarded the *Camera dei Deputati* as an anachronistic institution. The years that followed saw changes in the functioning of parliament, under the presidency of Alfredo Rocco, restricting the powers of the permanent commissions. Equally, there were irregularities in elections, denounced by Giacomo Matteotti (later assassinated); the removal of communist or *aventiniani* deputies; proposals for the creation of political assemblies and economic forums, as seen, for example, in the Carta del Carnaro, or the institution of a lower chamber and Senate composed of representatives of professional and syndicalist organizations. The culmination of this process was to make parliament superfluous, achieved with the institution of the *Camera dei Fasci e delle Corporazioni*, planned since 1936 by the Commissione Solmi, whose members represented a variety of fascist ideological positions, and who squabbled amongst themselves in the course of their work.[66]

In the case of the Franco regime in Spain, which throughout four decades of existence was continuously institutionalizing itself, the opening of the Cortes, in 1942, and their functioning, were always in tension with the dynamic of the Movimiento Nacional (the single party) and its various projects for *desarrollo político* [political development]. Franco was endowed with almost absolute executive and legislative powers, the political parties had been closed down, and there was a consensus on steering the regime towards an organic democracy (influenced by very varied political positions that ranged from the constitutional theories of Herbert Kraus to those of Maurice Hauriou). Even so,

---

[65] Mark Mazower, *The Dark Continent: Europe's Twentieth Century* (London: Penguin, 1999), pp. 16-31.
[66] Francesco Perfetti, *Fascismo e Riforme Istituzionali* (Florence: Le Lettere, 2013), pp. 9-92.

there were conflicts between *tradicionalistas* and *falangistas* over the position of the corporativist Cortes and the more or less secondary role envisaged for them, compared to the Consejo Nacional of the Falange Española Tradicionalista (FET) and the Juntas de Ofensiva Nacional-Sindicalista (JONS).[67] In the 1950s and 1960s, the power struggles between the 'political families' of Francoism, which remained divided over doctrinal visions, not only did not diminish but were exacerbated by changes to the system. Following the approval of the Reglamento de las Cortes, of 1957, and the Ley Orgánica del Estado (LOE), of 1966, the Cortes increased the supervisory and legislative powers and saw their composition changed. The biggest change was with the introduction in the Tenth Legislature of *procuradores familiares*, many of whom were from the liberal professions or business, who broke with the regime's canons of parliamentary politics and placed an unprecedented degree of pressure on the institution. They were for the most part *aperturistas* [reformists], and they disturbed the relationship of forces in favour of the Movimiento and the Organização Sindical, at a time when the latter, pledged to the creation of political associations (albeit of limited pluralism) were confronting the *inmovilistas* [Franco hardliners], who were defending the monolithic single party. At the end of 1968, the Government put at end to what was seen as an instrumentalization of the Cortes by the *procuradores familiares*, concentrating power in the hands of the Consejo Nacional del Movimiento. However, following the failure of the associative project in 1969, in the Cortes and the Consejo, a group of *aperturistas* critical of the Government moved to question the role of the parliamentary groups, which did fit into the scheme of an organic democracy. Despite the efforts of the *continuista* supporters, the legislative achievements of the *espíritu del 12 de febrero* (1974) and the action of an informal Grupo Parlamentario, which aimed to institute a democratic monarchy from within the parliamentary system, consolidated the *aperturista* project. At the time of Franco's death, and with the support of elements abandoning his ranks to join different areas of Government, it became clear that the future of the associations did not lie in their development within the Movimiento, but through a future system of parties. The radical reform of the parliamentary system, started in March 1976 with the publication of a new Reglamento for the Cortes, was tumultuous. It removed from the Consejo Nacional the monopoly of political associations, by allowing their transformation into political parties and the formulation of the Ley de Reforma Política. With its approval, on 18 November of that year, it started the process of self-dissolution of the representative institutions of the dictatorship, including the Cortes.[68]

The examples cited show profound differences from the Portuguese case,

[67] Miguel Ángel Giménez Martínez, *Las Cortes Españolas en el régimen de Franco: nacimiento, desarrollo y extinción de una Cámara Orgánica* (Madrid: Congreso de los Diputados, 2012), pp. 56–66, 84–92.
[68] Julio Gil Pecharromán, *El Movimiento Nacional (1937–1977)* (Barcelona: Editorial Planeta, 2013), pp. 265–315.

both in the arguments put forward to criticize parliamentarianism and in the institutions and forms of government set up, and even in the doctrinal and political differences between sectors supporting the regimes. They also reveal differences in political mobilization and in the political and intellectual climate. The fragility of the political elites in Portugal, highly dependent on the clientelistic structure of the state, more interested in the administration of the current political system and the neutralization of tensions within political groupings than in debating the guiding principles of the state, may help to explain this situation.

Final Considerations

Taking into account the above observations, it becomes more difficult to explain the evolutions of political systems in the inter-war dictatorships, particularly of parliamentary systems and of the relationship between the executive and legislative powers, in the optic of fascism and its influence in the overthrow of democratic regimes.[69] Theoretical formulations that explain the forms and evolution of parliaments in the inter-war dictatorships in terms of the creation of regime parties or of corporativism, in their different variants, seem too simplistic to account for historical reality. The discussions around regime parties have contributed to making parliaments places of legitimation for dictatorial authority, intended to guarantee the political monopoly amongst the elites, or to contain threats (principally military) against the regimes themselves. In the case of explanations based on the so-called 'political corporativism', it is taken as a contrivance that was an agent of the hybridization of institutions and an authoritarian alternative to liberal democracy, serving to repress organized interests and elites by creating organic legislative chambers.[70]

However, each of these interpretive elements rests on a valorization (not empirically demonstrated, in terms of agents, contents, bases) of the so-called institutional and transnational transfers, which leads to a disregard for the juridical tradition and the specific political systems in each state and the limits in the understanding of the actors themselves of foreign experiences, or to equate influences to imitative behaviour. We should not forget the importance of different national characteristics in the formulation of political and juridical practices, as well as the revolutionary tendency of the authoritarian and fascist regimes, where to institute a new order meant to free the state both from the

---

[69] It will be recalled that Juan Linz made a distinction between, on the one hand, the theme of the crisis of the democratic regimes and rise of authoritarian governments, and, on the other, the emergence of fascism, whether as a movement or as an ideology, and its influence in the overthrow of the democratic regimes. Juan Linz, *Obras escogidas*, ed. by J .R. Montero and T. J. Miley, vol. 1 — *Fascismo: perspectivas históricas y comparadas* (Madrid: Centro de Estudos Políticos y Constitucionales, 2008), pp. 181–87.
[70] An example of this theoretical position can be found in António Costa Pinto, 'O corporativismo nas ditaduras da época do Fascismo', in *Varia Historia*, 30.52 (Jan-Apr 2014), 17–49.

internal shackles that had, allegedly, been corrupting and degrading it and from external influences. The latter should not be confused with external relations and cooperation between governments, that very often justify the concealment of differences between regimes, particularly at times such as the period between 1918 and 1945, marked downstream by the Paris Conference and upstream by the new global conflict, the outcome of which was, for a long time, uncertain. Finally, it is appropriate to question to what extent the emphasis placed on the above-mentioned institutional transfers does not also lead to identifying authoritarian and antidemocratic regimes with fascism and totalitarianism, an identification already traced out in opposition positions at the time, and which became dominant after the end of the Second World War, made by people engaged (*engagés*) in ideological conflicts.

Historical and political analysis has over-valorized an alleged mimicry in the Portuguese authoritarian experience, as concerns its institutions and ideology, of foreign models. However, as shown here, the dominant features, which were determinant for the original political system of 1933 as well as its later evolution, are of a primarily internal character. In summary, it can be seen that in Portugal a rejection of the solutions typical of organic representation and a loyalty to a liberal framework were constants throughout the Salazar and Caetano regimes. Hence the choice of an imperfect bicameral system, with the creation of a new representative assembly alongside a chamber of organic representation, in which the former is always given greater weight than the latter. It also opted to give parliamentary deputies more significant functions than in any other authoritarian regime in Europe between the wars. This model of organization in parliament did not dispense, obviously, with the clear control of the Executive, but it did contribute to providing a high level of political stability in the regime, helping to pacify its political life — at least amongst its supporters — creating space and conditions for an enduring political compromise between the various interest groups within the Estado Novo. Parliament then, in the authoritarian regime, was a site of political negotiation, where political solutions were chosen, which, once defined, were presented as sources of legitimation for various sectoral policies. Its role was not, then, worthless in the ability that the regime manifested, over many years, in putting an end to the armed insurrection as the normal and efficient route to power.

Translated from Portuguese by Richard Correll

Memory of Resistance and the Resistance of Memory: An Analysis of the Construction of Corporatism in the First Years of the Portuguese Estado Novo

Francisco Carlos Palomanes Martinho

Universidade de São Paulo/ CNPq

> Deveríamos rir-nos da fragilidade da memória, ou pelo menos sorrirmos das artimanhas do seu esquecimento. [We should laugh at the fragility of memory, or at least smile at the wiles of its forgetting.]
>
> Lídia Jorge, *Combateremos a sombra* (Lisbon: D. Quixote, 2007)

Introduction

Lucien Febvre once said of the French Resistance that 'everything is terribly complicated in relation to men, their dreams, their ideas, their passions — and, ultimately, their activities'.[1] He was reflecting on the difficulties his fellow compatriots had in understanding collaboration with fascism during the Vichy regime. Years later, Pierre Laborie analysed French society under the collaboration regime of Marshal Pétain. According to this historian there predominated amongst the French a certain ambivalence, a *grey zone*, an area larger than those of adhesion or resistance, in which the majority of the population existed. They lived their daily lives without any defined engagement and sought strategies of survival in a country under French military occupation. They were not necessarily in favour, but also not necessarily against. As Febvre said: 'The majority of the French were not first pro-Vichy then supporters of the resistance, Pétainists and afterwards Gaullists, but they could be simultaneously for a more or less long period a little of both at the same time.'[2] Perhaps because ambivalence does not seduce, perhaps because we need pre-emptory affirmation of definitive utopias, all societies which have authoritarian experiences avoid dealing with such disagreeable and uncomfortable pasts. The exception is when studies of authoritarian regimes evoke the predominance

---

[1] Cited by Pierre Laborie. *L'Opinion française sous Vichy* (Paris: Seuil, 1990).
[2] Pierre Laborie, '1940-1944: os franceses do pensar-duplo', in Denise Rollemberg and Samantha Viz Quadrat (eds), *A construção social dos regimes autoritários: legitimidade, consenso e consentimento no século XX*, vol. i: *Europa* (Rio de Janeiro: Civilização Brasileira, 2010), pp. 31–44 (p. 39).

of opposition movements; in these cases, it is common to exalt the resistance and the heroic act of those who chose to confront arbitrariness. Authoritarian regimes tend to be seen as random, as accidents which occurred along the route in the middle of a 'natural tendency' of society: democratic and progressive.

It is not surprising, then, that in the case of the Portuguese *Estado Novo*,[3] which lasted almost half a century, there are more frequent studies of the resistance and the opposition than those which explain the commitment of the Portuguese, or a significant part of them, to the long-lived authoritarian regime.[4] The aim of this article is to analyse the efforts of the Portuguese *Estado Novo* to implement trade union policy between 1930 and 1934, in other words, the period of the preparation and organization of the statist trade union model, completed in 1933, and the first reactions to its imposition.[5] I therefore consider it possible to understand not only the reasons for the acceptance of and collaboration with national unions, but above all, the effectiveness of the institutionalization/modernization dynamic in the process of the construction of the *Estado Novo*. This is what we believe will be the principal contribution this article will make to the historiography of the period.

The Dilemma of Participation in the Antecedents of the *Estado Novo*

In February 1930 the government appointed a tripartite commission to discuss legislation about working hours, as well as to prepare regulations on the question. Representing worker organizations, the Trade Union of Industrial and Commercial Workers of Lisbon, linked to the anarchist CGT (*Confederação Geral dos Trabalhadores* — General Confederation of Workers), and the Association of Clerks of Lisbon, of socialist hegemony. The invitation opened the serious problem of whether or not to participate in negotiations with a government considered illegitimate. While, for the anarchist leaders participation was an affront to the principles which guided their action,

---

[3] On 28 March 1926 a coup d'état brought to an end the Portuguese First Republic (1910-1926) and set up a military dictatorship which in 1928 became a corporatist and civil/military dictatorship under the command of the then Minister of Finance, António Oliveira Salazar. The *Estado Novo* itself began only in 1933 with the implementation of a new constitution. For a chronology of the phases of the authoritarian Portuguese regime, see Manuel Braga da Cruz, *O partido e o Estado no salazarismo* (Lisbon: Presença, 1988), pp. 38-47.

[4] Some examples from the period dealt with here: João Freire, 'Os anarquistas portugueses na conjuntura do pós-guerra', in *O Estado Novo: das origens ao fim da autarcia (1926-1959)* (Lisbon: Fragmentos, 1987), pp. 9-26; Manuel de Lucena, *Evolução do sistema corporativo português*, 2 vols (Lisbon: Perspectivas e Realidades, 1976); Maria Filomena Mónica, 'Poder e saber: os vidreiros da Marinha Grande', *Análise Social*, 67-68-69 (1981), 505-71 ; João Arsénio Nunes 'Sobre alguns aspectos da evolução política do Partido Comunista Português após a reorganização de 1929 (1931-33)', *Análise Social*, 67-68-69 (1981), 715-31; Alice Ingerson, 'Consciência de classe em Vila Nova de Famalicão', *Análise Social*, 67-68-69 (1981), 863-84; Dawn Linda Raby, *Fascism and Resistance in Portugal* (Manchester: Manchester University Press, 1988).

[5] In relation to 18 January, which will not be analysed here, see Maria de Fátima Patriarca, *Sindicatos contra Salazar: a revolta do 18 de Janeiro de 1934* (Lisbon: Imprensa de Ciências Sociais, 2000); idem, 'O "18 de Janeiro": uma proposta de releitura', *Análise Social*, 123/124 (1993), 1137-52.

the majority of members of the Association of Clerks were favourable to participation. Avoiding precipitated deliberation, the decision taken was to convene various class groups to Lisbon to pronounce on the issue.[6]

The meeting was held on 25 February 1930, in the offices of the Union of CP (*Comboios de Portugal*) Railway Workers. The dominant tendency was opposed to entering talks with the government. The socialists, on the one hand, were not opposed to participation, but the anarcho-syndicalists and communists, on the other, were opposed due to questions of principle. They also called attention to the unequal representation between workers and employers, and noted that, even if this were not the case, the employers would always have an advantage since they could count on the votes of the state representatives.[7] Moreover, for both anarchists and communists, workers' victories had to be obtained through the class struggle and not via agreements with the state. The final decision was for non-participation. A new meeting was held on 6 March, this time in the Trade Union of Navy Arsenal Workers, with a communist hegemony. By twelve votes to five, a proposal from the representatives of the Trade Union of Typesetters, also close to the communists, was approved, for organizing an 'Inter-Syndical Commission to Defend Working Hours'.[8]

Although in a minority position, there was a current favourable to participation. For example, according to one participant from the Union of Industrial and Commercial Workers of Lisbon, it was 'just and reasonable' to climb the stairs of ministries as long as it was to meet the demands of workers in order to improve their living conditions. In relation to the accusation of collaborationism, he stated that 'the purity and coherence of principles should equally oblige non-participation in the arbitration tribunals to which almost all the unions sent representatives.'[9] For others, participation through legal means, once it respected the balance of forces, was the best way to defend workers' interests.[10]

After the establishment of the Inter-Syndical Commission to Defend Working Hours, it was quickly transformed into a union appendage of the Portuguese Communist Party (PCP),[11] after which the Inter-Syndical Commission (CIS) was formed. In this way a communist trade union confederation was created, which came into dispute with the anarchist CGT's control over the workers'

---

[6] Fátima Patriarca, *A questão social no Salazarismo (1930–1947)* (Lisbon: Imprensa Nacional–Casa da Moeda, 1995), pp. 22/24.
[7] In my study of Portuguese trade unionism, I sought to demonstrate that the anarchists' predictions did not come true, on the contrary, in the tripartite negotiations the employers were often isolated due to the general tendency of the representatives of the state to defend the demands of the National Trade Unions, cf. Francisco Carlos Palomanes Martinho, *A bem da Nação: o sindicalismo português entre a tradição e a modernidade (1933–1947)* (Rio de Janeiro: Civilização Brasileira, 2002).
[8] Fátima Patriarca, *A questão social no Salazarismo*, pp. 26–30.
[9] Idem, idem, pp. 34–35.
[10] Idem, idem, p. 36.
[11] In relation to the PCP, see João Madeira, *História do PCP: das origens ao 25 de Abril* (Lisbon: Tinta da China, 2013).

movement. In this episode of the creation of CIS, it seems to us to be interesting to observe that, once the opposition between the latter and CGT had been consolidated, both sought to deny the tenuous unity constituted at the beginning of 1930.[12]

Before starting the discussion about corporatist institutionalization, we have to make a brief mention of the important and undeservedly forgotten union current composed of the socialists. An attitude of provoked forgetting resulted from deliberate behaviour by anarchists and communists, as if the social fights of the periods were summarized in the duel waged by both.[13] Fundamentally, the socialist syndicalist strategy was to maintain the union movement within legality. This conduct earned them the epithet of 'collaborationists', as well discrediting them, in the eyes of some, in relation to their effective importance in the union environment. This is actually difficult to measure. Nevertheless, they not only existed, but directly intervened in the questions raised on a daily basis by Portuguese trade unionism. In the sphere of worker organizations, the socialists from Porto organized themselves in 1929 in the FAO (*Federação das Associações Operárias* — Federation of Worker Associations). In the rest of the country, socialist actions occurred in what were called 'Class Associations' which they either organized or exercised some influence in. Recognizing the need for a more wide-ranging organization, they defended the creation of the UGT (*União Geral dos Trabalhadores* — General Union of Workers). Although intended to bring together all the 'reformist' trade union structures in the country, it was never established.[14]

Corporatist Legislation: Choices and Options

The choices facing the different current within the trade union movement came to a head in 1933. On 23 September 1933, based on three Decree Laws,[15] the National Labour Statute (*Estatuto do Trabalho Nacional* — ETN) was established. Also created by Decree Law,[16] and subject to the Sub-Secretary of State for Corporations and Social Security, was the National Labour and Social Security Institute (*Instituto Nacional de Trabalho e Previdência* — INTP). A new form of relationship was thereby established between the state and the world of labour. Although the process of bringing together the state and workers began, as we have seen, in 1930, it was with the institutionalization of the *Estado Novo* and the agencies formally destined for a relationship of proximity with the

---

[12] Fátima Patriarca, *A questão social no Salazarismo*, pp. 38–40.
[13] Idem, idem, pp. 69–91.
[14] In the historiography about this theme, although only a minority deal with the socialists, it is worth referencing the pioneering study of Maria Filomena Mónica, *O movimento socialista em Portugal (1875-1934)* (Lisbon: Imprensa Nacional–Casa da Moeda, 1984).
[15] Decree 23.049, aimed at employers in commerce, industry, and agriculture; Decree 23.050, aimed at employees, workers, and professionals; and Decree 23.051, aimed at the rural world.
[16] Decree 23.053.

world of labour that the corporatization of the Portuguese state can be said to have effectively begun.[17] Of course, the strengthening of the unions was not isolated from a process of institutionalization and even the modernization of the regime in other areas considered strategic. This is the case, for example, in education, culture, politics, and development, as well as urban modernization, topics that fall outside the scope of this article.[18] The union movement thus had to deal with this new standard of relationship from then on, a new standard which defined ideological orientations, internal norms of functioning and, more importantly, attributed powers to the state which, between 1933 and 1944, were expanded by other decrees.[19]

According to Decree 23.050, workers in commerce and industry had to be organized in National Unions. These would be based on trades or professions and would operate in districts. In each district there would be a monopoly of union representation. At the same time, according to the ETN, the unions had to obey the principles which subordinated individual and collective interests to those of the national economy, to collaboration with the state and other classes, and with nationalism, which limited union actions to Portugal. Furthermore, union statutes had to clearly express their fidelity to nationalism, the renunciation of all activities contrary to the 'interests of the Portuguese Nation', as well as a repudiation of the class struggle.[20]

Workers had to respond to this new policy. However, this had to be done in accordance with a pre-imposed policy which, despite the leadership of the worker movement, already had repercussions amongst their 'representatives'. The choice could be both to consolidate and to isolate leaders, in the same way that it affirmed a project of trade union organization opposed to the models in

---

[17] This process of the consolidation of corporatist trade unionism can be seen in the statistics for the growth of entities recognized by the state, as well as the number of union members. In 1938, the number of existing unions was 232 against only 15 in 1933. For this year we do not have a figure for the number of members. In 1938 the total was 185,713. In 1944, the number of unions reached 311 while the total number of members was 431,431. In 1972, on the eve of the fall of the Estado Novo, the number of unions was 327 and the total members 895,370. Cf. José Barreto, 'Os sindicatos nacionais do Estado Novo'. Revised version of the article 'Sindicatos Nacionais', in António Barreto and Maria Filomena Mónica (eds), Dicionário de História de Portugal (Porto: Figueirinhas, 2000), pp. 436–45.

[18] In relation to the themes in question, amongst others, see Vítor Marias Ferreira, 'Uma nova ordem urbana para a capital do Império: a "modernidade" da urbanização e o "autoritarismo" do Plano Director de Lisboa, 1938-1948', O Estado Novo: das origens ao fim da autarcia (1926-1959). Volume II (Lisbon: Fragmentos, 1987), pp. 359–75; Pedro Lains, 'A economia portuguesa no século XX', in António Costa Pinto (ed.), Portugal contemporâneo (Lisbon: D. Quixote, 2004), pp. 117–36; Francisco Martinho, 'Entre o fomento e o condicionamento: a economia portuguesa em tempos de crise (1928–1945)', in Francisco Martinho and Flávio Limoncic (eds), A grande depressão: política e economia na década de 1930: Europa, Américas, África e Ásia (Rio de Janeiro: Civilização Brasileira, 2009), pp. 305–30; Nuno Teotónio Pereira; José Manuel Fernandes, 'A arquitectura do Estado Novo', in O Estado Novo: das origens ao fim da autarcia (1926-1959). Volume II (Lisbon: Fragmentos, 1987), pp. 323–57; Fernando Rosas, Salazarismo e fomento económico (Lisbon: Editorial Notícias, 2000); idem, 'O salazarismo e o homem novo: ensaio sobre o Estado Novo e a questão do totalitarismo', Análise Social, 157 (2001), 1031–54.

[19] Fátima Patriarca, A questão social no Salazarismo, p. 227.
[20] Idem, pp. 228.

force among the principal working class movements. Subordination to the state and the 'nationalist' commitment were presented as impediments that were too strong to be passively accepted. From the point of view of the left-wing worker leaders — anarchists, communists, and socialists — the general tendency was not to accept the determinations 'imposed' by the state. Nevertheless, the paths chosen by different union sectors about the corporatization process were not always the same.

The general exception to the rule were the currents on the 'right' of the trade union movement, immediately willing to accept the changes. Examples of this were the Trade Union of Workers and Employees in the Dairy Industry and the Trade Union of Civil Construction Employees, both from Covilhã, hegemonized by Catholics and a single press organ, the *Voz dos Trabalhadores* newspaper. Not only could great optimism in relation to the corporatist organization model be perceived here, but it was also affirmed that this model implied the end of liberalism and communism, 'the principal causes of disorder in the economic and moral world'. Furthermore:

> The French Revolution had suppressed the Corporations, 'the sole protection for the working class, with this being subjected to the at times tyrannical game of unchecked capitalism.' From now on it will no longer be like this. 'Trade unions, bodies that cooperate with the Corporatist State, will satisfy in common agreement the most urgent needs of the working classes and employers, until over time the corporatist regime is properly established, with vocational and apprenticeship schools, work grants, preparatory regulations, and the choosing of representatives for the Councils to defend their own professional interests.' [21]

The idea of the trade union as a body aimed at conflict — as the liberal tradition argued — was from then on denied in favour of a new organizational concept. It was not anti-union, but the defender of an idea of collaborative unions that constructed order. Their role from then on would be merely technical, to look after 'professional interests'. In the case of Catholics, it should be noted that a culture of this type had existed since the end of the nineteenth century, when the Church first sought to formulate an alternative to liberal capitalism and socialism. It also served to show that the constitution of corporatist syndicalism in Portugal was not only the fruit of political repression, but also of the immediate adhesion of sectors which acted in an organized manner in the union sphere.

The state had imposed the deadline of 31 December 1933 for the new boards of the various Portuguese trade unions to hold assemblies in order to adopt the new directives. Of the thirty-eight class associations who held assemblies by this date, fifteen of them refused to join the new corporatist order while twenty-three accepted it. Voting against Decree 23.050 were the following professional

---

[21] 'Sindicalizemo-nos', in *A Voz dos Trabalhadores. Órgão dos Sindicatos dos Empregados e Operários da Indústria de Lanifícios e da Construção Civil da Covilhã*, no. 38, 1 December 1933.

categories: journalists, metallurgical workers, railway workers, clerical workers, all types of commercial salesmen, hotel professionals, employees of *Carris* (public transport company), confectioners, drivers, telephone workers, tobacco workers, the Association of Tobacco Industry Workers, the Trade Union of Workers of the Navy Arsenal, the Union of State Employees, and Lisbon port workers. Voting in favour of integration into the corporatist order were: doctors, private school teachers, musicians, bullfighters, agricultural administrators, dental technicians, engineers of the Merchant Marine, officers of the Merchant Marine, port workers, stevedores, marine inspectors, dock workers from Lisbon Port, traffic staff, bakers, sugar-mill technicians, employees of Fósforos Lisbonenses [Lisbon Match Company], tobacco workers, civil construction workers, foremen, theatre machinists, insurance workers, recreational centre and club workers, as well as forty dissident workers from *Carris* and the Hotel Workers Union. It should be noted that, although the large majority of professional unions (doctors, private school teachers, etc.), were amongst those who voted in favour of the new decree, some important trade unions also decided to opt for the new corporatist order (bakers, port workers, civil construction workers, etc.), which could be a sign of the seductive capacity of the new law among poorer groups.[22] There was also a draw, in the case of the Association of Pharmacist Assistants. Associations which rejected the statist project or which did not hold assemblies were to be dissolved. In this case, groups of members sought to form organizational commissions so that they could found a National Union recognized by the state. Often the failure to hold assemblies was not exactly a rupture or act of disobedience, but rather was a sign of an advanced state of demobilization. In January 1934, various class associations sought to hold assemblies in order to obtain legal recognition in the manner imposed by the state, so that the entity could regain legal recognition.

An analysis of the documents reveals a complex scenario in which choices and options were made in a context of insecurity about the future. It was a game and, for each path adopted, the results were unpredictable. One of the first unions to choose to take sides in relation to Decree Law 23.050 was the Union of Journalists of Lisbon. For this reason, it prepared a technical report on the new legislation to be sent to the General Assembly for that group of workers.[23] This report initially showed that its authors were aware of the interests of the *Estado Novo* in the sense that the new legislation would alter the *modus operandi* of Portuguese trade unions:

---

[22] Comando Geral da PSP. Arquivo Histórico do Ministério para a Qualificação e o Emprego (AHMQE).
[23] Parecer da Direcção do Sindicato dos Profissionais da Imprensa de Lisboa acerca do decreto 23.050 para ser apresentado à sua Assembléia Geral, focando aspectos da reorganização dos Sindicatos Nacionais. É assinada por Artur Portela, Presidente, Belo Redondo, Vice-presidente, Julião Quintinha, Secretário-Geral, Carlos Nunes, Secretário-Adjunto, Manuel Nunes Júnior, Tesoureiro (12 fols). ANTT — AOS/CO/PC10A.

The reading of the decrees which established the new corporatist organization quickly certifies that the aim of the government is to take all the associational positions, as it has taken all political positions, only allowing the activity of the party group which it supports. There can be no doubt that it intends to extend and establish its influence within the professional collectivities, bringing together for the same political purposes, for the service of the Dictatorship and the *Estado Novo*, elements that are logically heterogeneous.[24]

It was written within a perception that they were heading towards a restriction of liberties, under which the professionals defined the direction to be taken. At the same time the union sought to affirm the strictly neutral nature of the entity, preserving its economic and cultural character. In this way, when press censorship was established and the Professional Identity Card was replaced by the Journalist's Identity Card, controlled by the state, protests were avoided, so that it was not confused with political activity.[25] In relation to the legislation itself, as well as criticizing the curtailment of a wider debate about its content, the report stated that ETN had established a collective contract, but did not oblige employers to accept it, which resulted in it being 'dead in the water'. Furthermore, although the legislation allowed the establishment of employer associations, even in a provisional manner, the old employer associations were maintained, in an obvious situation of 'injustice' in relation to workers.[26] It was an incoherence in the proposal of 'harmony' preached by the regime.

In relation to Decree 23.053, which created the National Institute of Labour and Social Security (INTP), the criticism was because the same decree also extinguished some courts which had judged labour conflicts. The Union of Journalists had often used these courts. It was thus seen as the loss of one more guarantee to workers.[27]

However, the main observations were made about Decree 23.050, responsible for the creation of National Unions, and imposing the date of 31 December as the final deadline for the modification of statutes and adhesion to the corporatist system. The first criticism was in relation to Article 9, which stipulated that Unions had to be subordinated to the interests of the national economy:

> It is evident that it would be more pleasant if we could defend our rights and privileges in harmony with the interests of the national economy, in perfect collaboration with the state and its agencies, when these can expand freely and with equity.
> However, what we cannot do is simulate ignorance of the effects of a similar doctrine, agreeing to our subordination to the bourgeois economic

---

[24] Idem, fol. 1.
[25] Idem, fol. 2.
[26] Idem. Also in Brazil the corporatist legislation had similar traits in worker and employer organizations. Cf. Ângela de Castro Gomes, 'Os paradoxos e os mitos: o corporativismo faz 60 anos', in *República, trabalho e cidadania* (Rio de Janeiro: FGV/CPDOC, 1991).
[27] Parecer da Direcção do Sindicato dos Profissionais da Imprensa de Lisboa (12 fols). ANTT — AOS/CO/PC10A.

structure, knowing that this, instead of meeting the common good, is built on the privileges of the economic interests of workers, and is often even prejudicial to the state itself.[28]

For the leaders of the Union of Journalists there prevailed the idea of a syndicalism based on struggle, constructed in liberal type societies, and fundamentally marked by disputes of an economic nature.

Article 10, which stipulated the national character of unions, thereby preventing them from affiliating to any international body or participating in congresses or meetings without the prior authorization of the government, was also discussed by the Union. Also in this case there prevailed the idea of a traditional union model, in contrast with the national and corporatist unions which the *Estado Novo* sought to implement:

> [...] we are almost forbidden from having professional or cultural relations with our foreign comrades, not being able to take a step in this direction without the authorization of the government, which thus imposes on us an inexplicable guardianship, as if any official entity would know better than us the relations that it is in our interest to maintain or that we would be capable of strengthening relations against national interests.[29]

The divergence with this article was because not only were international relations beneficial to workers, but they also did not necessarily clash with the so-called 'national interests'. An example of this was the Catholic Church which, as a body with an international nature, exercised activities in different countries without this characterizing an affront to the Nation 'and no government thought to inspect or condition the relations that Catholics and their agencies have abroad'.[30]

The observations about the state and the Catholic Church demonstrate the capacity of trade unionists to use the strongest elements of the *Estado Novo*'s discourse in defence of their own interests. What was involved was not a rupture with order, but a demonstration that this order provided for the elements dearest to the new regime, such as the Church and the state itself, rights that were contradictorily prohibited to unions and other civil bodies. The document then discussed Article 15 onwards, which dealt with statutory dispositions, considered as being so prejudicial that they 'made the existence of our union useless':

> Section c) of Article 15 stipulates that the statutes must contain a repudiation of the class struggle. The class struggle will only disappear when the economic anomalies and inequities which cause it disappear. Fighting for class demands is the principal action to be attributed to our Union. If forced to renounce this struggle, the principal purpose of the union will be

[28] Idem, fols 3–4.
[29] Idem, fols 4–5.
[30] Idem, fol. 5.

eliminated. It will not have a reason to exist, since for the other associative functions there already exist bodies for mutualism, social security, and the instruction and recreational societies.[31]

Similarly, they sought to emphasize the differences which separated unions from other forms of organizing labour, not destined to the defence of economic interests. It was also clear that the defence of these interests necessarily signified conflict and, as a result, what the new regime sought to eradicate: class struggle.

A differentiated conception of trade unionism thereby refused to adhere to the new institutional order. In the Oliveira Salazar Archive (AOS/ANTT), we found another objection to the imposition of the new corporatist order. This was a motion prepared by the group of railway workers, but unsigned — probably due to the restriction imposed on liberties at that time. Unlike the document mentioned above, this motion was not in the name of a trade union, but a group of workers.[32] Nevertheless, some similarities with the previous document were evident. In relation to the question of the so-called class struggle, which was abolished by section c) of Article 15, the Motion stated that 'the class struggle will remain no matter what, while the current capitalist system exists'. In addition, this group of trade unionists repudiated the restriction of liberties imposed by legislation, as well as the prohibition of support for strikes or international connections.[33]

In relation to Clause 1 of Article 15, which was binding on members of National Unions who were in full enjoyment of their civil and political rights, the criticisms of the members of the Union of Journalists were due to the fact that for them the political problems faced by each individual did not prevent them from being honourable and, moreover, this problem was outside the trade union organization.[34]

One of the limits imposed by the new legislation was on the General Assembly which could meet only once per year, for the purpose of electing its board. In relation to administration and the Union accounts, these were under the guardianship of INTP.[35] Thus the most important form of worker representation within the Union, the General Assembly, was weakened. Moreover, its deliberations had to be approved by the Sub-Secretary of State for Corporations. The predictable result was the weakening of union organization and subservience to the regime:

> So our dear members, see to what purpose associative action is reduced,

---

[31] Idem, fol. 6.
[32] Moção feita por um grupo de ferroviários não satisfeitos com a nova organização corporativa, criada pelo Decreto nº 23.050 de 23 de Setembro, representando, segundo eles, uma supressão das liberdades associativas e da luta de classes. (2 fols). ANTT — AOS/CO/PC10A.
[33] Idem.
[34] Parecer da Direcção do Sindicato dos Profissionais da Imprensa de Lisboa. Idem, fol. 7.
[35] Idem.

and the uselessness of our existence as a union. No autonomy is left to us, not even to freely elect our boards, whose members we necessarily know better than any other official entity.

In this way, in the future the Board of our Union will come to be only what our Governments wants. As in the corporatist organization there is the purpose of attributing political functions to Unions, we have to admit that the National Institute of Labour and Social Security seeks to assure in the Unions the influence favourable to the governments through boards of their confidence.[36]

Once again, in the analysis made above by union leaders, there was a clear dichotomy between a union with political purposes — and loyal to the regime — and a union with exclusively economic purposes — and gifted with autonomy. Another article deserving of critical annotations in the document was Article 20, complementary to the observations made above, which determined the loyalty of unions to public bodies:

> According to Article 20 the approval of statutes of National Unions would be withdrawn if they deviated from the purpose for which they were created, not fulfilling their statutes, not providing the government or bodies of public law with information requested about subjects of the specialist of the same unions, not duly performing the functions they have been or come to be entrusted with, holding or assisting strikes or suspensions of activity, or infringing the stipulations of this Decree Law, without prejudice to the personal responsibility of the administrative bodies and any other applicable penalties.
>
> As our members will verify, the simple fact of assisting any strike or suspension of activity — which can be legitimate and respectable occurrences, such as our 1921 strike — is the motive for dissolution and severe sanctions against the Board.[37]

A traditional definition of organizations with a corporatist nature can be found in Article 22. This determined that contracts and labour regulations signed by Unions should include the entire category of workers, and not only those who belonged to the Union. According to the document from the Journalists, this definition served even more to weaken the union organization, instead of strengthening it:

> Unless better stated, this doctrine does not appear to be of good logic. In the first place, because we understand that the individual, once he is not a member of the Union, should not use advantages or support sanctions which derive from union or corporatist action that he is not part of. Secondly, because that practice appears to us to be anti-union, since it could lead workers to be convinced that it is not in their interest to fulfil their moral and material interests of solidarity with the Union, and that it is not necessary to join in the sharing of advantages.[38]

---

[36] Idem, fol. 8.
[37] Idem, fol. 8–9.
[38] Idem, fol. 10.

Joining the Union was, for the agents responsible for the constitution of the corporatist order to the *Estado Novo*, an individual option. However, for the corporatist regime, there was a natural 'belonging', since there was just a single professional body. For this reason, the Union represented all those who were part of the same professional category.

The expectation of the *Estado Novo* was that there would be a spontaneous adhesion to the National Unions, like the other forms of corporatist organization, *Grémios*, *Casas do Povo*, and Orders. However, for this to occur, the opposition of various union sectors unwilling to accept state guardianship had to be confronted. For some, as in the case cited, the adhesion of new corporatist statutes was understood as an annulment of the autonomy of the Union:

> We cannot leave unrecognized, with the greatest serenity we have, that the statutes organized within this system will result in an instrument which will annul our associative life, due to their characteristics, while this utterly needless demand will represent an injustice that we cannot accept.[39]

At the end of the document, the measures of censorship imposed on the press and the restriction of liberties resulting from this are criticized:

> Allow us to explain, in ending this report, it is useful to emphasize that the continuation of the exercise of the Prior Censorship of the Press is strange, as it goes much beyond political reports, which as well as being in breach of the constitution, prevents press professionals from complying with their mission of informing the country, and is also in breach of Article 4 of Decree 23.048 (National Labour Statute), restricting the freedom of labour of journalists and causing them moral and material harm.[40]

At some moments the motion signed by the railway workers mentioned above has a more incisive and aggressive nature than the technical report presented to the journalists. According to the former:

> Considering that the organized working class has always rejected any type of collaboration with the state or with the business class because this was contrary to the interests of the workers, as is widely proven;
>
> Considering that this decree precisely imposes this collaboration under the direct action of the state, which is the same as saying the employers;
>
> Considering that this practice is antagonistic to the class struggle, in relation to our submission to the economic-capital structure, this is very harmful, since it is known that in their anxiety to maintain bourgeois privileges employers always harm employees;
>
> [...];
>
> RAILWAY WORKERS, meeting in a General Assembly, HAVE RESOLVED
> 1 Not to agree with this deliberation;
> 2 To advise all railway workers to obey the said laws in accordance with their conscience;
> 3 To charge the current Administrative Bodies to continue carrying out

[39] Idem, fol. 11.
[40] Idem, fols 11–12.

their positions and grants them full powers to act in accordance with the spirit of this motion.[41]

As can be noted, the document signed by the group of railway workers who were opposed to the new corporatist legislation not only had a more incisive discourse, but was also intended to persuade the railway workers in a General Assembly to decide not to adhere to the corporatist system. However, despite the differentiated methods, the content of both documents was the same: pessimism about the consequences which Decree Law 23.050 would have for workers and their representative entities.

Legality, Legitimacy, and Authority

In February 1933, the Minister of the Interior[42] received correspondence from the Board of the Association of Office Employees of Lisbon, requesting the reopening of their organization, closed four months previously, 'since nothing has been stated about the investigations which surely have been carried out'.[43] Perceiving the existence of an investigation on the part of the state, the workers only asked for the right to function, not questioning the legitimacy of the investigative procedure.

The state project which was beginning to be constructed consisted of a programme of inclusion combined with control over society as a whole and workers in particular. This was the reason for the investigative action of the Police. In these terms, the Police for the Social and Political Defence of Lisbon[44]

---

[41] Moção feita por um grupo de ferroviários... Ibid.
[42] Albino Soares Pinto dos Reis Júnior. A member of the political elite of the *Estado Novo* since its beginning, he was one of Salazar's most important councillors. Coming from the republican right, he soon aligned himself with the regime that was established in the 1930s. He was Civil Governor of Coimbra (1931–32) and Minister of the Interior (1932–33) in the period when the Policy of Defence and Social Policy was created. Despite his proximity to Salazar, in the post-war period he adopted a position closer to the reformist current led by Marcelo Caetano. Member of the Executive of the *União Nacional*, in 1933 he was nominated judge of the Supreme Administrative Court, being appointed its President three times. After 1935, he held various positions in the National Assembly, and was its president between 1942 and 1961. He presided at the Executive Commission of *União Nacional* and its V Congress, held in February 1970, as Salazar was impeded from doing so. He was appointed the same year president of the Consultative Commission of *Acção Nacional Popular*. Cf. Maria Inácia Rezola, 'REIS, Albino Soares Pinto dos (1888–1983)', in Fernando Rosas and José Maria Brandão de Brito (eds), *Dicionário de história do Estado Novo* (Lisbon: Círculo de Leitores, 1995), p. 826.
[43] Correspondence of the Fiscal Council of the Association of Office Workers of Lisbon, 19 February 1933, sent to the Minister of the Interior. ANTT/MI-GM, Maço 458/Cx 11.
[44] In relation to the police and repressive system of the *Estado Novo*, see Maria da Conceição Ribeiro, *A polícia política no Estado Novo, 1926–1945* (Lisbon: Estampa, 1995). We are not interested in an analysis of police actions during the *Estado Novo*, but it is interesting to note that it was characterized by an active role in combatting the adversaries of the regime, as well as maintaining relations with other European police bodies. In 1939, for example, a PVDE (Police for Surveillance and Defence of the State) agreement was signed with the Italian Police to establish aid and 'reciprocal collaboration in everything related to the fight against communism or which represents activities against the political systems of Italy and Portugal.' Cf: *Acôrdo Técnico entre a Direcção Geral da Polícia Italiana e a Polícia Portuguesa de Vigilância e Defesa do Estado*. ANTT/MI-GM, Maço 507/Cx. 65.

sent, in the same month, a report explaining the reasons for the closing of the offices of the association in question: 'The offices of the Association of Office Employees of Lisbon were sealed on 17 September of last year, after the arrest of the Lisbon Regional Committee of the Portuguese Communist Party, which was found holding a meeting there [...]'.[45] For the regime, it was necessary to reorganize a trade union model which would eliminate the ideological tradition of the previous class-based associations, even more so when dealing with a workers' organization that was not committed to the idea of nation as taught by the regime, since they were linked to international bodies: '[...] it also appears that this Association is a member of the Portuguese Section of International Red Aid, and also of the Inter-Union Commission, which is advised and directed by the Portuguese Communist Party.'[46] Also according to the report, after the meetings carried out in the offices of the Association of Office Employees, a revolutionary front was formed, composed of communist and anarcho-syndicalist factions: 'It sent its President, Viterbo de Campos, to the clandestine meeting of the Inter-union Commission, in which the foundations were approved on which the Single Front for Revolutionary Struggle, in other words union organizations, communists, and anarcho-syndicalists.'[47] Communism was, according to the regime's propaganda, at the same time a 'real danger' and a 'foreign threat'. It was thus seen as a threat that was not even European, being seen as an oriental phenomenon, alien to Western civilization. According to Faria:

> [...] an anti-communist sentiment radicalized the entire ideological discourse of the *Estado Novo* and we know how it combined various forms of intervention, principally by translating it into a complex network of actions and ideas of a political, economic, religious, cultural, military nature, etc., which affected all spheres of social life and remained encrusted throughout the political longevity of Salazarism.
>
> [...] Salazarism constantly fed on this anti-communism to create around itself unity and consensus against an alleged idea of invasion, danger, and chaos.[48]

Although it was not yet in the period understood as the *Estado Novo*, it was already evident that there was a need for a discourse of an external danger as a form of consolidating and achieving hegemony for the national project, and as a method of looking for consensus.

In April the representatives of the Board of Association of Office Workers of Lisbon sent further correspondence to the Ministry of the Interior calling for the reopening of the union in question. According to the correspondence:

---

[45] 'INFORMAÇÃO', 22 February 1933, from the Head of the Investigation Section of the Social and Political Defense Police. ANTT/MI-GM, Maço 458/Cx 11.
[46] Idem.
[47] Idem.
[48] Telmo Daniel Faria, 'O comunismo: um anátema estado-novista', in *Do Estado Novo ao 25 de Abril. Revista de História das Idéias*, 17 (1995), 229–62 (p. 231).

> The office workers, as Your Excellency the Minister is certainly not unaware, constitute an orderly class, always within the strictest legality, and they desire to raise and have respected their legitimate rights. For this reason, they founded in 1910, in accordance with the Law, their Class Association which always was characterized by the high level that has been characteristic of the resolution of questions inherent to its function.[49]

Contrary to official arguments, the representatives of office workers affirmed their strict commitment with legality. The problem was that this legalism implied the need for an organization which formally represented the interests of office workers, and this body did not exist:

> For six months, office workers have been without defence, have been prevented from having their Class Association meet, from formulating the complaints for those to whom they should be duly presented, from studying the problems of interest to their profession, from, in short, legally manifesting their right to life.
> If it continues, this situation could cause irreparable harm of a material order to the class of office workers, irrespective of others or a moral order which we do not need to talk about.[50]

The state, through the Chief of Staff of the Minister of the Interior, Manuel Ribeiro Ferreira, granted authorization to the President of the Board of the Association of Office Workers for the reopening of the entity, strictly to choose representatives for the Commission of Commerce, Industry, and Agriculture to be used to prepare a report about the regulation of the professions of book-keepers, accountants, and specialized book-keepers. The date and time of meetings were to be communicated in advance to the Police of Defence and Social Policy.[51] At the same time, the Chief of Staff of the Ministry of the Interior also informed the Director of Police that permission for the reopening of the Association of Office Workers was restricted solely to the choice of representatives of the Commission organized by the Ministry of Commerce, Industry, and Agriculture.[52]

Revealed in this episode is the prominent characteristic of corporatism in the regime which was beginning to be articulated in a more definitive manner. On the one hand, the punishment was maintained against a trade union entity ideologically linked to communism and therefore one that defended an anti-nationalist project. On the other hand, demands of a strictly professional interest had to be maintained, in order to preserve the value and the role of professional categories as a whole in the national construction project.

---

[49] Correspondence sent to the Ministry of the Interior, 3 April 1933, by the Fiscal Council of the Association of Office Workers of Lisbon. ANTT/MI-GM, Maço 458/Cx 11.
[50] Idem, fols 1–2.
[51] Correspondence dated 11 May 1933, from the Chief of Staff of the Ministry of the Interior, to the President of the Fiscal Council of the Association of Office Workers of Lisbon. ANTT/MI-GM, Maço 458/Cx 11.
[52] Correspondence 654-A, 11 May 1933, from the Chief of Staff of the Ministry of the Interior, Manuel Ribeiro Ferreira, to the Director of PDPS, 11 May 1933.

Strategies of Resistance, Survival, and Control

The decree laws which regulated the corporatist organization were received in an ambivalent manner by the Portuguese working class. As we have seen, there were those who immediately opposed the state project as they considered it authoritarian. At the same time there were also segments which were openly favourable to the new order of labour, either due to resignation to something difficult to change, or because they considered the state's action to be positive, to the extent that it could become an alternative framework for defending the interests of the workers themselves. Backed by the law they could act against the lack of interest of employers in meeting their demands. The state was thus present both for those who opposed the corporatist order, and for those who opted for adhesion.

In relation to the segments which preferred to resist the corporatization of the state, some alternatives were sought in order to guarantee survival strategies for anti-corporatist union organizations, some of them within the state itself. On the other hand, the state also sought to adopt strategies which could guarantee its control over the trade unions as a whole. In November 1933, the Chief of Staff of the Minister of the Interior, António Leite Cruz, sent correspondence to the civil governors warning that:

> [...] various worker organizations, not wanting to adapt their statutes to the new legislation of the corporatist state, have sought to maintain their current organizations, skilfully using for this the resource of transformation into recreational societies, whose authorizations are granted by the Civil Governors.[53]

He stated that the same had occurred with the bank workers of Lisbon, a majority of whom after passing a resolution favourable to the corporatization of the state, who saw part of their fellow professionals organize a *Grémio* (guild) of Bank Workers which, 'did not intend to be anything more than a legal mask, posing as a recreational association for an absolutely illegal class organization.' Moreover, Leite Cruz states that this *Grémio* of Bank Workers had already received authorization.[54] He also argued that certain precautions should have been taken at the moment of granting the authorizations, which included:

1) Rigorously ascertaining the intentions of the founders of the groups in question;
2) Not to consent to the names of these groups which caused any confusion with professional organizations, nor allow these to be exclusive to any class; and,

---

[53] Confidential Circular 1645, from the Chief of Staff of the Ministry of the Interior, 13 November 1933. ANTT/MI-GM, Maço 462/Cx 15.
[54] Idem. For an analysis of the Union of Bank Workers of Lisbon and their adhesion to the corporatist model see José Pedro Castanheira. *Os sindicatos e o salazarismo: a história dos Bancários do Sul e Ilhas* (Lisbon: Ed. Sindicato dos Bancários do Sul e Ilhas, 1983).

3) In the case of doubt, to consult the Sub-Secretary of State for Corporations and Social Security.[55]

The groups which opposed the implementation of corporatism at its very beginning demonstrated that the only possibility of survival was a measured adaptation to the new structure. And they sought to do this through the institutional 'breaches' permitted by the regime itself. It was thus from within the state that it could be resisted. Opponents to the union model imposed from above could at the very most confront the regime *through* the corporatist order they alleged they were combatting. It was a strategy which, instead of corroding the new order, ended up giving it legitimacy.[56]

Later Answers to Decree 23.050

Reception of Decree Law 23.050 was variable, as we have seen, although it was predominantly linked to choices in favour of adhesion to the new model of labour organization. At the beginning of February 1934, the National Union of Workers in the Bakery Industry, a group which the previous year had adhered to the new union structure, called a meeting. With the participation of 100 individuals in the assembly, the president of the section lamented the restricted number of those present, when dealing with 'such a numerous class'.[57] After this, he lamented the lack of mobilization of the category of workers, stating that many only joined the Union after gaining privileges, considering that those who acted this way were worse than employers, since the latter acted in accordance with their own interests. Furthermore, 'they did not know how to carry out their duties'.[58]

A constant fact in the life of Portuguese trade unionism in the first years of the *Estado Novo* was the struggle for respect for and compliance with official working hours. Common in assemblies was the presence of a representative of the state, either from the PSP (Public Security Police) or from INTP. However, the presence of an official representative did not inhibit workers from not only presenting in an explicit form their demands of a corporatist nature, but also from making constant denunciations of employers. On the contrary, the official presence gave security to these workers. The protector state once again was not only present but also, and above all, became the vector of workers' demands.

[55] Confidential Circular ...
[56] Once again the Portuguese case is similar to the Brazilian. The argument of the opposition 'within' the state machine only strengthened it over the years. In relation to this, see Leôncio Martins Rodrigues, 'O sindicalismo corporativo no Brasil', in *Partidos e sindicatos: escritos de sociologia política* (São Paulo: Ática, 1990), pp. 46–76; Francisco Carlos Palomanes Martinho, 'O estatismo sindical e a transição democrática: um estudo sobre o Sindicato dos Metalúrgicos do Rio de Janeiro', in José Ricardo Ramalho and Marco Aurélio Santana (eds), *Trabalho e tradição sindical no Rio de Janeiro: a trajetória dos metalúrgicos* (Rio de Janeiro: DP & A/Faperj, 2001), pp. 213–47.
[57] *Comando da Polícia de Segurança Pública — Secção de Informações do Comando*. ANTT/MI-GM, Maço 468/Cx. 21.
[58] Idem.

At the end of the session, the idea of the *Estado Novo* was explained as an important reference for the defence of workers against their employers:

> Afterwards, the president of the board asked the union of the class, protesting against the industrialists since these demanded 106 kilos of bread from 75 kilos of floor, in this way forcing them to shamelessly rob the public. They will only stop doing this when they have committed themselves to take the necessary measures. They ended up lamenting that the workers did not know how to take advantage of the situation of the *Estado Novo*, since this is the path of truth opened by Salazar [...].[59]

One of the national unions that was organized after 1934 was the Bakers' Union. The assembly which decided to create the union was held on 9 February, at which 400 members participated. The new statutes, in accordance with the spirit of Decree 23.050, were immediately accepted by unanimity.[60] Nevertheless, tension could be perceived between the former leaders, opposed to adhesion to the state model, and the new leaders. According to one of the participants of the assembly, the former board had mortgaged the union's furniture, while a motion demanding the return of its property was passed, which was signed by the organizing commission of the union. Otherwise, the intervention of the relevant authorities would be requested.

With the title of National Union, the Bakers held another assembly in March, this time under the presidency of Alfredo da Fonseca, secretary of the Ministry of the Interior.[61] The assembly counted on the participation of approximately 500 individuals. In addition to the optimism of the new organization of labour, in the assembly divergences were expressed in relation to the former board of the Class Association of Bakers:

> [...] Alfredo Dias Pires said that the new Union would have important benefits for the class of bakers, adding that the government was only interested in the welfare of workers. He accused the former board of the extinct class association of having caused its demoralization. He ended by praising His Excellency the President of the Ministry, due to the good will which it had always shown in protecting the working classes.
> [...]
> Hermínio Alexandre attacked the same board of the extinct association for the manner in which it always dragged the working class away from the path of order, considering themselves satisfied that the bread workers had been duly organized.[62]

The representativeness of the assembly demonstrated that, even before the implementation of corporatist policies, among Portuguese workers there were segments favourable to a trade union organization more sympathetic to dialogue with the state. Even considering that the former class association was

[59] Idem.
[60] Idem.
[61] Idem.
[62] Idem.

representative, the possible advantages of a trade union organization more inclined to public order should not be ruled out. This resulted in its adhesion to the corporatist model, principally at the beginning, when the expectations about changes in the living conditions of workers were considerable.

The following month, the National Bakers' Union met again. The meeting was held on 19 April 1934 and 150 members of the Union participated. In addition to constant complaints about employers, a proposal was presented by the board, approved unanimously, according to which the class would thank, 'in an orderly demonstration the constituent powers for the manner in which they had been attended', as well as a representation containing all the complaints.[63] Also approved was a proposal making the Sub-Secretary of State for Corporations, Pedro Teotónio Pereira,[64] an honorary member of the Union.[65]

Finally, in May a meeting was held which approved the letter sent to the Sub-Secretary of State for Corporations.[66] Although the letter was signed in the name of Joaquim Dias, it was passed in an assembly, so that it could represent the union as a whole. At the beginning the correspondence left clear the workers' commitment and support for the *Estado Novo* and the corporatist organization:

> The Corporatist state is, for us workers, a masterpiece by Your Excellency; it will consolidate the *Estado Novo*.
> Through the Corporatist State the working classes will satisfy many of their most legitimate aspirations which cost them years of struggle, suffering, and blood.
> Defending the Corporatist State is, to an extent, defending the interests of the working classes; thus its defence is imposed on all of them.[67]

While the struggles of the past were recognized by the workers as being an important period, albeit one marked by so much suffering, the *Estado Novo* and the corporatist organization which it gave form to, represented the final conquest of an objective. Resulting from this was the necessity and the obligation for the working class to defend it. However, to defend the corporatist

---

[63] Idem.
[64] An activist in Portuguese *Integralism* in his youth, he immediately became one of the most important collaborators of the *Estado Novo*. In 1933, he held the position of Sub-Secretary of State of Corporations and Social Security and in 1936, Minister of Commerce and Industry. The following year he was appointed a 'special agent' of the Portuguese government to the Francoist regime during the Spanish Civil War. In 1938, at the end of the War, he was appointed Portuguese Ambassador to Spain, organizer of the Portuguese-Spanish Treaty of Friendship and Non-Aggression, which formalized the recognition of the frontiers of the two Iberian states and affirmed the reciprocal friendship of the two countries. From 1945 to 1947, he was ambassador in Brazil. In 1958, after being representative of the Portuguese government in Washington and London, he was appointed Minister of Social Security. Cf. Fernando Rosas, 'PEREIRA, Pedro Teotónio (1902–1972)', in Fernando Rosas and José Maria Brandão de Brito (eds), *Dicionário de história do Estado Novo* (Lisbon: Círculo de Leitores, 1996), pp. 718–19.
[65] *Comando da Polícia de Segurança Pública — Secção de Informações do Comando*. Ibid.
[66] *Carta Aberta dos Manipuladores do Pão ao Ilustríssimo e Excelentíssimo Sub-Secretário de Estado das Corporações*. Idem.
[67] Idem.

state it was necessary to take action to uproot from the category those who were hostile to it, linked to the past of the organization and to struggles which at that moment no longer had any meaning:

> The Corporatist State is suffering from *'Meneur'* (i.e., agitators), a new type of serious attack; thus in the class of bakers and the distributers of bread in Lisbon, able criminal people have stealthily managed to establish themselves in the corporatist organization of the class and, like inconsistent puppets, expect to play great roles fulfilling the wishes of the puppet masters of these <u>old ones</u> who have caused us so much harm.[68]

It can immediately be deduced that these 'old ones,' underlined in the letter, were the left-wing groups which controlled the former class association in the period before the 1930s — 'old' groups, and therefore alien to the 'new order.' However, as well as these, the letter was also aimed at groups already connected to the corporatist state, who, bloated with this authority, exploited the Union. Thus:

> We already went to Your Excellency in order to formalize our complaint against the people who are there, because they are worse than those who were in charge in the old organization. It is worse, much worse! The people were dangerous to the Estado Novo, but did not repudiate what they were doing, and some are paying for silliness that they believe to be a healthy doctrine.[69]

The intention of this letter was to express discontent with the organizing committee of the new National Union which, stating that it was in line with the interests of the *Estado Novo*, did not hesitate in taking the advantages given to them. The leaders of the former class association were at fault because of their ideological projects, but they were recognized as individuals who believed in their projects and also believed that they were acting to the benefit of the class. 'However, the ones now, they are turncoats who make false confessions of faith, thus they are doubly dangerous. These are without the intellectual or moral capacity to propagate good, and are fertile in artifices to do harm.'[70]

However, the demarcation with the 'subversive' past came shortly afterwards, in reporting the real intentions of those who had participated in the organization of the new National Union. According to the letter, ties with what was worst from the past were evident:

> They have formed an organizing commission for the National Union, not with the noble intention of saving and redeeming a suffering and badly judged class; not to give form and life to the splendorous conception of the Corporatist State, which has been presented to the working masses of the country in the name of Your Excellency as a reformer and protector, one of the rare men who very infrequently emerge in the history of humanity,

[68] Idem.
[69] Idem.
[70] Idem.

have joined to free a friend who the police had arrested as a result of the last revolutionary strike. Was he an angel? No! He was a former deportee, the pensioner of the previous Union![71]

In the document a certain ambivalence can be perceived in relation to the past, in particular towards the old class association. At the same time that the efforts and honesty of the previous directors were praised, their ideological and antinational deviations were criticized. Similarly, the administrative incapacity of the group which proposed to organize the Nation Union of Bakers was also criticized:

> On the Board is there a treasurer? Yes, but simply an honorary one, because not having the capacity other than to idealize a bookkeeper, who writes the inventory, the cash flow, and current accounts, [...], the treasurer is actually a member of the Board who performed those functions in the previous union and the class accuses him of indulging himself with significant amounts, [...], which was done without hearing, without consulting the Board.[72]

Also according to the correspondence, the organizing commission had breached the law, falsifying the documents necessary for the new union organization:

> They circumvented the Law of the Corporatist State, specifically when this required the foundation to send the name of one hundred members, because some of these names are pure fantasy; neither are they members nor do they belong to the class!
>
> Without respect for the statues and for the Law, when the presidency of the Board became open, a great child was imposed in this place as the secretary of the general assembly and in his place promoted a strange friend; about the latter, we did not dare investigate the police records of this person, as we were afraid.[73]

Order was an inviolable principle and for this reason the irregularities which had occurred in the National Union of Bakers had to be eliminated. The Unions, although linked to law and order, were also seen as instruments of struggle and for the guarantee and defence of collective interests and in this way they entered permanently into conflict with the employer class. Despite the ambiguity towards the old members of the class association, an idea of fidelity to the Corporatist State was common, without, however, abandoning mobilization against private privileges, both of employers and parts of their own class. Despite the political engineering, to a large extent successful, constructed by the regime, the fact should not be denied that unionized workers were adapted to the political project in accordance with their conveniences. They thus had relative autonomy in terms of their behaviour.

The bakers remained mobilized throughout 1934, defending the *Estado Novo*

---

[71] Idem.
[72] Idem.
[73] Idem.

at the same time that they demanded their rights. Two questions remained on the agenda: the problem of fines and the question of working hours. In a meeting held in August, the members of the Union approved two representations to be delivered to the Minister of the Interior and the Sub-Secretary of State for Corporations and Social Security. In both of these, changes were requested in regard to fines and more rigorous compliance with working hours.[74] In relation to fines, the problem had existed since the beginning of the year. In the meeting on the third of February, there were expressions of discontent about the fines applied to workers, when these should have been applied to the employers, since these determined the measures for the baking of bread.[75] As far as can be seen, the problem still continued in October. Moreover, like various other categories of workers, working time was a chronic problem, since inspection on the part of the state was difficult.[76] According to the legislation, bakeries now had to operate during the day, considered by workers to be an advance and a conquest of the Corporatist State.[77] However, there remained the need for rigid inspection for this to be actually implemented.

Also in August, the National Union of Bakers met again. The tensions experienced since February continued, for which reason the board of the Union resigned with new members being chosen to replace them. As well as the resignation of the board, the problem of fines continued, causing reactions of insubordination to order by some members of the category: 'José Gonçalves declared that he thought the fines which are being applied to the bakers to be exaggerated, and counselled the transgressors not to pay the fines, since, in his understanding, only in this way would they see their complaints responded to.'[78] In a meeting accompanied by a representative of the PSP and an Inspector from the Sub-Secretariat of Corporations, the motion of rebellion presented by the trade unionist should be highlighted. Once again this type of attitude disqualified the myth of a monolithic state at the service of interests of its bureaucracy or its dominant class. In the meeting of the following month, September, the key issue continued to be working times:

> Alfredo Dias Pires, who spoke first, after reading an article about bread, recently published in the newspaper *O Século*, said that working hours were being studied by the competent authorities, although the millers were exerting pressure for the bakers' demands not to be met. Next, he read a document referring to working hours, in which were named various countries where eight hours a day were worked with one day's rest per week. He ended by saying that only in Portugal did bakers have difficulty in getting to work eight hours.[79]

[74] *Comando da Polícia de Segurança Pública...* Idem.
[75] Idem.
[76] Idem.
[77] Idem.
[78] Idem.
[79] Idem.

In turn, the board of the Union was also the target of criticism by the assembly, due to its slowness in dealing with questions related to the demands of bakers: 'Hermínio Alexandre said that the board of the Union had still not satisfactorily informed the class of the progress of its submissions to the relevant authorities. He attacked the millers as they were the cause of why the question of working hours had not been resolved.'[80]

It thereby became necessary for new submissions be made to the authorities in order to satisfy the bakers' interest. While resorting to the state signified an attempt to guarantee rights, it also represented a defence against the permanent accusations made by employers that saw bakers, and indeed all mobilized professional categories, as enemies of order.[81]

Finally, the last meeting of the Lisbon bakers was held in October.[82] The problems related to working hours raised tensions among the workers to such an extent that at the beginning of the assembly the chairperson asked that those present remain calm when discussing this subject, and then let the INTP representative, Castro Fernandes, chair the session. In addition to the struggle for an eight hour working day, the bakers also sought to put into effect their right to have a day of rest on Sundays. The demand of the Lisbon union was consistent with those of the other regions: 'Josué Teixeira, a delegate from the bakers of Setúbal, read a document from his class association supporting the eight hour working day and a day of rest on Sunday, in addition to demonstrating solidarity with his comrades from Lisbon.'[83]

What appears here is the horizontal behaviour of workers, connected to common objectives. Obviously these are workers from the same professional areas. However, the connections and the solidarity demonstrated reflect collective behaviour which, as mentioned above, went beyond the expectations of the *Estado Novo*. In fact, in the clashes which occurred during the period studied between the state and employers, what can also be noted is that the proximity between workers and official agencies was often very intense. This can be seen in the affirmations of Castro Fernandes, the INTP representative:

> Castro Fernandes praised the working classes for the seriousness with which they dealt with things, and stated that the National Institute of Labour had taken over the defence of these classes.
>
> After having shown the great advantage that the eight hour working day would bring, he said that in Portugal there was no tyranny, but rather a desire to protect all those who worked and did not know how to defend themselves.[84]

Sunday was thus to be preserved as a day of rest, with another day not being

---

[80] Idem.
[81] Idem.
[82] Idem.
[83] Idem.
[84] Idem.

accepted even if they were paid double.⁸⁵ In these episodes, which occurred in relation to the struggle of the state to implement corporatism, the bakers demonstrated behaviour that was constant amongst all the professional categories studied in this paper: a political position favourable to the *Estado Novo* and an interpretation of corporatist legislation which helped achieve their objectives. Thus they did not submit to what was immediately determined by the state or to what this state expected of them.

The Corporatist State: First Impressions

Linked to INTP, SAS (*Serviços de Acção Social* — Social Action Services) was created to accompany the activities of the National Unions. Created under the auspices of the December 1933 National Labour Statute, it sought to ensure that corporatist organization became fully functioning as quickly as possible.

In July 1934, the Services Director of SAS wrote to the Sub-Secretary of State for Corporations presenting an initial balance of the agency's actions. Based on these documents, it is possible to determine the opinion of state agents about the possibilities of the consolidation of corporatism in Portugal. According to the author, various consultations were made about corporatist organization and the procedures necessary for its implementation. Consultations not only about the National Unions, but also about *Casas do Povo* and *Grêmios*. Even the class associations which did not transform themselves into National Unions presented complaints and requests which, when considered fair, were met. Due to the non-functioning of the Labour Courts, the *Assistentes* carried out various conciliatory interventions, which in general were successful. In addition, SAS also drafted the first collective labour contract, between the *Sociedade Sines Lmdᵃ* company and the National Union of Tejo Dockworkers, while also preparing a contract to be signed by the National Union of Coopers and the Wine Exporter Guilds.⁸⁶

Despite the evident advances, some difficulties were encountered. One was in relation to monitoring of working times but, despite some interventions being made, notably in the Borges e Irmão and Espírito Santo banks, the efficiency of this service left a lot to be desired.⁸⁷

The Director of SAS then highlighted the most constant difficulties in the implementation of his services. The first was the resistance encountered in many actual government departments, causing delays and difficulties in the resolution of various subjects. Second, was employer resistance to collaboration with the agencies of the Corporative State, not only creating bottlenecks for the development of the new union structure, but also persecuting leaders of the

---

⁸⁵ Idem.
⁸⁶ 'RELATÓRIO CONFIDENCIAL', by the Services Director of SAS [illegible signature], 10 July 1934. AHMQE, fols 1/2.
⁸⁷ Idem., fol. 2.

National Unions. Finally, the third difficulty was due to the fact that Unions were not carrying out the new role assigned to them, with many intending to continue to use previous forms of conduct, 'just surreptitiously'.[88] In relation to this problem, on the part of the Director of SAS, there were no great surprises, as he pointed to paths that could overcome the former impasses experienced by the corporatist organization:

> However, this difficulty does not constitute any surprise to us, since there could not be any intention of having ready to be placed before all the unions a prepared elite, real leaders.
>
> As a result, continual vigilance of the unions and the systematic indoctrination of their members was necessary. The first part would as far as possible be carried out by these Services, which would immediately start to carry out regular inspection visits of the National Unions of Lisbon; [...][89]

Despite the efforts and strategies adopted, the SAS representative in Lisbon also stated that an accentuated dismay hung over workers due to the difficulties highlighted above. According to union leaders these had caused a fall in the initial enthusiasm, which at that moment no longer made sense. In addition, at that time some National Unions had begun to lose members, a fact of unequivocal concern for the architects of the corporatist organization.[90]

Conclusion

The analysis of the initial period of Portuguese corporative syndicalism does not allow us to assess its greater or lesser effectiveness. The majority of works about the question lead us to believe in its fragmentation and, as a result, in its ineffectiveness. This is the case of the studies, for example, by Manuel de Lucena and Fátima Patriarca. Patriarca even states that the regime was concerned with 'isolating and fragmenting, in other words, weakening the union organization.'[91] Outside of Portugal, research carried out by Philippe Schmitter and Howard Wiarda has also pointed in this direction.[92] The question, though, is 'weakening' in relation to *what* or to *whom*. If a comparison is made with the periods of Constitutional Monarchy or the First Republic, we can point in this case to the effectiveness of the corporative unions. The fragility and incapacity of significant conquests in the former two periods are, on the one hand,

---

[88] Idem.
[89] Idem, fols 3–4.
[90] Idem, fols 4–5.
[91] Manuel de Lucena, *Evolução do Sistema Corporativo Português*, vol. I: *O Salazarismo* (Lisbon: Perspectivas e Realidades, 1976), p. 234: Fátima Patriarca, *A questão social no Salazarismo*, pp. 283–84.
[92] Philippe C. Schmitter, *Corporatism and Public Policy in Authoritarian Portugal* (London and Beverly Hills: Sage, 1975); idem, *Portugal: do autoritarismo à democracia* (Lisbon: Imprensa de Ciências Sociais, 1999); Howard J. Wiarda, *Corporatism and Development: The Portuguese Experience* (Amherst: University of Massachusetts Press, 1979).

striking.[93] At the same time, as Barrington Moore Jr demonstrated in his study of workers in the Ruhr, fragmentation is not a synonym of demobilization, nor do large conglomerates signify greater mobilization.[94] The fact is that, daring to disagree with the above mentioned authors, the institutionalization of unions led workers to the recognition of these organizations, and at the same time, the recognition of employer opposition, highlighted by state agents themselves. Furthermore, to the extent that the conquests, even if timid, were directed at the entire category of workers, and not only union members, the relatively small number of unionized workers stopped being a significant problem.[95]

Finally, in relation to the attitudes of men and women who experienced the Portuguese dictatorship and corporatism, it is worth remembering Febvre's phrase, once again cited by Laborie: 'history is a form of organizing the past so that it does not weigh too much on the shoulders of men'.[96] It is thus licit to state that those who live through or study dictatorships organize the past in such a way that it becomes more palatable in the eyes of contemporaries. Far from hiding the past, it appears to us more licit to seek to understand the reasons for acceptance. It is not for us to either construct a memory of resistance nor to resist the memory. *Que no es lo mismo, pero es igual*. It is true that there were confrontations, but it is also true that the longevity of Salazarism gave the social movements a certificate in incompetence if we say that the choice for resistance was the predominant option. What we can call a *grey zone*, returning to the beginning of the text, is exactly this: a space of conflict and acceptance; of Salazarism and anti-Salazarism: everything at the same time. Without wanting to exhaust the theme, and causing more doubts than reaching conclusions, Adam Przeworski's proposal seems stimulating to us:

> Individuals face choices and one choice might be to become a worker and another choice might be to cooperate with other workers. But they do have choices, and we must analyze the entire structure of choice as given to individuals, not to workers. For it may be that there exist conditions under which their choice is to become workers and cooperate with

---

[93] In relation to trade unions and unions prior to the emergence of the *Estado Novo*, see Manuel Villaverde Cabral, *O operariado nas vésperas da República (1909-1910)* (Lisbon: Presença, 1977); João Freire, *Anarquistas e operários: ideologia, ofício e práticas sociais: o anarquismo e o operariado em Portugal, 1900-1940* (Lisbon: Afrontamento, 1992); Alexandre Samis, *Minha pátria é o mundo inteiro: Neno Vasco, o anarquismo e o sindicalismo revolucionário em dois mundos* (Lisbon: Letra Livre, 2009).
[94] Barrington Moore Jr, *Injustiça: as bases sociais da obediência e da revolta* (São Paulo: Brasiliense, 1987), Chapter 7: 'Militancy and apathy in the Ruhr before 1914', pp. 316-80.
[95] Not by chance, when he was already General Secretary of the Portuguese Communist Party, Álvaro Cunhal, at the beginning of the 1940s, defended the entrance of communists into the National Trade Unions. This question is discussed in greater detail in Francisco Martinho, *A bem da Nação: o sindicalismo português entre a tradição e a modernidade (1933-1947)* (Rio de Janeiro: Civilização Brasileira/FAPERJ, 2002). In relation to the decision of communists to enter the National Unions, see 'A frente única e o trabalho nos sindicatos nacionais', in *O PCP e a luta sindical: documentos para a história do Partido Comunista Português* (Lisbon: Avante!, 1975), pp. 21-26.
[96] Pierre Laborie, 'Memória e opinião', in Cecília Azevedo and Ana Maria Mauad (eds), *Cultura política, memória e historiografia* (Rio de Janeiro: Editora FGV, 2009), p. 97.

capitalists against other workers and the optimality of this strategy may be incomprehensible if we truncate the choice set by viewing individuals as ready-made workers.[97]

For Fátima Patriarca, *in memoriam*.

---

[97] Adam Przeworski, *Capitalism and Social Democracy* (Cambridge: Cambridge University Press, 1987), p. 97.

Portuguese Origins and the 'True' Brazil: The Corporative Vision of Oliveira Viana

Luciano Aronne de Abreu

Pontifícia Universidade Católica do Rio Grande do Sul

The 1920s were a decade of vivacity in Brazil. Not only in regards to disputing hegemonic models of cultural production and political and social order, but also the proposal of different ways of overcoming its problems and building a 'true' Brazilian nation, as it was called by the conservative intellectuals of the 'geração dos anos 1920–40' [1920–40 generation].[1] On the one hand, different workers' strikes (1917), the founding of the Brazilian Communist Party (1922), the Modern Art Week in São Paulo (1922), and the *tenente* revolts (1922) are seen as examples of growing discontent with the Brazilian political and social realities of the time. On the other hand, different politicians and intellectuals tried to speak on the nation's behalf and answer its demands in the National Congress, the press, or even through the publishing of 'scientific' works. They tried to induce a broad discussion in order to build a new social and political order in the country. A 'true' and unified modern nation.

This study, however, does not intend to analyse the aforementioned movements and their claims,[2] but only to understand the foundations and meaning of the 'true' Brazilian nation, its Portuguese origins, and its corporative future, based on the work of Francisco José de Oliveira Viana,[3] regarded by historiographers

---

[1] Daniel Pécaut, *Os intelectuais e a política no Brasil: entre o povo e a nação* (São Paulo: Ática, 1989), p. 22.
[2] There is an extensive bibliography on these subjects in Brazil. For example, refer to: César Augusto Bubolz Queirós, 'Estratégias e identidades: relações entre governo estadual, patrões e trabalhadores nas grandes greves da Primeira República em Porto Alegre (1917–1919)' (unpublished doctoral thesis, UFRGS, Porto Alegre, 2012); Luigi Biondi, 'Entre associações étnicas e de classe: os processos de organização política e sindical dos trabalhadores italianos na cidade de São Paulo (1890–1920)' (unpublished doctoral thesis, UNICAMP, 2002); Neide Luzia de Rezende, *A Semana de Arte Moderna* (São Paulo: Ática, 2006); Edgar Carone, *Tenentismo: acontecimentos, personagens, programas* (Rio de Janeiro: DIFEL, 1975); Vavy Pacheco Borges, *Tenentismo e revolução brasileira* (São Paulo: Brasiliense, 1992).
[3] Francisco José de Oliveira Viana was born on 20 July 1883, in Saquarema, Rio de Janeiro, and died in Niterói, Rio de Janeiro, on 28 March 1951. Having finished high school at the Colégio Pedro II (Rio de Janeiro), he went to the Free Law School of Rio de Janeiro, where he graduated in 1905. He acted as a lecturer in Criminal Proceedings and Social Law in the Law School of Niterói. In public administration, he worked as Director of the Institute for the Development of Rio de Janeiro (1926); member of the Advisory Council of the State of Rio de Janeiro (1931); Legal Advisor for the Ministry of Labour, Industry and Trade (1932–40); member of the Special Commission for Federal Constitution Review (1933); member of the Commission for Law Revision in the Justice Ministry (1939); and Minister of the Federal Court of Auditors (1940). During his professional career, he also acted as a columnist in many media outlets, such as: *A Ordem* (Saquarema), *Diário Fluminense* and *A Capital* (Niterói),

as the 1920–40 intellectual generation's main representative.[4]

It should be noted that even though the historiography dedicated to the analysis of his work is extensive, there are almost no biographies of the author,[5] and a great many of these studies highlight the authoritarianism and racism in Oliveira Viana's thought, sidelining other topics and focusing only on these matters. Owing to his contribution to Getúlio Vargas's government and his support for the dictatorship of 1937, Oliveira Viana's work was targeted by left-wing and liberal intellectuals, especially after his death in 1951. According to José Murilo de Carvalho, slandering Oliveira Viana became one of his favourite sports, calling the author 'racista, elitista, estatista, corporativista, colonizado, nas críticas mais analíticas. Reacionário, quando a emoção tomava conta do crítico' [racist, elitist, statist, corporatist and colonized, in the more analytical criticisms. Reactionary, when criticism gave way to emotion].[6] Carvalho concludes: 'Oliveira Viana foi mandado aos infernos' [Oliveira Viana was sent to hell].[7]

Recently, however, especially from the 1990s onwards, perhaps because of the end of a long period of military dictatorship, historians and social scientists have revisited Oliveira Viana's works looking for the roots of Brazilian authoritarianism. Yet, such studies did not seek to rescue the author from the hells he was banished to, as observed by José Murilo de Carvalho in his own analysis, but to have him and his work go through 'um julgamento menos marcado por circunstâncias políticas passadas' [a judgement less marked by past political circumstances].[8]

A Revista da Semana, Correio Paulistano, A Manhã, Jornal do Comércio, O País, Revista do Brasil, Correio da Manhã, O Estado de São Paulo and also the *Revista de Estudos Jurídicos*. He also took part in many institutes and academies, such as: International Institute of Anthropology (Instituto Internacional de Antropologia); Portuguese Society of Anthropology and Ethnology (Sociedade Portuguesa de Antropologia e Etnologia); Portuguese Academy of History (Academia Portuguesa de História); Institute of Anthropology and Ethnology of Porto (Instituto de Antropologia e Etnologia do Porto); Brazilian Historic and Geographic Institute (Instituto Histórico e Geográfico Brasileiro); and Brazilian Academy of Letters (Academia Brasileira de Letras). Regarding his extensive and diverse intellectual production, the following should be highlighted as his main works: *Populações meridionais do Brasil* (1920); *Evolução do povo brasileiro* (1923); *O ocaso do Império* (1925); *Problemas de política objetiva* (1930); and *Instituições políticas brasileiras* (1949). For a bibliography of the author, refer to: Vasconcelos Torres, *Oliveira Viana: sua vida e sua posição nos estudos brasileiros de Sociologia* (Rio de Janeiro and São Paulo: Livraria Freitas Bastos, 1956). For an overview of his theories, refer to: Jarbas Medeiros, *Ideologia autoritária no Brasil* (Rio de Janeiro: FGV, 1978). For an analysis of his theories and his influences and relations to other intellectuals of the same generation, refer to: Daniel Pécaut, *Os intelectuais e a política no Brasil*; Maria Stella Bresciani, *O charme da ciência e a sedução da objetividade: Oliveira Viana entre intérpretes do Brasil* (São Paulo: UNESP, 2005).

[4] This study will only analyse Oliveira Viana's works from 1920 to 1945, which is the end of the Getúlio Vargas's Estado Novo — an authoritarian and mildly corporative political regime. Only the first editions of works from *Populações Meridionais do Brasil* to *Problemas de Direito Sindical* will be analysed.

[5] As of today, the only exception is the biography published in 1956, by Vasconcelos Torres, who was an admirer of Oliveira Viana and had easy access to sources through the author's family.

[6] José Murilo de Carvalho, *Pontos e bordados: escritos de história e política* (Belo Horizonte: UFMG, 1999), p. 203.

[7] Ibid.

[8] Ibid., p. 204.

Even though authoritarianism and racism may still be the focus of much of this analysis, scholars of his work started distinguishing between Oliveira Viana's diagnosis of Brazil's delayed development — its colonial past and lack of solidarity — and his prognosis for the building of a new authoritarian and corporative society. For example, Ângela de Castro Gomes noted that 'em seu diagnóstico o "insolidarismo" da sociedade brasileira, raiz mais profunda de seu atraso, tinha que ser entendido e vencido' [in his diagnosis, the lack of solidarity in Brazilian society, the deepest root of its backwardness, had to be understood and overcome], this being the key to explaining 'a complexidade, a longevidade e a profundidade dos nossos problemas' [the complexity, longevity and depth of our problems].[9] The author argues that Oliveira Viana suggests an alternative guideline that is at the same time 'uma forma de ação e de prognóstico político e intelectual' [a form of action and intellectual and political prognosis], having suggested a corporatism 'entendido como uma práxis, isto é, como um conjunto de ideias indissociáveis da ação' [conceived as a *praxis*, i.e. a set of ideas indistinguishable from action].[10]

It is not my intention here to cite every one of these studies, but merely to point out the main trends or interpretive currents regarding Oliveira Viana's theories and works. Among those, one can highlight three authors still considered to be important references for discussing the diagnoses and prognoses that Oliveira Viana made of the Brazilian society. These are Wanderley Guilherme dos Santos, who analyses Viana's thinking in terms of instrumental authoritarianism, Bolívar Lamounier, who focuses on state ideology, and José Murilo de Carvalho, who looks at Viana's Iberism. We will start our discussion in this article by looking briefly at these three contributions.

According to Wanderley Guilherme dos Santos, until the Revolution of 1930 liberal criticism of the political system emphasized the contradiction between constitutional liberalism and the common practices in political life being personalized, based on clientelism and relations with the so-called *coroneis* [colonels]. These practices did not result from constitutional issues, but rather from misconduct and deviation of principles by parties and their own leaders, concerned with their personal gain instead of the nation. However, the author noted that, still in the 1920s, Oliveira Viana had expressed clearly and for the first time the real dilemma of Brazilian liberalism — that a political system could not exist in the country without a liberal society, as Brazil 'não possui uma sociedade liberal, mas, ao contrário, parental, clânica e autoritária' [did not have a liberal society, but, on the contrary, one based on familial, clan and authoritarian principles].[11] According to Wanderley Guilherme dos Santos,

[9] Ângela de Castro Gomes, 'Oliveira Viana: do insolidarismo ao corporativismo', in Francisco Palomanes Martinho and Flávio Limoncic (eds), *Intelectuais do antiliberalismo: projetos e políticas para outras modernidades* (Rio de Janeiro: Civilização Brasileira, 2010), pp. 201–31 (p. 207).
[10] Ibid., p. 208.
[11] Wanderley Guilherme dos Santos, *Décadas de espanto e uma apologia democrática* (Rio de Janeiro: Rocco, 1998), p. 34.

Oliveira Viana concludes that Brazil 'precisa de um sistema político autoritário cujo programa econômico e político seja capaz de demolir as condições que impedem o sistema social de se transformar em liberal' [needs an authoritarian political system which has a political and economical programme capable of demolishing the conditions preventing the social system from becoming liberal].[12] As opposed to doctrinaire liberalism, seen as theoretical and unattached to real political practices, Oliveira Viana proposed what Wanderley Guilherme dos Santos calls instrumental authoritarianism, i.e. imposing an authoritarian political regime in the country so as to overcome its problems and to build a liberal society in the long term.

On the other hand, Bolívar Lamounier believes Oliveira Viana searches in the past for a diagnosis for the current problems, and at the same time, tries to legitimate the building of an authoritarian political and institutional model in the country. Thus, his authoritarianism would not be merely instrumental, a means to an end, but the more fitting political regime for the Brazilian reality. He argues that Oliveira Viana and other intellectuals linked to the authoritarian tradition in political thought had political action in mind, clearly intending to persuade the political and cultural elite of the time and to influence events. The transformation of the political line of thought at that time, as noted by Lamounier, should be perceived 'como a formação de um sistema ideológico orientado no sentido de conceituar e legitimar a autoridade do Estado como princípio tutelar da sociedade' [as a formation of an ideological system directed towards conceptualizing and legitimating the authority of the state as society's tutelary principle].[13] Defined by Lamounier as the concept of 'state ideology' as opposed to 'market ideology', this system is credited by the author with 'o intento de domesticar o mercado, e particularmente o princípio de mercado atuante nas relações políticas' [the intent to tame the market, specially the market principle acting in political relations].[14] Among its features, Lamounier highlights the prevalence of the state principle over the market principle, an organic-corporative view of society, technocratic objectivity, an authoritarian view of social conflict and the disorganization of civic society, absence of political mobilization, elitism, and what the author calls a benevolent Leviathan: the State (Leviathan) is seen as 'o guardião e a força vital de uma sociedade igualmente benevolente, "cordial" e cooperativa. Ele é benevolente porque a reflete em suas boas qualidades, e porque a corrige, severa, mas afetuosamente, nas más' [the guardian and vital energy of an equally benevolent, 'cordial' and cooperative society. It is benevolent because it reflects it in its good qualities and because it corrects its faults, harshly, but lovingly].[15]

---

[12] Ibid.
[13] Bolívar Lamounier, 'Formação de um pensamento político autoritário na Primeira República: uma interpretação', in Boris Fausto (ed.), *História Geral da Civilização Brasileira*, tomo III: *O Brasil Republicano*, vol. 2, ch. 10 (Rio de Janeiro: Bertrand Brasil, 2006), p. 384.
[14] Ibid., p. 385.
[15] Ibid., p. 400.

Despite acknowledging Oliveira Viana's connection to the conservative tradition of the Viscount of Uruguai,[16] and stating that these intellectuals[17] 'podem ser apropriadamente chamados de autoritários instrumentais, na medida em que o autoritarismo para eles era apenas um meio que certas sociedades, em certas circunstâncias, tinham que empregar para atingir o objetivo, a sociedade liberal plenamente desenvolvida' [may aptly be called instrumental authoritarians, in so far as their authoritarianism was only one means that certain societies, under certain circumstances, had to employ in order to achieve their objective, a fully developed liberal society],[18] José Murilo de Carvalho believes that his utopia can be defined by his concept of Iberism. Negatively, Iberism can be understood, according to Carvalho, 'como a recusa de aspectos centrais do que se convencionou chamar de mundo moderno. É a negação da sociedade utilitária individualista, da política contratualista, do mercado como ordenador das relações econômicas' [as a rejection of central aspects of what is conventionally called the modern world. It is the denial of an individualistic and utilitarian society, of a contractualistic political system, and of the market as the organizing principle of economic relations]. Positively, however, it can be understood as 'um ideal de sociedade fundada na cooperação, na incorporação, no predomínio do interesse coletivo sobre o individual, na regulação das forças sociais em função de um objetivo comunitário' [an ideal of a society based on cooperation, incorporation, the predominance of the collective interest over the individual, regulation of social forces in the service of a common goal].[19] Between the appreciation of a rural and patriarchal past and its conformation to the modern industrial and working-class world, José Murilo de Carvalho believes Oliveira Viana's utopia was building 'uma sociedade harmônica, incorporadora, cooperativa. O

---

[16] Paulino José Soares de Souza, Viscount of Uruguai (1854), was born in Paris on 4 October 1807, and died in Rio de Janeiro, on 15 July 1866. He studied until senior year in the Law School of Coimbra. After being sent to prison in Portugal for political reasons, he returned to Brazil and finished his studies in the Law School of São Paulo (1831). Professionally, he acted as Juiz de Fora (external judge, appointed by the monarch) and then Ombudsman of the District of São Paulo, making it as far as Associate Justice of the Court of Appeals (1852) and retired as Minister of the Supreme Court of Justice (1857). Politically, he held the following positions: Provincial Deputy (1836) and President of the Rio de Janeiro Province (1836), Minister of Justice (1840), Minister of Foreign Affairs (1843–44 and 1849–53), Senator of the Empire for the Conservative Party (1849) and Counsellor of State (1853). In 1862, he published his main work, 'Ensaio sobre o Direito Administrativo', a summary of his political thought, highlighting the discussion of differences in political centralization and administrative decentralization, both essential for overcoming the Brazilian development delay. For more information, refer to: Ivo Coser, *Visconde do Uruguai: centralização e federalismo no Brasil (1823–1866)* (Belo Horizonte: UFMG, 2008).
[17] According to José Murilo de Carvalho, Oliveira Viana's references to the organic intellectuals of the Empire, or the ones he considered having ideals built based on the national reality, included Olinda, Feijó, Paraná, Vasconcelos, Uruguai, Euzébio, Itaboraí and Caxias. To this extent, Carvalho states: 'Excluding Feijó, who was an authoritarian, we have the elite of the Imperial conservatism, the builders of the monarchic order. Oliveira Viana used to call them conservative-authoritarians [...]'. For more information, refer to: Carvalho, *Pontos e bordados*.
[18] Carvalho, *Pontos e Bordados*, p. 213.
[19] José Murilo de Carvalho, 'A Utopia de Oliveira Viana', in Élide Rugai Bastos and João Quartim de Morais (eds), *O pensamento de Oliveira Viana* (Campinas: UNICAMP, 1993), pp. 13–42 (p. 23).

corporativismo, o sindicalismo, a legislação social vinham trazer a resposta' [a harmonious, incorporated, cooperative society. Corporativism, unionism, and social legislation would bring the solution].[20]

Despite their different focuses on instrumental authoritarianism, state ideology, and Iberism, Wanderley Guilherme dos Santos, Bolívar Lamounier and José Murilo de Carvalho unanimously highlight Oliveira Viana's look to the past, his authoritarian thought, and his proposal of a corporative future for Brazilian society. Each in his own manner, these authors not only analyse Oliveira Viana's diagnosis for the Brazilian developmental backwardness, but also point out his prognosis of overcoming and building a new corporative society. In this sense, as aforementioned, I intend to advance the discussion of Oliveira Viana's diagnosis and prognosis for the construction of a 'true' Brazilian nation, or in other words, Brazil's Portuguese origins and its corporative future. Therefore, I emphasize the nationalistic meaning of the references to the past as well as to the future of Oliveira Viana's thought, both his diagnosis and prognosis for the developmental delay instead of his Iberian or authoritative features.

The Portuguese Origins of the Originality and Faults of Brazil

Searching for their own way of being and existing, Oliveira Viana and other contemporaries[21] had established an intricate web of ideas, preconceptions, and assumptions about the Brazilian colonial past, seeking its origins. In this regard, Maria Stella Bresciani points out that most interpreters of Brazil locate the foundation for their interpretation of the Brazilian past in the contrast between itself and others, with tones of resentment derived from a perception of two fundamental defects: 'o da natureza inadequada e o dos homens menos qualificados, daí os resultados pouco elogiáveis' [that of its inadequate nature and that of its poorly qualified men, hence the uncommendable results].[22] In this way, according to Bresciani, negativity and neediness were consolidated as a commonplace subject[23] in every academic and literary work about Brazil: 'nossa identidade se constitui na falta, naquilo que não tivemos, na ausência de predicados, na incapacidade de triunfar. Há um vazio a ser preenchido, se possível for' [our identity is built upon the absence, upon that which we do not have, upon the lack of predicates, upon the incapacity to succeed. There is a void to be filled, if possible].[24]

---

[20] Carvalho, *Pontos e bordados*, p. 223.
[21] Intellectuals like Paulo Prado, Sílvio Romero, Euclides da Cunha, Sérgio Buarque de Holanda, and Gilberto Freire can be cited as examples. In this regard, refer to Bresciani, *O charme da ciência*, ch. 2.
[22] Bresciani, *O charme da ciência*, p. 104.
[23] According to Maria Stella Bresciani, 'commonplace' should not be read as a cliché or a banality, but as 'common' places, i.e. a 'shared group of ideas, notions, theories, beliefs and assumptions, allowing for the exchange of words and arguments about an effective political community' (Myriam R. D'Allones, apud Bresciani, p. 41). In this regard, refer to Bresciani, *O charme da ciência*.
[24] Ibid., p. 108.

However, the ambiguous character of these interpretations about the national past should be observed, associating the Brazilian nation's originality both to the negative and positive points of its Iberian origins. Negatively, the Portuguese culture of direct personal relationshops would result in a 'lukewarmness of the forms of organization that result in solidarity and ordering'; its repulsion of the 'work ethic and cult' would result in a lowering of the 'active virtues' of manual labour in favour 'inactive virtues'; Portuguese blind obedience would result in our 'disposition to follow orders'; the Portuguese liking for routine would impede technical progress on the *latifundia*; and their lack of racial pride would make Brazilians a mixed people. Positively, though, sensibility, mobility and the Iberian's unique capacity to adapt would be its main qualities.[25]

However, Oliveira Viana's ambiguity about the past should not be mistaken for a negative view of the Portuguese origins. On the contrary, he idealized the colonial past stating that colonization in Brazil was started by the highest Portuguese nobles and then followed by commoners who would ruralize the colonial society, based upon latifundia. Following Independence, the dispersion of latifundia and the concentrated power of the landed aristocracy would be taken negatively by Oliveira Viana as obstacles to unifying and building the Brazilian nation. According to Bernardo Ricupero, Oliveira Viana's analysis of latifundia changes according to the historical moment analysed. During the colonial period, latifundia would be 'o principal instrumento de adaptação do colono europeu ao ambiente americano' [the main instrument for adapting the European colonist to the American environment]; while after Independence, given its self-sufficiency, it would be regarded as the 'impedimento mais sério para a tarefa de unificação nacional que então se imporia' [most serious obstacle to the task of national unification that was then pressing].[26] In this regard, although referring widely to Oliveira Viana's interpretation of the colonial past, Arno Wehling noted that it would represent the possibility for him to confirm his central thesis: 'a força do clã rural, a inorganicidade social e a plasticidade dos estadistas portugueses que, ao contrário dos políticos "idealistas" do Império, que perseguiam a unidade, adaptaram-se à diversidade das formas regionais de poder' [the strength of the rural clan, social disarray and the plasticity of Portuguese statesmen who, unlike the 'idealist' politicians of the Empire, who sought unity, adapted themselves to the diversity of regional forms of power].[27]

---

[25] These features were summarized from Maria Stella Bresciani comparing Sérgio Buarque de Holanda's, Oliveira Viana's and Gilberto Freire's views of the Portuguese colonizers. The intention is to indicate features commonly associated to the Portuguese origins, but not delving deep into the analysis. In this regard, refer to: Bresciani, *O charme da ciência*, ch. 2.

[26] Bernardo Ricupero, 'O Conservadorismo Difícil', in André Botelho and Gabriela Nunes Ferreira (eds), *Revisão do pensamento conservador: ideias e políticas no Brasil* (São Paulo: HUCITEC, 2010), p. 83.

[27] Arno Wehling, *O Estado colonial na obra de Oliveira Viana*, in Élide Rugai Bastos and João Quartim de Morais (eds), *O pensamento de Oliveira Viana* (Campinas: UNICAMP, 1993), p. 80.

In this regard, Oliveira Viana's view of the past was not that of a historian seeking to rebuild facts and meaning. On the contrary, as Oliveira Viana's history was the 'political master', it should answer problems of its own time and then turn to the future, to the construction of a new nation in Brazil. In this sense, his ambiguity towards the past may be due to the instrumental quality of his references, according to diverse theses and projects defended throughout his extensive and varied work. On one hand, Oliveira Viana highlights the Iberian qualities of Brazil's identity and its rural historical formation, without delving into its past. On the other hand, after 1930, he would defend implementing a corporative model in Brazil, capable of preserving traditional values of its identity, overcoming the dispersal of latifundia, and building a truly harmonic and connected nation, while recognizing the needs resulting from the construction of a modern Brazilian nation and the need to surpass it.

The society formed in colonial times was, in Oliveira Viana's words. 'dispersa, incoerente, revolta, gira em torno do domínio rural. O domínio rural é o centro de gravitação do mundo colonial. Na disseminação geral da população, lembra um pequeno núcleo solar com as suas leis e a sua autonomia organizada' [dispersed, incoherent, rebellious, and centred around the rural domain. The rural domain is the centre of gravity of the colonial world. In the general dissemination of its people it reminds us of a little solar system, with its laws and its organized autonomy].[28] Originally, according to Oliveira Viana, this society and the forming of latifundia resulted from the high mobility and capacity for adaptation of the Portuguese people and the unique conditions of the American environment, marked by its extraordinary spaciousness, as he referred to the Brazilian territory's geographic characteristics.

In this sense, Oliveira Viana highlights the noble and racially superior feature of the first Portuguese colonizers, which would explain the grandeur observed in the territorial nobility of São Paulo and Pernambuco, where there would be 'um escol considerável de fidalgos de sangue, descendentes autênticos das mais notáveis e ilustres casas da península' [a considerable elite of blue-blooded noblemen, authentic descendants of the most notable and illustrious houses of the [Iberian] Peninsula].[29] There would also be another layer of colonizers, formed by 'elementos plebeus, lavradores do Minho, de Trás os Montes, das Beiras, da Estremadura — homens sóbrios e honrados, embora de poucas posses [...]. É remediada, a princípio, depois é abastada' [plebeian elements, farmers from the Minho, Trás os Montes, the Beiras, Estremadura — sober and decent men, although of modest means [...]. It is comfortable, at first, later it becomes wealthy].[30]

---

[28] F. J. Oliveira Viana, *Populações meridionais do Brasil* (São Paulo: Monteiro Lobato & Cia., 1920), p. 56.
[29] Ibid., p. 11.
[30] Ibid., p. 13.

In the first centuries of colonization, this noble elite would suffer a shock with the 'mundane ways' of their court and urban life and the 'rough and rugged' medium they were now entering, between the peninsular spirit (centripetal) and the new American tendencies (centrifugal). Slowly, especially after the third century of colonization, the noble class would be absorbed by the common class, and urban life would retract in the colony, making colonizers organize their social life in their own way, not seen yet by the Portuguese.[31] In this new rural society, Oliveira Viana believes, 'das tradições da antiga nobreza peninsular nada lhes resta, senão o culto da família e da honra' [of the traditions of the ancient peninsular nobility nothing is left to them, other than the cult of family and honour].[32]

Contrary to 'the luxury and silks of the first and second centuries', however, Oliveira Viana says rural life was imposed on Brazil by mere circumstances, fixating the feeling on the psychology of Brazilian society, whose preferences were linked to a rural domain and its cattle, sugarcane and coffee fields, sugar mills and widespread slavery. In this way, the Brazilian would call himself 'um homem do campo à maneira antiga. O instinto urbano não está na sua índole; nem as maneiras e os hábitos urbanos' [a countryman in the old style. The urban instinct is not in his disposition; nor urban ways and habits].[33] Still, as aforementioned, the Brazilian rural nobility would reflect in its 'feelings and volitions' the most 'instinctive and structural' qualities of the Peninsular soul, which would form 'ainda hoje o melhor do nosso caráter' [still today, the best of our character].[34] In this way, says Oliveira Viana, the main qualities of the rural Brazilian man are his fidelity to his word, rectitude, respectability and moral independence.[35] However, it should be noted that these values would not be shared by the common classes in which 'pela profusa mistura de sangues inferiores' [by a profuse mix of inferior blood], 'uma desorganização sensível na moralidade' [a notable disorganization in morality] is the norm.[36]

These points on values and Iberian character of Brazilian identity would be strengthened by Oliveira Viana in *Pequenos Estudos de Psicologia Social* (1921), where the author states that national character is 'intact and incorruptible', guarding 'the purity of early temper'. Once again, these values were linked to the rural features of Brazilian society, even in more cultured and civilized urban areas. In this regard, as Oliveira Viana noted, 'of our twenty-one [state] capitals, most are composed of nothing but large villages, offering a frankly rural complexion by their people's nature and costumes'. Besides, most of the population of the cities 'is formed of individuals out of the rural world that circles and envelops it'. Finally, the author recalls, the urban population of south and north comprise 'mais ou menos, dois milhões e meio de almas, cabendo,

---

[31] Ibid., pp. 14–16.
[32] Ibid., pp. 18–19.
[33] Ibid., pp. 21–22.
[34] Ibid., p. 39.
[35] Ibid., pp. 43–44.
[36] Ibid., p. 40.

por isso, os vinte milhões restantes (cerca de 90%) à massa rural' [more or less two and a half million souls, the remaining 20 million (about 90%) thus belonging to the rural mass].³⁷ The author also criticizes his contemporaries for the tendency 'das classes superiores e dirigentes do país a se concentrarem nas capitais' [among the upper and ruling classes of the country to concentrate themselves in the capitals], which would result in a 'crise intensa e extensa nos seus meios profissionais de subsistência' [intensive and extensive crisis in the professional means of subsistence] and on the apparent 'degeneração do caráter nacional' [degeneration of the national character].³⁸

In that context, however, according to Oliveira Viana, Brazil's 'renewing reaction' would not be to militarize the people, as advocated by defenders of compulsory military service, or the implementation of a corporative model, as he would defend years later, but to return to old virtues. In his words: 'é na renovação desse velho culto nacional da terra opima e nutridora, culto em que se formaram e definiram os atributos melhores e mais preciosos da nossa índole étnica. É nisto que está a grande obra a empreender-se para "regenerar" o nosso caráter e para "nacionalizar" a nossa alma' [it is in the renewal of this old national cult of a fertile and nurturing land, a cult in which the best and most precious attributes of our ethnic temperament were formed and defined. It is in this that lies the great work to be undertaken to 'regenerate' our character and to 'nationalize' our soul].³⁹

In this sense, according to the author, even if most Brazilians were living more or less rurally and domestically, the people from Minas Gerais (the *Mineiros*) would best demonstrate 'os aspectos mais brandos da nossa índole nacional' [the softer aspects of our national character].⁴⁰ That is because, according to him, 'os contingentes peninsulares entram na formação da gente mineira em condições muito particulares — mais densos, menos dispersivos, mais puros. Daí o serem os mineiros, dentre os vários grupos regionais das nossas populações, talvez aquele em que mais se conservam os aspectos lusitanos da nossa cultura' [the peninsular contingents affect the formation of Mineiros in very particular ways — denser, less dispersive and purer. Hence it is that the Mineiros, among various regional groups of our population, are perhaps the ones who most conserve the Portuguese aspects of our culture].⁴¹ In other words, concludes Oliveira Viana, the Mineiros' traditionalism would represent the typical expressions of national character and, therefore, keeping them 'dentro das formas evolutivas da civilização' [inside civilization's evolutionary forms] would be 'o ideal de um povo consciente da sua personalidade e orgulhoso do seu espírito' [the ideal of a people conscious of its personality and proud of its spirit].⁴²

---

[37] Oliveira Viana, *Pequenos estudos de psicologia social* (São Paulo: Revista do Brasil — Monteiro Lobato & Co., 1921), p. 18.
[38] Ibid., loc. cit.
[39] Ibid., p. 21.
[40] Ibid., p. 30.
[41] Ibid., p. 50.
[42] Ibid., p. 52.

In *Evolução do Povo Brasileiro* (1923), as in his earlier works, Oliveira Viana highlights rural character and racial fusing as important characteristics of colonial Brazilian society, both resulting from the great adaptive capability and miscegenation of the Portuguese people. By arriving in Brazil and finding 'uma população de aborígenes ainda na idade da pedra polida' [an aboriginal population still in the Polished Stone Age],[43] they were forced into leaving their commercial spirit behind in order to invest in agricultural exploitation. From their small peninsular properties, the Portuguese originated in Brazil a society based upon latifundia, from the aristocratic origins of the first colonizers and the metropolis's goal of exploiting riches, and not exactly colonizing the territory.

On one hand, the aristocratic origins of the first colonizers would have made the environment less suitable for small properties and small cultures, as 'esta é essencialmente democrática. O pequeno proprietário é um trabalhador braçal e realiza, com as forças da própria família, os serviços necessários à cultura' [this is essentially democratic. The small landowner is a manual worker and fulfils, with the efforts of the family itself, the duties necessary for cultivation]. Noblemen, on the other hand, come from a traditionally feudal society where 'só o serviço das armas é nobre, só ele honra e classifica. Falta-lhes aquele sentimento da dignidade do labor agrícola' [only the practice of arms is noble, only it brings honour and distinction. They lack that feeling for the dignity of farm labour].[44] However, seeking to exploit its riches, the metropolis would only concede *sesmarias* [allocations of land] to 'pessoas que possuam meios para realizar a exploração delas e fundar engenhos' [people who possessed the means to undertake their exploitation and to set up plantations].[45]

Therefore, land would have become an element of social distinction and classification of the colonial society, and the domain of the plantations, as they were complex and costly, was limited to 'tipos mais representativos das grandes qualidades da raça: é aí que estão os homens de mais capacidade, de mais prestígio, mais bem dotados para a vida pública' [the best examples of the great qualities of the race: thus these are the ones who are the most capable, the most prestigious and best-endowed for public affairs].[46] Among them were slavers and slaves, who constituted the base of production on great properties, shepherds, who had in herding a way of taking land, and 'domain tenants', described by Oliveira Viana as poor white and mixed-race free men that gravitated around the plantation masters, 'formando um bloco de grande coesão que constitui o clã fazendeiro' [forming a block of great cohesion that constituted the farming clan].[47] In this sense, plantations would harbour a

---

[43] Oliveira Viana, *Evolução do povo brasileiro*, 2nd edn (São Paulo: Cia. Editora Nacional, 1923), p. 48.
[44] Ibid., p. 52.
[45] Ibid., p. 53.
[46] Ibid., p. 62.
[47] Ibid., p. 66.

great quantity and diversity of people and races,[48] and would form a 'pequena sociedade, complexa, heterogênea, poderosamente estruturada' [little society, complex, heterogeneous and powerfully structured], with autonomous cores and providing the colonial society with 'um aspecto ganglionar e dispersivo, de extrema rarefação' [an extremely rarefied, ganglionic and dispersive aspect].[49]

In his subsequent work, especially after 'O Idealismo da Constituição' (1927), Oliveira Viana would not be concerned any more about highlighting colonial origins, cultural character, and the superiority and adaptive capabilities of the Portuguese colonizers, but rather the needs emerging from the construction of the Brazilian nation after its independence. Thereafter, references to the colonial past in the author's work were gradually focused on current problems and the need to overcome them with the future in mind, even though he would not stop cherishing and idealizing that past.

On one hand, the author reiterates his founding and idealized view of the past and the Iberian origins, stating that from a 'mais íntimo, mais concreto, mais objetivo, mais científico, das nossas coisas, do nosso meio, da nossa história, de todo esse glorioso esforço pesquisador, uma nova cultura americana, própria, nativa, genuína, surgirá e florescerá [...]' [more intimate, more concrete, more objective, more scientific (knowledge) of our affairs, our environment, our history, from all this glorious research effort, a new American culture, unique, native, and genuine, will sprout and blossom [...]]. This culture, according to Oliveira Viana, 'será o florão mais radiante da nossa grandeza. Nela iremos encontrar as fontes mais puras do nosso idealismo de onde manará, para satisfazer a nossa sede de renovação, uma corrente perene, rica de inspirações genuinamente americanas' [will be the most radiant flower of our grandeur. In it we will find the purest sources of our idealism, from which will flow, to satisfy our thirst for renewal, a perennial current, rich in genuinely American inspirations].[50] On the other hand, the author returns to the bad example set by the Portuguese to criticize Brazilian Republicans and their idealism. In this case, Oliveira Viana cites Eça de Queiroz, for whom 'os males de Portugal

---

[48] I do not intend to go further into Oliveira Viana's discussion about racial issues in the formation of Brazilian society. In this regard, the author defines Brazil as a 'wide field for racial fusion', where white, black, and indigenous people would 'breed and breed again in every aspect, two by two, three by three, in every corner of the known world' (*Evolução do povo brasileiro*, p. 107). On the Portuguese, the author points as a defining aspect their complex ethnic formation, characterizing two distinct groups by the time of the colonization: 'one blond, tall, slim, with nomadic and conqueror habits; the other brown, small, slim or short, with sedentary and peaceful habits.' About the former, Oliveira Viana believed that 'the blond and slim types prevail on the aristocratic class: military and feudal nobility of the peninsula. The brown, slim or short types were the base for the popular and middle classes' (Ibid., pp. 109–10). In Brazil, the first colonizers were of the blond slim group, a more adventurous type, who originated its rural aristocracy. The later colonization currents were formed by individuals 'of the Celtic-Iberian race, brown and short', who will only emigrate 'when the new habitat offers assurances and opportunity for easy triumph' (Ibid., p. 116). For more information, refer to: Oliveira Viana, *Evolução do povo brasileiro* (São Paulo: Monteiro Lobato, 1923), second part.
[49] Ibid., p. 65.
[50] Oliveira Viana, *O idealismo da Constituição*, 1st edn (Rio de Janeiro: Terra de Sol, 1927), p. 148.

eram devido, uns, ao próprio temperamento do povo português, outros, "traduzidos do francês"' [some of Portugal's evils were due to the temper of the Portuguese people themselves and others were 'translated from the French']. In the same sense, he believes the Republicans were 'excelentes tradutores de males estranhos; péssimos intérpretes dos nossos próprios males' [excellent translators of foreign evils; terrible interpreters of our own evils].[51]

In this regard, the political and engaged character of Oliveira Viana's work and the work of other intellectuals of his generation should be noted. His criticism to the idealism of the elite and his overcoming in the name of the construction of a 'true Brazilian nation' were not accidental, but frequent in his work.

Since *Populações Meridionais do Brasil* (1920), for example, the author used to say that 'há um século estamos sendo como os fumadores de ópio, no meio de raças ativas, audazes e progressivas. Há um século estamos vivendo de sonhos e ficções, no meio de povos práticos e objetivos. Há um século estamos cultivando a política do devaneio e da ilusão diante de homens de ação e de prêa [...]' [for a century we have been like opium smokers, amidst active, daring and progressive 'races. For a century, we have been living on dreams and fictions, amidst practical and objective peoples. For a century we have been cultivating a politics of reverie and illusion in the face of men of action and guts [...]].[52] As an alternative, it would be up to Brazil to make 'the courageous resolution of changing educational, political, legislative, and governmental methods.' In other words, says the author, 'devemos doravante jogar com fatos, e não com hipóteses, com realidades, e não com ficções, e, por um esforço de vontade heroica, renovar nossas ideias, refazer a nossa cultura, reeducar o nosso caráter' [we should from now on deal with facts, not with hypotheses, with realities, and not with fictions, and, by a heroic effort of will, renew our ideas, remake our culture and re-educate our character].[53]

For this, as aforementioned, Oliveira Viana argues that the past would be the best instrument to get to know our environment, our affairs, and our people, at the same time recognizing and cherishing the Iberian origins and identifying needs resulting from it; this could lead to some kind of diagnosis for the nation's problems and conditions in order, from now on, to deal with facts and not hypotheses. In this sense, by referring to post-Independence times, Oliveira Viana would start to view his colonial heritage in a negative way, especially latifundia, the lack of social solidarity, and absence of the State, as directly connected matters, and thus perceived in mutual relation.

Latifundia, as pointed out by Bernardo Ricupero, would be viewed by the author as the major obstacle to unifying the nation. In his own words, Oliveira Viana says 'we are latifundia', but it 'insulates men; disseminates them; absorbs

---

[51] Ibid., pp. 26–27.
[52] Viana, *Populações meridionais do Brasil*, p. xi.
[53] Ibid., p. xii.

them; it is essentially anti-urban', it withers the 'neighbourly society', and reinforces family bonds, which would absorb 'toda a vida social em derredor. O grande senhor rural faz da sua casa solarenga seu mundo. Dentro dele passa a existência como dentro de um microcosmo ideal: e tudo é como se não existisse a sociedade' [all the social life around it. The rural lord makes his manor house his world. Inside it he passes his life as if in an ideal microcosm: and everything is as if society did not exist].[54] Latifundia, therefore, would have a simplifying function in the colonial society, due to its independence and economic self-sustainability. As Oliveira Viana sums up, 'nem classe comercial, nem classe industrial, nem corporações urbanas. Na amplíssima área de latifúndios agrícolas, só os grandes senhorios rurais existem. São os grandes domínios como que focos solares: vilas, indústrias, comércio, tudo se ofusca diante da sua claridade poderosa' [neither a commercial class, nor an industrial class, nor urban corporations. In the vast area of agricultural latifundia, only the rural landlords exist. The great domains are like solar systems: towns, industries, commerce, everything is dazzled before its mighty light].[55]

Socially, the result would be the formation of loose and unstable relations among lords and free workers, renters or settlers, besides preventing the formation of a European middle class in Brazil, as clarified by Oliveira Viana. On one hand, the landlord did not need these workers because he possessed slaves; on the other hand, due to the pleasantness of the tropical climate and the available land, 'a vida se torna empresa fácil' [life becomes an easy business], and these workers could easily change places.[56] In this sense, institutions of social solidarity would be scarce in Brazil, making farming families the only type of solidarity for four centuries. According to the author, besides the insulation of latifundia, the nonexistence of other types of pressure would be yet another critical factor for lack of solidarity in colonial times: 'nenhuma pressão poderosa — vinda do alto: do poder; vinda de baixo: da classe inferior; vinda de fora: do inimigo interno e externo — obriga os nossos mansos e honestos matutos, desde o primeiro século até hoje, a mutualizarem os seus esforços na obra de defesa comum' [Since the first century until today, no powerful pressure forces our meek and honest backwoodsmen to join efforts to work on common defence, be it from the top: the powerful; from the bottom: the inferior classes; or from outside: the domestic and foreign enemies]. As Oliveira Viana sums up, 'fora da pequena solidariedade do clã rural, a solidariedade dos moradores, especialmente a solidariedade dos grandes chefes do mundo rural, os fazendeiros, jamais se faz necessária' [besides the small solidarity of the rural clan, the solidarity of denizens, and specially of the chiefs of the rural world, the farmers, it is never needed].[57]

---

[54] Ibid., p. 41.
[55] Ibid., p. 130.
[56] Ibid., p. 137.
[57] Ibid., p. 173.

In this case, the solidarity of clans is further reinforced by white anarchy and the absence of the state in the colonial society. According to Oliveira Viana, the concentration of inferior classes around rural nobility did not come into being for herding, religion, or for military reasons, but for protection against the so-called white anarchy that dominated the whole of Brazilian rural society, from top to bottom. In other words, the state and its institutions were incapable of protecting citizens without means in that society. Factionalism of justice and partiality, the arbitrariness of great landowners and factionalism of municipal corporations were examples of this anarchy. Thus, says the author, 'as instituições de ordem política e administrativa, ou mesmo instituições de ordem privada e social não amparam os cidadãos sem fortuna; não os ampara a solidariedade parental ou a solidariedade de classe; essa função só é exercida de forma eficiente pelo fazendeiro local' [the political and administrative institutions, or even private and social institutions, did not support citizens without means; family solidarity or class solidarity did not support them; this function would only be exerted efficiently by the local farmer]. The landlord has 'como seu mais vivo pundonor, rebater a injúria por ventura feita aos seus rendeiros pelo proprietário vizinho ou pela autoridade local' [as his highest honour, to counter the affront perhaps made to his tenants by the neighbouring landowner or the local authority]. His clients had 'o dever da fidelidade absoluta, mantido com nobreza cavalheiresca por esses humildes campônios: desde o dever de prestar, se for preciso, auxílio material na defesa do patrono até a obrigação iniludível de votar no candidato do chefe' [the duty of absolute fidelity, kept with knightly nobility by these humble peasants: from the duty of giving material aid in the patron's defence, if needed, up to the unavoidable obligation to vote for his candidate].[58]

The absence of the state could also have aggravated the situation in many regions of colonial Brazil, given the conditions of exploration and occupation of their territory, as colonial expansion happened faster than the expansion of public powers. In Oliveira Viana's words 'entre nós o poder público tem uma marcha mais remorada do que a massa social, cujos movimentos incumbe a ele regular e dirigir. Há uma visibilíssima discordância, ainda hoje sensível, entre a área demográfica e a área política, entre a área da população e o campo de eficiência da autoridade pública' [among us, public power moves at a slower pace than the social mass, whose movements it is responsible for regulating and directing. There is a clearly visible discordance, still notable today, between demographics and politics, between the population and the efficiency of the public authority].[59]

In other words, as suggested before, Oliveira Viana's diverse views of the Brazilian colonial past — sometimes negative, sometimes positive — are not exactly paradoxical, as they share coherence with his view about context and

[58] Ibid., p. 163.
[59] Ibid., p. 210.

conditions for the creation of a Brazilian nation in the nineteenth century, and his ideal for a new and 'true' nation to be built in the twentieth century. In this sense, latifundia, lack of social solidarity (limited to clans), and absence of the state were not negative aspects in themselves, but related to each historical movement analysed. If these characteristics were positive and suitable to the Portuguese colonial needs in colonial times, in monarchist and republican times, in contrast, they formed a negative heritage in terms of national unity. In these terms, how would it be possible to harmonize our Iberian origins and heritage of the past, which cannot be denied, with building a nation and overcoming its delay in relation to more practical and objective peoples?

In monarchist times, says Oliveira Viana in his debut work, this political function was exerted by the Crown, which was supposed to secure the nation's and central power's definitive triumph over local chieftains (clan lords). According to him, in the fourth century [of colonization], the monarch is the 'agente mais prestigioso, mais enérgico, mais eficaz do sincretismo nacional. O poder central deve a ele, com a sua unidade e a sua ascendência, a sua consolidação e estabilidade' [most prestigious, energetic, efficient agent of national syncretism. Central power owes its consolidation and stability to him, in his uniqueness and ascendancy].[60] In that context, still marked by a strong provincial separatism and vivacious local *caudillismo*, the crown would be the 'regulador supremo do jogo dos partidos, o grande dominador dos clãs, o repressor da caudilhagem nacional' [supreme regulator of the play of parties, the great dominator of clans, the oppressor of national *caudillismo*].[61] In contrast with the British liberal formula of 'The King reigns but does not rule', the conservatives in Brazil have brought alive a new principle 'mais adequado à nossa índole e à nossa civilização política: o princípio do poder pessoal do monarca. É a fórmula dada por Itaboraí nessa frase enérgica e imperativa, em que responde o programa dos liberais: — o Rei reina, governa e administra' [more adequate to our character and our political civilization: the principle of monarch's personal power. The Viscount of Itaboraí responds to the liberal agenda with this energetic and imperative formula: — the King reigns, rules and administers].[62] More so than monarchy, the unity of the Brazilian nation would be secured by the monarch, 'o único que compreende a realidade das nossas coisas, a nossa incultura política, a artificialidade dos nossos partidos, a impossibilidade de praticar-se aqui, na sua pureza, o belo regime, que fez a glória da nação inglesa e ainda hoje lhe garante estabilidade' [the only one who comprehends the reality of our affairs, our lack of political culture, the artificiality of our parties, the impossibility of practising here, in its purity, the beautiful regime which is the glory of the English nation and still today

---

[60] Ibid., p. 249.
[61] Ibid., p. 254.
[62] Ibid., p. 258.

guarantees its stability].[63] Finally, in Oliveira Viana's opinion, Dom Pedro II gave Brazil half a century of progress, peace, tranquillity, and order. By his personal power, he 'corrige a hostilidade, a intransigência, o exclusivismo das facções políticas. Pelo equilíbrio do seu espírito culto e prudente, modera as impaciências e os excessos reformadores, tão nocivos e perturbadores nos povos novos, como o nosso' [corrects hostility, intransigence, the exclusiveness of political factions. By his spiritual, refined, and prudent balance, he moderates the impatience and excesses of the reformers, so harmful and disturbing in young peoples such as ours].[64]

As for monarchist institutions, Oliveira Viana states in *Evolução do Povo Brasileiro* (1923) his view that 'essa construção não é má; porque sob ela o país se abriga durante mais de meio século, e cresce, e prospera, e se robustece, e se prestigia aos olhos do mundo' [this construction is not evil; because under it the country shelters itself for over half a century, and grows, and prospers, and invigorates itself, and gains prestige in the eyes of the world].[65] According to him, the work of independence and Empire statesmen is cyclopean, being compelled to modify 'tanto os métodos de política como os aparelhos de governo do período colonial, e o fazem com capacidade admirável' [both political methods and government apparatus from the colonial era, doing so with remarkable capability], in a 'luta heróica e contínua em prol da unidade nacional contra a formidável ação dispersiva dos fatores geográficos' [heroic and continuous struggle for national unity against the formidable dispersive action of geographic factors].[66] Once again, however, the author reiterates the monarch's central role in maintaining the institutions of monarchy, arguing that the imperial statesmen were motivated by the principle of intangibility of the King, its essential piece: 'com ela, jogando-a com habilidade, eles realizam as duas grande missões do poder central no país: a unificação da nacionalidade e a organização da sua ordem legal. Sem ela, não teriam realizado a primeira e, portanto, não teriam realizado a segunda: e seríamos hoje, talvez, um amontoado de pequenas repúblicas desorganizadas' [playing skilfully with it, they accomplished the two great quests of central power in the country: national unification and the organization of its legal order. Without it, they would not have accomplished the first and so would not have accomplished the second: we would be today, perhaps, a bunch of small disorganized republics].[67]

Of the monarch's person, Oliveira Viana says in *O Ocaso do Império* that Dom Pedro II 'não era um rei molengão e, menos ainda, um rei preguiçoso: atento, meticuloso, exigente, cioso da exação e da regularidade' [was not a soft king, even less so a lazy king: attentive, meticulous, demanding, solicitous for exaction and regularity], who would have performed more seriously than

[63] Ibid., p. 262.
[64] Ibid., loc.cit.
[65] Viana, *Evolução do povo brasileiro*, p. 217.
[66] Ibid., pp. 217–18.
[67] Ibid., p. 223.

anyone in his constitutional vocation: 'foi durante cinquenta anos o melhor empregado público do Brasil, o paradigma da classe, flor, exemplo e espelho de todos eles' [for fifty years he was the best public employee in Brazil, the paragon of his class, flower, example and mirror of them all].[68] In balancing his actions, the author states that 'bem sentimos hoje quanto foram injustas para com ele (o Imperador) as gerações, no meio das quais viveu. [...] Nós, os de agora, lhe somos gratos pelo seu esforço indefeso de meio século em favor da bondade, da justiça e da paz. O juízo que lhe fazemos hoje, dele e do seu Reinado, é que ele, como nenhum outro brasileiro, bem mereceu a Pátria' [we can sense today how unfair generations in the midst of which he lived were to him (the Emperor). [...] We, the ones living today, are grateful to him for his tireless effort over half a century in support of goodness, justice, and peace. The judgement we make today, of him and his Reign, is that he, like no other Brazilian, deserved the Country].[69]

By comparing institutions and actions of colonial and monarchist statesmen, despite their cited differences, Oliveira Viana points out a common point: 'ambos jogam com dados da realidade objetiva' [both played with data of the objective reality].[70] Although the former had only fiscal goals and the latter wanted to keep the Empire integral and re-establish its legal order, 'uns e outros inspiram-se, porém, em dados concretos e experimentais, e mantém sempre um permanente contato com as nossas realidades' [some are inspired by concrete and experimental data, always keeping in touch with our realities].[71] Republican statesmen acted differently, however, being modelled by exotic patterns. In this sense, Brazilian republicans would not have responded in an adequate way to the problem of conciliating our Iberian origins and heritage with the construction of a 'true nation' in Brazil, overcoming its delay.

In this regard, while criticizing the utopian idealism[72] of Brazilian republicans, Oliveira Viana states that they could have presented 'um belo edifício, sólido e perfeito, construído com a mais pura alvenaria nacional, e deram-nos um formidável barracão federativo, feito de improviso e a martelo, com sarrafos de filosofia positiva e vigamentos de pinho americano' [a beautiful edifice, solid, and perfect, built with the purest national masonry, but instead presented a formidable federative shed, impromptu and hammer-made, with battens of positive philosophy and beams of American pine].[73] This happened because the Republic was proclaimed during the exceptional instability and

---

[68] Oliveira Viana, *O ocaso do Império* (São Paulo: Melhoramentos, 1925), p. 55.
[69] Ibid., p. 208.
[70] Viana, *Evolução do povo brasileiro*, p. 238.
[71] Ibid., loc. cit.
[72] According to Oliveira Viana, there are two forms of idealism: 'the utopian idealism, which disregards experimental data, and organic idealism, formed of reality and supported only on experience, guided by observations of people and environment' (*O idealismo na evolução do Império e da República* (São Paulo: Biblioteca de O Estado de São Paulo, 1922), p. 17). About these different types of idealism and causes of utopian idealism in Brazil, see elsewhere in the same work.
[73] Ibid., pp. 79–80.

disorganization of the monarchy, breaking its old political and partisan frames, without a truly and generalized republican feeling between people and elite. Actually, according to Oliveira Viana, the absent feeling 'não era o da crença na República, mas sim o da descrença nas instituições monárquicas [...]; mas o certo é que essa descrença na monarquia não importava necessariamente a existência do sentimento contrário, de fé nas instituições republicanas' [was not of belief in the Republic, but rather of disbelief in monarchist institutions [...]; certainly, this disbelief in the monarchy did not necessarily mean the opposite feeling, of faith in republican institutions].[74]

Among the popular masses, 'almost totally unlearned and dispersed in barbarism in forests and wildernesses', the discussions on governmental forms, constitutional institutions, monarchy, republic or democracy were mere 'abstractions that transcended their rudimentary mentality'. If the masses had to believe in some institution, 'esta seria a monarquia, ou antes, o monarca, o Imperador, entidade feita de carne e osso, que eles sabiam estar vivo e presente na Corte — mandando; e não na República, uma palavra apenas, coisa vaga, abstrata, estranha, inacessível à sua limitada compreensão' [it would have to be monarchy, or rather the Emperor, a flesh and bone entity, who they knew was alive and present at the Court, ruling; not in a Republic, a mere word, a vague, abstract, alien thing, beyond their limited understanding].[75]

New democratic and republican governmental forms, however, would only find fertile ground among the 'cultivated elite in capitals and important cities, in the patriarchy of fortune and culture, in the management of parties, universities and literary centres', and yet limitedly until 1888. Apart from Rio Grande de Sul, says Oliveira Viana, most republican hubs were disorganized and incoherent in the rest of the country up until the beginning of 1889: 'estavam a seis meses do dia do seu triunfo — e ainda eram uma congênere de batalhadores escoteiros, agindo em pequenos pelotões isolados, à maneira dispersiva das guerrilhas!' [they were six months from their day of triumph — and still they were like Boy Scout fighters, acting in small isolated platoons, in the scattered way of guerrillas!].[76] Hence, his conclusion that the country was not ready for the Republic — not even the republicans.

Thus, republicans' utopian idealism could be due to their unreadiness and disorganization for implementing a new regime, but a certain attraction to the American political organization could also be added to this. In this sense, Oliveira Viana ironically states that the republican mentality was based on the belief in the power of written formulas, without considering elements of the Brazilian reality and its people. To these dreamers, he said, 'pôr em letra de forma uma ideia era, de si mesma, realizá-la. Escrever no papel uma constituição era fazê-la para logo coisa viva e atuante: as palavras tinham o poder mágico

---

[74] Viana, *O ocaso do Império*, p. 105.
[75] Ibid., pp. 106–07.
[76] Ibid., p. 127.

de dar realidade e corpo às ideias por elas representadas' [to put an idea into writing was, in itself, to achieve it. Writing a constitution on paper was to make it at once living and active: words had the magic power of giving reality and body to ideas represented by it].[77] However, the constitution of 1891 would not exactly summarize the Brazilian reality, but instead what was more liberal of the ideologies of the time: French democracy, English liberalism, and American federalism. Once again ironically, Oliveira Viana says that those who grouped around republican propagandists 'waited for the good fortunes of Republic, democracy, and federation with the same mystical excitement of peasants who walked alongside Jesus in Galilean streets waiting for God's Kingdom'. However, after its implementation 'para logo se levantou um sussurro de desapontamento do seio da turba fanatizada — e esse desapontamento se acentuou, com o tempo, numa permanente desilusão' [at once there arose a whisper of disappointment from the midst of the fanatical crowd — and that disappointment became accentuated, with time, into a permanent disillusion].[78]

Such delusion and failure of the republican ideals in Brazil were precisely due to the disagreement between idealism of constitution and national reality, considering that it would be based on assumptions without plausible objectivity, such as 1) existing public opinion; 2) opinion expression through parties. Oliveira Viana believed that 'somos um povo em que a opinião pública, na sua forma prática, na sua forma democrática, na sua forma política, não existe' [we are a people in which public opinion, in its practical form, in its democratic form, in its political form, does not exist].[79] Equally, in Brazil, there were no true political parties, which at that time only represented the interest of individuals (clan lords) and not the collective interests of the nation.

The only form of organization the governments found were factional clans, as referred by the author: 'Estes é que acabam dominando-os inteiramente e reduzindo-os, por fim, a simples instrumentos dos seus interesses e ambições. Eis porque o governo do povo, idealizado pelos sonhadores da constituinte, se torna aqui apenas o governo das coteries politicantes' [Those end up dominating them entirely, and finally reducing them to instruments of their interests and ambitions. This is why the people's government, idealized by the dreamers of the constituent assembly, becomes merely the government of political coteries].[80] The alternative to this model, however, would not come from a political or constitutional reform, but from the implementation of a new regime, 'conveniente e adaptado ao nosso povo' [convenient and adapted to our people],[81] as colonial and monarchist statesmen would have done in the past. Such a regime, like what will follow, would have to be based on the organized opinion of working classes, councils, and unions.

[77] Viana, *O idealismo da Constituição*, 1st edn, p. 25.
[78] Ibid., pp. 28–29.
[79] Ibid., p. 44.
[80] Ibid., p. 59.
[81] Ibid., p. 68.

The Corporative Solution and the Nation's Future

Contrary to the electoral and representative democracy implemented in Brazil by republican idealists, Oliveira Viana says true democracy is defined as 'the ruling of opinion', which may even lack elections and voters. According to him, 'eleições e eleitores não são coisas principais numa democracia; são meios para atingir o fim — e não são nem o meio único, nem o melhor dos meios. O que é principal numa democracia é a existência de uma opinião organizada' [elections and voters are not the main things in a democracy; they are means to reach an end — and they are not the only means, or the best of means. The main thing in a democracy is the existence of organized opinion].[82] However, opinion and democracy were non-existent in Brazil due to its lack of class solidarity or sentiment for collective interests. Thus, the condition for building truly democratic governments in the country would precisely be to organize public opinion: 'ou isto, ou a democracia republicana no Brasil será apenas um eterno sonho' [either this, or republican democracy in Brazil will be merely an eternal dream].[83]

On one hand, as aforementioned, the price of the colonial past, marked by dispersion and isolation of latifundia, would have built this lack of class solidarity, the absence of consciousness of collective interests and a state dominated by the local oligarchy and the clan lords' interests. On the other hand, however, the construction of a 'true' democratic nation in the country would require, at the same time, preserving and overcoming its colonial and monarchist heritage. The first case, the colonial past, would address preserving the origins and values of its Iberism, as defined by José Murilo de Carvalho, and overcoming the resulting dispersion and lack of social solidarity. The second case, the monarchist past, would not address re-evaluating monarchy as a government regime, but recovering the monarchist solution to the colonial dispersion in republican times, that is, imposing the central power over local chieftains not only by the action of the King but now a Single President,[84] as stated by Oliveira Viana.

A simple political or constitutional reform would not be enough to build a truly democratic and patriotic government in Brazil, given the ever-increasing technical character of modern society and the mass phenomenon, according to Oliveira Viana. Wide social and economic reforms were needed in the country, which would confer the electoral mass independence of opinion, in the absence

---

[82] Ibid., p. 90.
[83] Ibid., p. 61.
[84] According to Oliveira Viana, a one-party regime would not suit Brazil, given its history of a lack of solidarity, but a presidential regime would. In his words, the author states: 'ideally, the Estado Novo is not a Single Party regime, but a Single President regime. A single party would mean the establishment of an annoying oligarchy in the midst of the national community. What we need is a Single President. That is, a President that would not share his authority; a President without a boss; a sovereign President, who would exert his power in the name of the nation, subordinate and dependent only on it'. Oliveira Viana, *O idealismo da Constituição*, 2nd edn (Rio de Janeiro: José Olympio, 1939), p. 207.

of which it remained dependent on the oligarchies. In this sense, the most efficient means to ensure independence of opinion would not be universal suffrage, direct elections, the secret vote, or local self-government, but instead the 'difusão do espírito corporativo e das instituições de solidariedade social' [diffusion of the corporative spirit and of the institutions of social solidarity].[85]

In other words, the 'true' Brazilian nation would be established in a social or corporative democracy, also advocated as an Authoritarian Democracy,[86] reconciling the Iberian origins with the needs of the modern world. In this sense, in terms of objective politics,[87] we should highlight the importance given by the author to Technical Councils and unions in disseminating the corporative spirit, stimulating class solidarity and organizing opinions in Brazil. According to him, an important movement of the industrial and commercial classes alongside the government could be observed on the 1920s, what could be 'o primeiro passo para a constituição, com caráter permanente, junto ao poder, dos órgãos consultivos das nossas classes econômicas. Tudo está em reiterar esse expediente, torná-lo uma praxe, fixá-lo em costume, organizá-lo em tradição' [the first step towards a constitution, of a permanent character, close to power, of the advisory bodies of the economic classes. Everything lies in reiterating this expedient, making it a practice, fixing it in mores, organizing it in tradition].[88]

Until that time, the public administration had already created three supposedly technical, yet merely advisory Councils: National Council of Education (1911); National Council of Labour (1923); and National Council of Industry and Commerce (1923). Later, especially after the 1930s, various other councils and institutes were created in Brazil, such as the National Council of Coffee (1931), Institute of Sugar and Alcohol (1933), Technical Council of Economy and Finances (1937) and National Council of Oil (1938).[89] As defined by Oliveira

---

[85] Viana, *O idealismo da Constituição*, 1st edn (1927), p. 66.
[86] According to Oliveira Viana, the expression 'authoritarian state' is somewhat redundant, 'because the concept of state itself implies the idea of authority.' In this sense, the Estado Novo implemented in Brazil was in reality an 'Authoritarian Democracy, that is, a democracy founded on authority as its essential principle, not on liberty'. Viana, *O idealismo da Constituição*, 2nd edn (1939), p. 149.
[87] According to Oliveira Viana's line of thought, 'objective politics' are politics based on real and objective conditions of the country, contrary to political idealism. In this regard, also refer to note 12, about concepts of utopian idealism and organic idealism.
[88] Viana, *O Idealismo da Constituição*, 1st edn, p. 104.
[89] Although defined as technicians, it should be noted that these Councils were created in the interior of Brazilian public administration, becoming bound and directly under the government during its period of activity. The whole composition of these Councils, as defined by law, depended on the indication or recognition of its representatives by the government. As an example, the composition of the Nation Council of Labour was divided as follows: two representatives of working classes, two representatives of patronal classes, six experts of known repute regarding organization of work and social security, and two representatives of the upper bureaucracy — graduate employees of the Ministry of Agriculture and the Ministry of Industry and Commerce. Regarding the composition and activity of Technical Councils in Brazil, especially between the decades of 1930 and 1980, refer to Cássio Alan Abreu Albernaz, 'Timoneiros dos rumos da nação: carreiras e trajetórias da elite estatal do planejamento do desenvolvimento econômico e industrial no Brasil (1934–1982)' (unpublished doctoral dissertation, Pontifícia Universidade Católica do Rio Grande do Sul, Porto Alegre, 2012).

Viana, these councils were 'colaboradores técnicos da obra administrativa dos governos' [technical collaborators in the government's administrative work],[90] by way of both reports and advice later submitted for discussion and approval by the National Congress. On one hand, the authority and weight of these reports and advice come from these Councils' own compositions, as they were composed of '"competências", de "especialistas", de "técnicos", colhidos, por força da própria lei, a) nas esferas da alta administração; b) nos centros da cultura especializada; c) principalmente no seio das associações de classe' ['competences', of 'experts', and of 'technicians' gathered by the law itself a) in the upper circles of the administration; b) in specialized cultural hubs; c) mainly in the midst of the class associations].[91] On the other hand, however, the efficiency of Technical Councils in Brazil was limited by prejudices in the mentality of national elites, among which 'o mais grave, o mais absurdo, o mais anacrônico é a crença na competência da onisciência dos Parlamentos e na sabedoria infusa dos homens que, em virtude do mecanismo do nosso sistema representativo, acontecem chegar ao poder' [the gravest, most absurd, most anachronistic is the belief in the competence of the omniscience of Parliaments and the wisdom of men who, due to our representative system's mechanism, happen to have come to power].[92]

At least until the coup of the Estado Novo (1937), however, these Councils were no more than a technical collaborator of the government, as defined by Oliveira Viana, secondary and subordinate to the decisions of Executive and Legislative Powers, who complied, or not, with their reports and advice. Still, in times of electoral and representative democracy in Brazil, complying with the reports or advice of these Councils represented a supposedly technical argument for the Executive to justify its political decisions and favour the Parliament's approval of its administrative projects.[93] Such activity, however, was far from what Oliveira Viana envisaged, assigning Technical Councils and unions with the role of stimulating class solidarity and organizing opinion in Brazil. Thus, the best way to democracy is not fighting to elect members of the Parliament, but 'desenvolver os Conselhos Técnicos e as organizações de classe, aumentar a sua importância, intensificar as suas funções consultivas e pré-legislativas, generalizar e sistematizar a praxe da sua consulta da parte dos poderes públicos' [developing Technical Councils and class organizations, raising their importance, intensifying their advisory and pre-legislative roles, generalizing and systematizing the practice of their being consulted by the public powers].[94]

[90] Oliveira Viana, *Problemas de política objetiva* (São Paulo: Companhia Editora Nacional, 1930), p. 186.
[91] Ibid., p. 187.
[92] Ibid., pp. 192–93.
[93] Regarding the political use of technical institutions in Vargas's administration, with reference to the composition and activity of the Administrative Department of the Public Service (Departamento Administrativo do Serviço Público — DASP), refer to Luciano Aronne de Abreu, *Um olhar regional sobre o Estado Novo* (Porto Alegre: EDIPUCRS, 2007).
[94] Viana, *Problemas de política objetiva*, p. 201.

In relation to unions, it should be noted that their constitution's legal definition was guided by the 'new legal methods' recommended by Corporate Law, characterized 'pelo seu estrito objetivismo, pelo rigoroso realismo social da sua análise e das suas construções' [by their strict objectiveness, the rigorous social realism of its analysis and constructions].[95] To this extent, although not intending to further develop the analysis of such concepts and legal principles,[96] the controversy between jurist Waldemar Ferreira and Oliveira Viana about the creation of Labour Justice in Brazil is important to highlight, especially regarding its regulating jurisdiction and conflict resolution criteria.

For the first, its normative aspect is contrary to the principles of traditional Law and the Constitution itself, for giving power to the Judiciary to edit general rules, that is, legislating, and because any sentences determined by judges would only bind litigants themselves, not third parties. For the second, on the contrary, his divergences with Waldemar Ferreira were not only about judicial technique, but about two legal concepts: 'the old individualistic concept' and the new concept 'nascida da crescente socialização da vida jurídica, cujo centro de gravitação se vem deslocando sucessivamente do indivíduo para o grupo e do grupo para a nação, compreendida esta como uma totalidade específica' [born from the growing socialization of legal life, whose centre of gravity has been successively displaced from the individual to the group, and from the group to the nation, understood as a specific totality].[97] In this context, the dominant interest was not blind obedience to the Constitution, but the efficiency of the public service. Hence the need for decentralization of powers of the modern state and the need for creating corporative administrative entities, 'com poderes para decidirem as questões afetas à sua jurisdição, não pela aplicação da regra jurídica, como nos tribunais judiciários, mas mediante critérios de pura eficiência prática' [with power to decide matters within their jurisdiction, not by applying the legal rule, as in courts, but by criteria of pure practical efficiency].[98] This was the case for the aforementioned Technical Councils and unions and Labour Justice[99] itself, which it was intended to create.

---

[95] Oliveira Viana, *Problemas de direito sindical*, Coleção Direito do Trabalho, 1 (Rio de Janeiro: Max Limonad, 1943), p. xvi.
[96] On legal principles and concepts of Corporate Law and the constitution of Labour Justice in Brazil, refer to: Oliveira Viana, *Problemas de direito corporativo* (Rio de Janeiro: José Olympio, 1938).
[97] Ibid., p. 7.
[98] Ibid., pp. 54–55.
[99] About Labour Justice, Oliveira Viana notes that it was not created to judge legal matters or techniques, but collective economic conflicts, even though this expression is redundant because 'every collective conflict is essentially economic' (*Problemas de direito corporativo*, p. 105). Thus, the sentences should also be collective and normative. In this sense, another singularity of Labour Justice would be its criteria for the formulation of sentencing. According to Oliveira Viana, there would not be, in a collective dispute, 'any pre-established point, pre-constituted evidence, legal text or contract to invoke which the judge should be subordinate to in order to determine his decision. There is just the fact, to which he must establish a regulation, as effective as if he was a legislator' (p. 114). The Labour Judge would ponder economic conflicts as a referee or expert 'who does not make a decision based on pre-established rulings, on practices based on jurisprudence, on the logic of similar cases, on principles of written law; but according to the interest of social justice, according to what seems equitable to each case' (pp. 115–16).

Unions, according to what was idealized by Oliveira Viana, should exert a guardian role over society, to teach Brazilians to develop solidarity of spirit and to organize the opinion of the country. Considering the decentralization of powers in the modern state and defining unions as corporative administrative entities, the author notes that unions are responsible for interacting harmoniously with the State, which had invested them with public authority powers.

This because, after the implementation of the Estado Novo (1937) in Brazil, the format of a single union by category was instituted,[100] directly bound to the State, with powers to represent and enter into collective conventions for a whole class, not only associates. Thus, says Oliveira Viana, 'desde que uma convenção coletiva é a lei da profissão ou da categoria, ela só pode emanar de uma única fonte, que é o sindicato único, autorizado legalmente a representar a categoria' [as long as a collective convention is the law of the profession or class, it can flow only from a single source, which is the single union, legally authorized to represent the category].[101] The author would argue: 'o sindicato não é outra coisa senão a associação profissional de direito privado, elevada, por uma seleção especial do Estado, à dignidade de representante da categoria toda, e, em consequência, provida de poderes bastante para, em nome do Estado, administrá-la' [the union is nothing other than the professional association of private interests, elevated, by a special selection of the State, to the status of representative of the whole category, and, consequently, given powers adequate to administer it in the name of the State].[102] This would be the origin of the Brazilian syndicalist system in relation to European models in general, and the Italian model in particular, given the differences in geography and population density between Brazil and Italy.[103] In territorial terms, contrary to the Italian provincial model, the professional and economic interests of

---

[100] About the principle of union unification, Oliveira Viana writes a list of thoughts in regards to its advantages in relation to the opposite principle of union freedom. Although it is not my intention to go into the analysis and arguments of this matter, it must be highlighted that, according to him, the single union by category would be the most suitable format for the Brazilian case, both for organization and for practicality. Oliveira Viana says: 'In reality, multiple unions of a same category of a same area would bring up the following difficulties: a) it would — greatly and uselessly — prevent connections between both classes — employer and employee [...]. b) it would hinder the application and efficiency of collective conventions [...]. This plurality of collective conventions and work regimes, originated in the plurality of unions, would in turn prevent the transformation of such conventions into professional regulations (Viana, *Problemas de direito sindical*, p. 52). For more information, refer to this same work.

[101] Ibid., pp. 4–5.

[102] Ibid., p. 114.

[103] Seeking to showcase the originality of the Brazilian syndicalist system and its suitability to the conditions of national reality, Oliveira Viana extensively develops comparisons with the Italian model. Besides highlighting that the Brazilian model is not 'a mere copy of the Italian system', the author was also concerned about stating the non-fascist and non-totalitarian character of the Brazilian model. In this regard, Oliveira Viana states, in sum: 'the dominating thought of our new syndicalist legislation, although serving an authoritarian regime, is to preserve autonomy and associative freedom of categories, reducing the State intervention to the strict necessary for the preservation of the Nation's general interests [...]' (Viana, *Problemas de direito sindical*, pp. 160–61). To learn more about this subject, refer to chapters XI, XII and XIII of the same.

Brazil were to be organized in three circles — local, state-wide, and national, with Unions, Federations, and Confederations as their representative bodies. Oliveira Viana concluded that, if it were not so, 'teríamos organizado um sistema sindical constituído de entidades profissionais de mera existência administrativa, artificiais, portanto, e sobre as quais seria ilusório e mesmo ridículo pretendermos assentar os fundamentos do nosso futuro edifício corporativo' [we would have organized a syndicalist system constituted of professional entities with a merely administrative existence, and thus artificial, upon which it would be illusory and even ludicrous to aim to base our future corporate edifice].[104]

Following what was described about the supposedly original and suitable corporate and syndicalist model proposed by Oliveira Viana, it would be possible to argue that it would allow Brazil to correct the wrongs of its colonial past — dispersion of latifundia and lack of social solidarity; to recover the monarchist solution of imposing central power over local oligarchies; and still allow the future constitution of the country as a modern nation. For this, it would be the unions' responsibility not only to exert their traditional roles as representatives and defendants of a profession, but also essentially to educate citizens on how to develop a consciousness regarding the common interests of society and build a new and true Brazilian nation, while also breaking and preserving the past in the name of a new unified and modern nation.

---

[104] Ibid., p. 200.

Brazilian Integralism and the Corporatist Intellectual Triad

LEANDRO PEREIRA GONÇALVES and
ODILON CALDEIRA NETO

Pontifícia Universidade Católica do Rio Grande do Sul and
Universidade Federal do Rio Grande

Integralism and Corporatism: Internal Debate

To understand the discourse and practices of Brazilian Integralism, it is fundamental to take into consideration the fact that they spoke to an insecure audience waiting for a great leader to protect them. Their leaders projected a paternalistic view of themselves, in which the harmonious family — the foundation of society — was an inspiration for the Integralist society, without divisions. They spoke as if they knew the causes of the woes of the modern world and believed they could protect the nation from future dangers. Prophetically, they stood as the only ones capable of establishing order against the evils which ravaged society, such as liberalism and communism.

Brazilian Integralism was formed in the beginning of the 1930s, under Plínio Salgado, and was rapidly supported by numerous intellectuals, politicians, religious leaders, and other members of Brazilian society. In 1932, *Manifesto de Outubro* was published proposing the formation of a great national movement and explaining the movement's political positions: a conservatism-based nationalism, having property maintenance as a form of social organization, and repulsion of cosmopolitanism as the mainstay of a strong and organized society amidst an authoritarian context.[1]

The Brazilian Integralist Action (Ação Integralista Brasileira — AIB), resulting from the political, social, and economic tensions in 1920s and 1930s Brazil, cannot be viewed or understood as a movement of even and monolithic doctrines and origins; however, there is no doubt that the main political composition of Integralism was on the line of thought of the leader, Plínio Salgado, and was later resignified and arrogated by other leaders and intellectuals.[2]

---

[1] *Manifesto de outubro de 1932* (Rio de Janeiro: Secretaria Nacional de Propaganda, 1932).
[2] In my view the following four authors form the fundamental starting point for research into Integralism in the fields of history and the social sciences: Hélgio Trindade, *Integralismo: o fascismo brasileiro da década de 30*, 2nd edn (Porto Alegre: Difel/UFRGS, 1979); José Chasin, *O integralismo de Plínio Salgado: forma de regressividade no capitalismo hiper-tardio*, 2nd edn (Belo Horizonte: Una,

AIB intellectuals and political proposals were oriented by the necessity for creating an authentic movement based upon a nationalist ideal, founded on Christianity, and with an *avant-garde* discourse. It is possible to identify the influence of Lusitanian Integralism (*Integralismo Lusitano* — IL — which, in turn, was based on the radical right-wing nationalism of the *Action Française*),[3] which aimed to be a practical answer to the papal encyclical *Rerum Novarum* (Pope Leo XIII) as much as reflecting practical and doctrinal aspects of Italian Fascism, especially the single-party perspective and State Corporatism.[4]

Undoubtedly, Plínio Salgado was the main political figure of AIB. Born in a traditional and conservative family from the countryside of São Paulo, he had migrated while still young to the capital, where he excelled in 1920s Modernism; he eventually established, over the next decade, the first political mass movement in Brazil. He proposed a normalizing order which suppressed individual will for the sake of a greater good: a unified Brazil under an Integral State. He deemed it necessary to devise strategies for popular mobilization, to be carried out by means of the types of public oratory and rhetoric common to rallies, and a complex body of propaganda, in press, radio, and film media.[5]

Besides Plínio Salgado, the second greatest figure in the leadership of the movement was Gustavo Barroso. Born in Fortaleza (state of Ceará) in 1888, he had been President of the Brazilian Academy of Letters, and founder of the National Historical Museum. In regards to Integralism, he was nominated general commander of the militia and Superior Council member, and was one of the main proponents of antisemitism in Brazil.

The third name in the Integralist hierarchy was that of the young lawyer Miguel Reale; a fellow countryman of Plínio Salgado, he was born in São Bento do Sapucaí (state of São Paulo) in 1910, and was responsible for indoctrinating the movement and organizing the Integralist youth, and was considered one of its main ideologists. After the AIB, he became a reference in Law and was known for elaborating the Three-Dimensional Theory of Law, in which the trifecta of fact, value, and legal norm make the concept of Law, presented in his 1940 thesis, *Fundamentos do Direito*.[6] He is now considered the father of the New Brazilian Civil Code of 2003 for having been entrusted with writing the new code.

1999); Gilberto Felisberto Vasconcellos, *Ideologia curupira: análise do discurso integralista* (São Paulo: Brasiliense, 1979); Marilena Chauí, 'Apontamentos para uma crítica da Ação Integralista Brasileira', in *Ideologia e mobilização popular*, ed. by Maria Sylvia Carvalho Franco (São Paulo: Paz e Terra, 1985).

[3] Olivier Compagnon, 'Étude comparée des cas argentin et brésilien', in *Charles Maurras et l'étranger, l'étranger et Charles Maurras: L'Action française — culture, politique, société II*, ed. by Olivier Dard and Michel Grunewald (Bern: Peter Lang, 2009).

[4] Leandro Pereira Gonçalves. 'Entre Brasil e Portugal: trajetória e pensamento de Plínio Salgado e a influência do conservadorismo português', 668f. (unpublished doctoral dissertation, Pontifícia Universidade Católica de São Paulo, 2012).

[5] See Leandro Pereira Gonçalves and Renata Duarte Simões (eds), *Entre tipos e recortes: histórias da imprensa integralista* (Guaíba: Sob medida, 2011) vol. II.

[6] Miguel Reale, *Teoria do Direito e do Estado*, 5th edn (São Paulo: Saraiva, 2000).

Even with an intellectualizing force behind it, Integralism was not a homogeneous system of thought and its intellectuals kept their own particularities, especially related to views on State Corporatism. It is possible to infer that this happened for diverse reasons. First, by the existence of an area of dispute among the main intellectuals of the movement who, despite agreeing on various doctrinal aspects and apparently consenting to Plínio Salgado's leadership, had different and sometimes conflicting interpretations of the Sigma Doctrine.

Besides, the three main intellectuals were products of their social environments, their views on Integralism differing by the degree of their formation, as well as the social roles of each of them. If Gustavo Barroso was already a renowned intellectual and member of the Brazilian Academy of Letters, Miguel Reale was still a young intellectual in formation. In turn, Plínio Salgado was an autodidact, and active in literary production and the defence of Christianity. Their common ground was surely conservatism and political activism.

Although the doctrine disseminated by the National Chief went virtually undisputed by the members,[7] other intellectuals like Gustavo Barroso and Miguel Reale created other currents of thought.[8] Plínio Salgado, highest in the Integralist ranking, presented himself as a doctrinal Catholic character, an advocate for spiritual revolution, acting for the invigoration of the Brazilians' souls, and rescuing national roots.[9]

Miguel Reale makes his legal-political thought evident, making himself indispensable to the movement and to the moment, and to anyone who seeks in Integralism a reflection upon Brazilian-specific problems.[10] In turn, the antisemite and militant Gustavo Barroso, who instead of accusing Zionism for its ethnic-racial character aimed his criticism at the influence Jews had had in Brazil since its independence, especially in economic terms, linking the poor situation of the 1930s to a past of debts and loans from Jewish bankers.[11]

Therefore, this study aims to identify theoretical and conceptual aspects of corporatism in thought, discourse, and practices of the intellectual trifecta of the movement and their actions in favour of an Integral State, interrupted by Vargas's coup in 1937, marking the beginning of the Brazilian Estado Novo, but disturbing Integralist expectations for the implementation of an Integral corporatism. The uninterrupted discourse of incontestable and organic harmony in the movement did not mean absence of different dispositions and political strategies in Integralism, and it is in this sense that resides the

---

[7] Chapter II: 'Do Movimento e sua Direcção'; Article 11 in *Protocollos e Rituaes:* regulamento (Niterói: Edição do núcleo municipal de Niterói, 1937), p. 7.
[8] Historiographically, excluding some works referenced in this article, the great majority of studies aimed to view the features of these Integralist intellectuals. Thus, this study seeks to contribute with a comparative analysis for the historiography of Integralism and corporatism.
[9] Gonçalves, 'Entre Brasil e Portugal'.
[10] Ricardo Benzaquen de Araújo, *In medio virtus: uma análise da obra integralista de Miguel Reale* (Rio de Janeiro: Centro de Pesquisa e Documentação de História Contemporânea do Brasil, 1988).
[11] Marcos Chor Maio, *Nem Rotschild nem Trotsky: o pensamento anti-semita de Gustavo Barroso* (Rio de Janeiro: Imago, 1992), p. 65.

issue of Integral and Corporatist State in the Integralism of Plínio Salgado, Gustavo Barroso, and specially Miguel Reale, a thought which disseminated the foundations of this model, appropriated and resignified in the work of other Integralist ideologists.

The Technical Corporatism of Miguel Reale

It is possible to find in Miguel Reale's thought an intellectualized and normative matrix of Brazilian Integralism, especially in regards to State organization, the union issue, and functions of regulatory bodies, among others. Although young and having joined the AIB at the age of twenty-two, he had been a militant in other political organizations of different shades, which helps to understand the origin and specificity of his Integralism.[12] Moreover, he was a student at the Law School of São Paulo, an intellectual and political hub of the nation, an area rich in ideas and attended by the political elites.

This Integralism comprised an essentially conservative, authoritarian, hierarchic tone,[13] especially if taken as an AIB internal current of thought. 'Democratic' spaces should be located at the base, whereas vocational and individual capabilities would be critical factors to escalating roles and powers. An example of this was the perspective on education in a possible Integral State; in Reale's view, access to education should be universal and free in its initial stage, but only the fittest and best-rated could follow intellectual formation.

Miguel Reale's notion of Integralist corporatism involves the necessary observation of his criticism of socialism and liberalism, considered foundations and expressions of the modern crisis, especially its manifestations in Brazil. According to Reale, a nation is constituted as 'um organismo ético, político, cultural e econômico [...] uma comunhão de língua, de história, de tradições, de costumes, de hábitos, de virtudes e de defeitos, uma consciência comum de querer' [an ethical, political, cultural, and economical organism [...] a fellowship of language, history, tradition, customs, habits, virtues and flaws, a common conscience of desiring].[14] In this way, solidarity within the nation would occur in a naturally harmonious way, between intelligence, manual labour, and capital.[15]

[12] As presented by Adriano Ferreira, the process of construction of a critical view of the communism of Miguel Reale was made while still submerged in Marxist political philosophy (see Adriano de Assis Ferreira, 'O marxismo de Miguel Reale', *Prisma Jurídico*, 5 (2006), 45–58). On Reale's disconnection from 'liberal socialism' (i.e. a non-Trotskyist or Stalinist socialism), the Integralist phase and the ultimate social liberalism, see José Maurício de Carvalho, 'Miguel Reale, do integralismo ao liberalismo social, a defesa da liberdade' *Cultura (Revista de História e Teoria das Ideias)*, 31 (2013), 349–60.
[13] For Alexandre Ramos, it is necessary to understand that, besides being essentially conservative and technical, Miguel Reale's Integralist thought was marked by an intensely Utopian perspective: Integral society. See Alexandre Pinheiro Ramos, 'Estado, Corporativismo e Utopia no pensamento integralista de Miguel Reale (1932–1937)', *Revista Intellectus*, 2 (2008), 1–22; João Fábio Bertonha, 'O pensamento corporativo em Miguel Reale: leituras do fascismo italiano no integralismo Brasileiro', *Revista Brasileira de História*, 33.66 (2013), 269–86.
[14] Miguel Reale, 'Perspectivas Integralistas' in *Obras políticas: 1ª fase, 1931–1937* (Brasília: Editora Universidade de Brasília, 1983), p. 15.
[15] By evidencing the issue of working beyond the perspective of manual and mechanical activity,

Based on this assumption, liberal democracy would be widely incapable in its representative ambitions, which would be both cause and effect of the distance between popular needs and aspirations of State obligations, especially laws. Instead of conceiving the individual inside their capacity of being social (as the 'essential and ultimate element of society'), liberal democracy would result in the atomization of the individual, so that individualism would undermine an individual's own comprehension as belonging to natural groups within society.

Thus, natural groupings would be incapable of understanding and assimilating individuals that constitute their universe. On the other hand, there were also criticisms of *Bolshevism* due to its complete absorption of the individual instead of individualization

> O integralismo combate o bolchevismo, porque o bolchevismo cria uma casta de exploradores do Trabalho em nome de uma doutrina negada pela experiência; — porque suprime o que há de nobre no homem sufocando as energias individuais que querem se expandir, reduzindo o indivíduo a um autômato, posto ao serviço do Estado, que tudo absorve. [...] o bolchevismo mecaniza o trabalho, quando é preciso dignificá-lo, intelectualizá-lo, fazendo com que o trabalhador tenha no Estado o lugar que de direito lhe cabe.[16]
>
> [Integralism goes against Bolshevism because it creates a caste of exploiters of Labour in the name of a doctrine denied by experience — because it suppresses the nobility in a man, suffocating his individual energies that want to expand, reducing him to an automaton in the service of the State, which absorbs everything. [...] Bolshevism mechanizes labour, when it is necessary to dignify and intellectualize it, ensuring that the worker has in the State the place that by right is due to him.]

Although not denying the role of the individual or, in theory, denying the absorption by the State and organizations, Miguel Reale's Integralism asserts that an individual is only fully understood when organized by unions, corporations, and their political representations (through corporate chambers).

As for representations, political parties would be incapable of manifesting the collective will of individuals. More than that, they would characterize bodies of artificial, transitory, heterogeneous, ephemeral life and be connected to the forces and urges of the great centres in Brazil. The political life of the coast of Brazil (or of cosmopolitism itself) would be artificially projected and imposed on citizens and on the political life of the countryside, the Brazilian *Sertão*, generating a dependent and parasitic relationship.

Besides, the political parties' disaggregating aspect would prey on society's natural groups: 'Dividem a Nação em vinte e uma naçõezinhas, dividem cada

---

Miguel Reale has the notion of a more complex world which is also tributary to social origins and the author's own activities. Thus, intellectual work is highlighted along with capital related activities. About the issue of complexity of the world in the Integralist view and the political career of Miguel Reale, see Araújo, *In medio virtus*.

[16] Reale, 'Perspectivas Integralistas', p. 29.

província em muitos partidos, desagregam a comunidade municipal, penetram no seio da família e lançam o esposo contra a esposa, o filho contra o pai [They divide the Nation into twenty-one little nations, divide each province into many parties, disaggregate the municipal community, penetrate to the heart of the family and set husband against wife, son against father].[17] In contrast, this disaggregating panorama and its due resolution would go *sine qua non* through the authoritarian Integralist democracy, formed with special attention to corporative bodies — thus developed for such mechanisms, but also emanating from them.

The guiding modern foundations of the nation were the same as the ones that existed in unions, at least in an Integralist view, as they would fulfil different roles to conceive its comprehensiveness, be they political (hierarchical indication of representatives for municipal and national chambers), economic (determination of collective agreements and others), cultural (education, sports, leisure etc.) and moral (conflict resolution).

Unions, organized vertically ('from municipality union to national confederations'),[18] and separately constituted as employers, employees, and technician unions would comprehend different corporations, from certain labour or production areas ('Coffee, Cotton, Transport Corporations etc.').[19]

The Integralist State would be responsible for understanding human complexity, satisfying material, intellectual, and spiritual needs, rather than merely organizing society around its dispositions and according to their field of work. Regarding the State's role in regards to the spiritual element, there are needs 'que nascem da consciência do inexplicável, isto é, da compreensão profunda de que há uma razão para esta vida, um motivo para este sofrimento, uma finalidade para o homem acima das contingências do próprio homem' [that grow from the conscience of the inexplicable, that is, from the deep understanding that there is a reason for this life, a cause for this suffering, a purpose for man above his own contingencies].[20]

Although spiritual primacy is not disconnected from a normative perspective of the State, it is not central to Miguel Reale's Integralism, at least as it is in other authors and ideologists work, like Gustavo Barroso and Plínio Salgado, among others. According to Reale, Integralism should fulfil a modernizing role, even if under conservative and authoritarian aegis.

An authoritarian and centring aspect of State should take place through the organization of unions. To Reale, the State would be responsible for supporting a single union per work class in each municipality. Thus, the State would also be responsible for inspecting unions, while also giving powers, such as voting rights in Municipal Council elections. In this way, the relation would be built upon rights and duties.

[17] Miguel Reale, 'ABC do Integralismo', in *Obras políticas: 1ª fase*, p. 194.
[18] Ibid.
[19] Reale, 'Perspectivas Integralistas', p. 23.
[20] Reale, 'ABC do Integralismo', p. 197.

The relation between State and society, mediated by class organizations (in the higher levels, corporations), would fulfil a need that resulted from national conditions. Miguel Reale states, supported by Oliveira Viana's work, that 'o Estado no Brasil não pode prescindir de uma ampla colaboração individual' [the Brazilian State cannot do without a wide individual collaboration].[21] Beyond this process, aiming at Integral totality, the State would be responsible for regulating the production of some industries, in the sense of preventing unbridled exploitation of produce (sugar, coffee, cotton) and prioritizing the modernization of the countryside, according to the needs and demands of each region. Thus, an Integral Brazilian State would comprehend a kind of Corporative Federalism while sounding out and resolving regional specificities.

Miguel Reale's corporatism has a hint of introspective imperialism, in the sense of achieving national autonomy, planning economic and political inequities among the regions, thus not needing to conquer exterior territories (since what was arranged was enough). This introspection would fit corporatism, which could 'resolve' disputes between provinces, between regional political parties, and disputes between capitalist concerns and class struggles encouraged by communism.[22]

For thematic, contemporary and political reasons, there could be a certain similarity between Integralist corporatism and other organizations and movements of a fascist nature. However, it aimed to avoid that by emphasizing instead the specificity of Integralism, elaborating its own praxis, while confirming the possible deficiencies of Italian fascism ('relativist, pragmatic, and empirical').[23] The Italian model would thus have a much less finished aspect than Integralism, as it would not comprise the *spiritualist* disposition of the Brazilian man as against the *vitalism* of the Italian corporatist.[24]

Integralist corporatism was beyond other European peers, besides the Italian model, for two reasons: absence of '*space* anguish'[25] (territorial needs and disputes) and 'a null heritage of hate and resentment'. In it resides the central piece of criticism of the German model which, despite offering organizational, political, and financial lessons, would not contribute to Integralism in regards to theories of racial superiority.[26]

As a criticism of liberal individualist atomization and communist absolute absorption, Reale states that the centralization of an absolute leader (the Italian *Caesarist* model) and the strenuous militarized discipline (the German case) would deprive the Integralist model of its individual and group autonomy. Thus, Integralists would be 'more democratic than European fascists'.

---

[21] Miguel Reale. 'Nós e os fascistas da Europa', in *Obras políticas: 1ª fase*, p. 232.
[22] Miguel Reale. 'Corporativismo e Unidade Nacional', in *Obras políticas: 1ª fase*, p. 237.
[23] Reale, 'Nós e os fascistas da Europa', p. 228.
[24] Regarding the spiritualist issue, Reale states that Integralism is 'spiritualist, truthfully spiritualist. A revolution for Brazil, without serving a particular belief, but serving every belief because it serves the eternal values of the Christian spirit.' Reale, 'Nós e os fascistas da Europa', p. 231.
[25] Ibid.
[26] Ibid.

Criticism of fascism and the search for Integralist specificity runs parallel to criticizing and refusing to approach other inspirational currents and political organizations. Regarding Charles Maurras, Reale states that Integralism distances itself due to the absence of a monarchical centrality (due to 'republicans'), Catholic intransigence (Integralism is Christian in different denominations), among other factors.[27]

Stating that there was 'nada de extraordinário, por conseguinte, que sejamos brasileiros, nacionalistamente brasileiros, e, ao mesmo tempo, apresentemos valores que se encontram também em movimentos fascistas europeus, como o de Mussolini, de Hitler e Salazar' [nothing extraordinary in our being Brazilian, nationalistically Brazilian, and, at the same time, displaying values that can also be found in European fascist movements, like that of Mussolini, Hitler, or Salazar].[28] Reale's corporatist proposal is located in a wide panorama, engraved in a certain zeitgeist. It would fit Integralism to tone its specificity, referring to a certain spirituality of universe and lexicon of green shirts, especially in Plínio Salgado's Integralism.

Plínio Salgado and the Spiritual Corporatism

Plínio Salgado, as National Chief of the AIB, presented himself as a doctrinal Catholic character, advocating for spiritual revolution, acting for the invigoration the soul of Brazilians, and rescuing national roots through the implementation of the Integral State. Revolution, aiming to establish a corporatist model, targeted elements like materialism, which became the movement's main critique. Plínio Salgado's discourse intended to create an intellectualized mechanism to establish a fight against communism because spiritualism would be achieved in society by creating an aversion to materialism and an appreciation of the unconscious based on God.

This revolution wanted to organize a corporatist, authoritarian, and radical society, based on the principles of Christianity. This Christian conception and a strong religious discourse made Integralism a political organization favoured not only by the Catholic Church but also by other religious groups. The importance that other Catholic movements gave to Integralism must be highlighted, especially regarding the trilogy God, Nation, and Family, viewed as the centrepiece of Christian faith in Brazil.

One of the most relevant components for understanding the spiritually

---

[27] Brazilian Integralism owes its republican option to Miguel Reale. Inside the AIB there existed various divergences regarding political segmentation, especially between Plínio Salgado, Gustavo Barroso, and Miguel Reale. The latter was head of the National Department of Doctrine and, in turn, had the control of many political mechanisms in the movement. In contrast to Plínio Salgado, Reale did not regard monarchist movements favourably: 'Republicanism and a certain prejudice to France would explain his attitude to Action Française and Integralism, both monarchical.' Trindade, *Integralismo*, p. 251.

[28] Reale, 'Nós e os fascistas da Europa', p. 227.

revolutionary project of Plínio Salgado was initially analysed in 1931, in an address presented at the Law School of São Paulo, inserted in the work *A quarta humanidade*, titled *Politeísmo — Monoteísmo — Ateísmo — Integralismo*. In this analysis, the author suggests humanity had produced three types of society: 'A Primeira Humanidade veio da caverna até a criação do Politeísmo; a Segunda vem do Politeísmo ao Monoteísmo; a Terceira vem do Monoteísmo ao Ateísmo [The First Humanity stretches from the cave up until the creation of Polytheism; the Second comes from Polytheism to Monotheism; and the third comes from Monotheism to Atheism].[29] A fourth humanity needed to be built, the Integralist humanity, which would come to into being through an Integral revolutionary process in order to implement a corporatist model of state.

Spiritually based revolution operates 'segundo os impositivos do Pensamento e este processa sua evolução segundo seu plano próprio, e seu próprio ritmo, conquanto aparentemente se revista de forma estruturada pelas próprias características de um período considerado' [according to the impositions of Thought, which processes its evolution according to its own plan and rhythm, although apparently it aligns itself structurally by the characteristics of a determined period].[30] With the creation and ascension of Integralism, Plínio Salgado defined that 'Revolution has begun',[31] and that the movement was preparing the unconscious for a spiritual revolution of corporatist nature.

Practically all of his and other theorists' work have mentions or citations of the Catholic Church, e.g. Gustavo Barroso's *Integralismo e Catolicismo*,[32] besides various materials edited by the National Propaganda Office, like *Os Catholicos e o Integralismo* (1937),[33] with many passages of prominent figures of Brazilian Catholicism exalting Integralism and thereby Plínio Salgado, who constantly addressed messages exalting the doctrine: 'Maria Santíssima é a grande salvadora das nações. O seu culto é o ponto inicial da ressurreição dos povos' [Holy Mary is the great saviour of nations. Her cult is the starting point for the resurrection of the peoples],[34] he stated, in a salvationist way, in *Maria: salvação do mundo!*

The Integralists' discourse regarding Catholicism was a one-way street. Such issues did not go unnoticed by the Vatican, who developed a series of investigations of Plínio Salgado and the AIB. In the *Archivio Segreto Vaticano*, there are documents showing that the Vatican, under Pope Pius XI, turning

---

[29] Plínio Salgado, 'Politeísmo — Monoteísmo — Ateísmo — Integralismo', in *A quarta humanidade*, 5th edn (São Paulo: GRD, 1995), p. 9.
[30] Plínio Salgado, *Psycologia da Revolução*, 2nd edn (Rio de Janeiro: José Olympio, 1935), p. 21.
[31] Plínio Salgado, 'Revolução Integralista', in *Palavra nova dos tempos novos* (Rio de Janeiro: José Olympio, 1936), p. 45.
[32] Gustavo Barroso, *Integralismo e Catolicismo*, 2nd edn (Rio de Janeiro: ABC, 1937).
[33] Tristão Athayde et al., *Os Catholicos e o Integralismo* (Rio de Janeiro: Secretaria Nacional de Propaganda, 1937).
[34] Plínio Salgado, *Maria: salvação do mundo!* (APHRC/FPS — Public and Historical Archives of Rio Claro/Plínio Salgado Fund-011.001.002).

its attention to Plínio Salgado's religious discourse.[35] The first document was written by Dom Gastão Liberal Pinto, Bishop of São Carlos, SP, and sent to Brazil's Apostolic Nuncio Dom Benedetto to be assessed and published, but it never was published.[36] The second was written by a specialist at the Nuncio's request.

Both texts were sent by Nuncio Benedetto to the Pope's State Secretary, Eugenio Pacelli, the future Pius XII, and, in this material, the AIB appears to be not well regarded, as opposed to Plínio Salgado's and his colleagues' discourse, which set both Integralism and Catholicism as elements for congregation. However, Plínio Salgado's words and the Integralist doctrine were useful for the period the world was in, viewing the AIB as the Brazilian fascism, and so aiding in the combat against the enemies of Christianity, communism, especially through the existence of Catholic dogmas in the foundation of Plinian thought, as in the solid discourse of the Catholic Social Teaching.[37]

Anti-communist discourse and the defence of Christian dogmas overcame any criticism of Plínio Salgado's thought. Plinian Integralism was based on approximating the Integralist discourse to Catholic discourse, towards a constitution of a spiritual corporatism of a Catholic nature, promoting gradual withdrawal from the fascist corporative discourse with its political nature and secular outlines. Inspiration in the doctrine and practice of Italian Fascism was moderated by the existence of the Catholic Social Teaching, having corporatism as a representative of evident convergence between the Catholic Church and Integralist politics, notably Plinian. Despite some divergences, reciprocity prevailed, as there were other interests beyond the religious. A core of ideas and political organization was created in defence of corporatism, anti-communism, anti-liberalism, and other convergent interests between the Catholic Church and the AIB.

The political principles of Integralism were established in this spiritual corporatist framework, which was addressed in the *Manifesto de outubro* in 1932, seeing the need for a nation organized into professional classes for the purposes of federal representation. Corporatism was still understood as a gathering of families, established in the defence of municipalism, viewed as the only way to make the vote free and conscious through the election of class representatives to the Municipal Chambers, established in an organic democracy.[38]

---

[35] *Breves observações sobre a ortodoxia da doutrina integralista perante a Igreja Católica* (Sacra Congregazione degli affari ecclesiastici straordinari anno 1938 — Pos. 529–531 — FASC. 50) e *Ortodoxia della Dottrina integralista nel Brasile?* (Sacra Congregazione degli affari ecclesiastici straordinari anno 1938 — Pos. 529–531 — FASC. 50)

[36] Later published in Gastão Liberal Pinto, 'Carta de Dom Gastão Liberal Pinto aos Bispos do Brasil sobre o integralismo: breves observações sobre a ortodoxia da doutrina integralista perante a Igreja Católica', *Boletim do Centro de Pesquisas e Estudos da História da Igreja no Brasil* (São Paulo), 22.3 (1984), 3–9.

[37] Analysed from Leandro Pereira Gonçalves, 'O integralismo de Plínio Salgado e a busca de uma proposta corporativista para o Brasil', in *A vaga corporativa corporativismo e ditaduras na Europa e na América Latina*, ed. by António Costa Pinto and Francisco Carlos Palomanes Martinho (Lisbon: Imprensa de Ciências Sociais, 2016), pp. 255–83.

[38] *Manifesto de outubro de 1932* (Rio de Janeiro: Secretaria Nacional de Propaganda, 1932).

With this purpose in mind, Plínio Salgado's Integralism established a process advocating the extinction of political parties, because for him people had the real representation, which was corporative, building on that ground a Brazilian Nation through Integralism.[39] It would be expressed in the Integral State, which would establish a political-social regime based upon the national-corporative doctrine and moral order, the spiritual cooperation of all forces defending the ideas of God, Nation, and Family.[40] For Plínio Salgado, the nation should be structured on corporative union bases.[41]

Intolerance and Corporatism in Gustavo Barroso

Before adhering to the Integralist movement in 1933, Gustavo Barroso was not effectively part of any fascist organization in Brazil and seemed to be more focused on philology rather than intense political activity. Indeed, his greatest intellectual and professional attributes were in the areas of literature, history, museology, journalism, and memoirs. On joining the AIB, Gustavo Barroso was the youngest 'immortal' to preside over the Brazilian Academy of Letters, which brought him respect among intellectuals and other parts of Brazilian society.

Having no background in extreme right-wing political organizations was no bar to his affiliation and settling into Integralist institutions. The very practice and discourse of Integralism, which anticipated the construction of an *authentically* Brazilian political ideal and movement, thus without the wrongs of the old ways of making politics, helped Barroso in his almost immediate establishment as the second figure in the green-shirt hierarchy, below only the *national chief* Plínio Salgado and just above Miguel Reale.

Just as his adhesion to Integralism marked Gustavo Barroso's first experience with right-wing radicals, it also initiated *Barrosian* Integralism, that is, production and publishing of his intensely antisemitic literature. In Plínio Salgado, Integralism assumes a conservative and Christian form; in Miguel Reale, it assumes a modernizing and authoritarian form; in Gustavo Barroso, Integralism became radically intolerant due to his antisemitism and other related aversions (e.g. his anti-masonic views).[42] Not by chance was Barroso the first Brazilian to comment on and translate the apocryphal historical falsification of *The Protocols of the Elders of Zion* (*Os Protocolos dos Sábios de Sião*), among other antisemitic titles and propaganda.[43]

---

[39] Plínio Salgado, *O que é o integralismo*, 4th edn (Rio de Janeiro: Schmidt, 1937), pp. 133–37.
[40] 'Estatutos da Ação Integralista Brasileira: 1º Congresso Integralista Brasileiro', in Plínio Salgado, *O integralismo perante a nação*, 2nd edn (Rio de Janeiro: Livraria Clássica Brasileira, 1950), p. 44.
[41] *Manifesto-Programma: de janeiro de 1936 — Concretização da Doutrina do Manifesto de Outubro de 1932* (Rio de Janeiro: Secretaria Nacional de Propaganda, 1936), p. 8.
[42] Specially regarding the issue of the anti-masonic aspect of the Integralist thought of Gustavo Barroso, see Luiz Mário Ferreira Costa, 'Maçonaria e antimaçonaria: uma análise da "História secreta do Brasil" de Gustavo Barroso' (unpublished masters thesis, Universidade Federal de Juiz de Fora, 2009).
[43] Maria Luiza Tucci Carneiro, *O veneno da serpente: reflexões sobre o anti-semitismo no Brasil* (São Paulo: Perspectiva, 2003).

Almost all of Gustavo Barroso's Integralist work was dedicated to disseminating an antisemitic discourse and to trying to understand the ramifications and dilemmas of this issue in Brazil, as a central or a secondary aspect. Issues like labour unions, the role of a possible Integralist State, or even the purpose of corporatism in the Brazilian nation were, according to Barroso, accomplished through sanitizing the mischievous activity of Jewish people in Brazil.

The 'historical meaning', in the *barrosian* view, brings to the question a decoupage of the ramification of a certain Jewish spirit (or Jewish infiltration), expressed in diversities such as the Renaissance, the Reformation, Islam, liberalism, and communism. Human desegregation, be it social, cultural, political or economical, walked hand in hand with Jewish activity.

In *O quarto império*, a theoretical rather than doctrinal work,[44] humanity's history is divided into four empires in a plot which elaborates on the degeneration of unity and solidarity among races and societies. The second empire, the She-wolf empire, comes after the lamb empire, establishing force upon order, and, more specifically, the Islamic distortion (influenced by Judaism) upon the medieval Christian order, until then harmoniously structured on family, respect for property, social organization, and corporate work.

> A Europa medieval vivia à sombra da Cruz. O Estado Cristão reconhecia o Direita Natural, baseava a economia na ética, entendia a Justiça, a Riqueza, a Realeza e o Pontificado como delegações provindas de Deus. A Família, a Propriedade, as Corporações firmavam a vida social.[45]
>
> [Medieval Europe lived in the shadow of the Cross. The Christian State recognized Natural Law, based its economy on ethics and understood Justice, Wealth, Royalty and the Pontificate as delegations coming from God. Family, Property, and Corporations were the basis of social life.]

Gustavo Barroso does not consider the notion of social organization of labour through corporations to be a mimicry of medieval guilds. This, however, does not mean that there was not an inspiration, especially for the Christian stratum on this matter. Anyhow, Barroso intended to dissociate any mimicry, even criticizing absolutism by citing António Sardinha (in *Ao ritmo da ampulheta*),[46] the main reference of Lusitanian Integralism, who understood power exercised in an absolute way to be nothing short of a transgression of limitations to the divine right of *all power* — this transgression being due to the influence of Roman Law, also criticized by Barroso.

The lamb empire (or empire of justice and peace), conceived as the fourth

---

[44] It is obviously not implied that this is a synthesis of Gustavo Barroso's Integralist thought, since it is assumed that intellectual trajectories are constantly being changed and reinterpreted by a same author, and only its totality can approach a synthetic analysis.
[45] Gustavo Barroso, *O quarto Império* (Rio de Janeiro: Livraria Jose Olympio Editora, 1935), pp. 86-87.
[46] Ibid., p. 79.

empire, would be the one to launch the capricorn empire, marked by confusion and disorder in every respect. Integralism would be nothing more than the practice and representation of a great movement in which Integralism could not only fit in but also be well-finished — and this solution would adopt corporatism as its organizing principle.

According to Gustavo Barroso, the ideal Integralist State would be based on Thomism, influenced and supported by Catholic Social Teaching, thus using strong and continuous religious arguments for sustaining its idea, foundation, and urgency. In this sense, Barroso approaches his literature to the prevalent Integralist current, led by Plínio Salgado. The Integralist State should recognize and solve more urgent needs and characteristics of municipalities in great dimensions (nationally) since they are understood as the 'gathering of families'.[47] Within municipalities, professional classes had organizational autonomy to comprehend the role of Municipal Chambers and election for mayors. Thus, municipalities would be both the epicentre and the laboratory of the corporatist ideal of the Integralist State.

However, the antisemitic tone of Barrosian Integralism was not absent, characterizing his view of Integralism and his rhetoric behind the need for corporatism. In *Cristianismo, Comunismo, Corporativismo*,[48] the author analyses dangers and solutions of diversities in the Modern States (in this case, States with fascist courts and communist states).

Although he also criticizes liberalism — a stage to precede the communist ascension — Barroso understands and emphasizes communism as essentially mischievous to nations and people, for removing spirituality and edifying materiality and class struggle as central issues. To Barroso, more than just a modern political ideology, communism was a Jewish creation guided by some kind of proletarian messianism, where the proletariat would experience ascension to heaven while on the Earth.

Unable to ascend to heaven (in its Christian, especially Catholic conception) for having denied Jesus Christ as Messiah, the Jewish people would incessantly seek a new opportunity, a new envoy, even if it were a collective one. They would project the liberation on the proletariat because they are capable of understanding the similarity between the oppressed and dispossessed, in the 'Jewish self-conception' and the workers' condition. Thus, earthly bliss would come to replace celestial and divine impossibility. In this sense, Barroso's anticommunism acquires clear religious and antisemitic contours. In addition, it aims to structure this issue in terms of Catholic Social Teaching, especially Pope Pius XI's encyclical *Quadragesimo Anno* (1931), which addresses the impossibility of associating Christianity with communism or socialism.

Similarly, and by citing encyclicals like *Rerum Novarum*, Barroso understands

---

[47] Gustavo Barroso, *O que o integralista deve saber* (Rio de Janeiro: Civilização Brasileira S/A, 1935), p. 30.
[48] Gustavo Barroso, *Comunismo, Cristianismo, Corporativismo* (Rio de Janeiro: ABC Ltda., 1937).

the indispensable character of Integralist corporatism as a solution to the danger of communism (especially *his* understanding of communism), liberalism, and so on. Thus, Barrosian Integralism's corporatism takes on an essentially antisemitic character and underpinning.

By reproducing Plínio Salgado's Integralist State definition ('a State that comes from Christ, is inspired by Christ, acts for Christ, and goes to Christ'),[49] Gustavo Barroso understands and aims to express not only his obedience to the Integralist movement's hierarchy, but also the principle which makes Brazilian Integralism the best blueprint for a Christian corporatism and model of the State.

While Italian corporatism is overly rigid and authoritarian in its relation between Party and State and the German model is built on an essentially military foundation, António Salazar's Portuguese Corporatism would be one of the best models with regard to State practice. According to Barroso, this would be due in great part to a visible inspiration by the French counterrevolutionary school, especially the leader of *Action Française* ('Charles Maurras' influence is visible'),[50] and the Catholic Social Teaching and fundamental values of Portuguese traditionalism.

The specificity, originality, and perfection of Brazilian corporatism (a complete synonym of Integralist corporatism) would reside, according to the author, in trying to understand corporations socially and culturally, beyond their economic function. Thomist inspiration would be the reason for the perfection of Integralist corporatism — *man was not made for economy, but the economy was made for man*. Thus,

> O Estado Corporativo Integral é um Estado completo, que incarna todo o espírito corporativista cristão do século XX. É um organismo que impõe uma ordem social espiritualizada, repelindo, no campo econômico, a usura, a especulação, e a escravização do homem pelo homem. Ele assenta nos direitos naturais da pessoa humana e nas virtudes morais, políticas e econômicas. É o Estado Forte, sobretudo moralmente forte. Seu poder é legitimamente constituído sobre alicerces corporativos, na crítica brilhante de Miguel Reale. Resulta das próprias corporações, não as cria.[51]

> [The Corporatist Integral State is a complete State, which embodies the whole Christian corporatist spirit of the twentieth century. It is an organism that imposes a spiritualized social order, repelling, in the economic field, usury, speculation, and the enslavement of man by man. It is based on the natural rights of the human person and on moral, political and economic virtues. It is a Strong State, especially morally. Its power is legitimately built upon corporative foundations, in Miguel Reale's brilliant critique. It results from the corporations themselves, it does not create them.]

Barroso continuously aimed to remove any possibility of aligning the Integral

---

[49] Ibid., p. 46.
[50] Ibid., p. 88.
[51] Ibid., p. 101.

State to any dictatorial concept (as it is perennial, while dictatorships are transitory) or to totalitarianism. Inside the *perfect* aspect that faced different conceptions of Integralism — although constantly making laudatory references to Miguel Reale and Plínio Salgado (exalting the brilliance and novelty of their political and doctrinal propositions) — it is possible to view intellectual and political disputes inside the Integralist movement.

Especially regarding Miguel Reale's views on forms of union organization, Gustavo Barroso criticizes elements of this Integralist current and perspective by stating that Reale's understanding was wrong in stating unions were public entities in the Integral State.[52] According to Barroso, it was necessary to understand unions as private bodies, since they are entities with foundations, interests, and needs as inherent as families. Establishing a public character for unions could result in an extremely authoritarian State, 'as hateful as the communist state'.

In reality, this procedure denotes an internal perspective and logic of Integralism and other political organizations. Disputes over conceptions and powers determined different political, ideological, and discursive perspectives. Aside from particular issues, like the character of the unions, Barroso's corporatism distanced itself from Reale's in his continuing antisemitism, and likewise Plínio Salgado's. More than differences inside the panorama of State, these questions help to explain internal currents in the AIB and how they aimed, each in its own way, to converge in a common end, which never came.

The Corporatism of the Estado Novo: An Integral Corporatism?

From its foundation, Integralism followed a path of political growth and fortification, however, its corporatist proposition was not successful. Meanwhile, with the political changes that resulted from the coup of the Estado Novo (1937) and the proposition of a corporative project surrounding Brazilian societies' organizations with Getúlio Vargas's authoritarianism, Integralists started to view possibilities to advance their ideals, including cooperating with the government.

Referring to 10 November 1937, Anor Bluter Maciel, lawyer and Professor of Economic History of the Americas in the School of Political and Economic Sciences of Porto Alegre, and a founding member of the AIB's nucleus in Rio Grande do Sul, states that, despite the radical change in Brazil's political ways, nothing happened in the national structure, especially because ideas in the Estado Novo's law represented aspirations of the AIB's doctrine from 1932 onwards, such as suppressing political parties and the organization of national labour.[53]

---

[52] Gustavo Barroso, *Integralismo e Catolicismo*, p. 98.
[53] Anor Butler Maciel, *Subsídios para o estudo da estrutura política do Estado Novo* (Porto Alegre: Edição da Livraria do Globo, 1937), p. 3.

The implementation of the Estado Novo brought about a new question among Integralists: 'would this be the moment of power?' With the presence of some Integralists in the dictatorial organization of 1937, Plínio Salgado and his followers started to have a glimpse of power. However, Getúlio Vargas used many centralizing principles: 'historiadores assinalaram ter sido o Estado-Novo Getuliano uma jogada para afastar Plínio Salgado do caminho do poder' [historians have stressed that Vargas's Estado Novo was a ploy to distance Plínio Salgado from the road to power].[54] Their relationship was always unstable.

The contact with Getúlio Vargas was made through having common enemies, instead of a political convergence of elements based on corporatism. The quest for supreme power was a generator of divergences and Vargas skilfully manipulated them, using their yearning for power, especially Plínio Salgado's.

It was notorious that the Integralists, especially their chief, knew about the coup and the constitutional charter. In correspondence with Ribeiro Couto, Plínio Salgado analysed the difficult period between the coup of the Estado Novo, in November, and the Integralists' attack on the Guanabara Palace, a prominent government building at the time, in May 1938. It was the final moment of that 'friendly relationship with the government' — from this moment on, Integralists were harshly persecuted by the Estado Novo, and their leader Plínio Salgado was exiled to Portugal.[55]

In the correspondence, he said that his son-in-law, Loureiro Júnior, was at his side in every moment of this period, keeping up with the negotiations.

> Ele trabalhou a meu lado nos transes mais difíceis da vida nacional, com uma discrição rara, assistindo a tudo o que aconteceu em 37 e 38, desde a elaboração da Carta Constitucional, que foi discutida e trabalhada em minha casa, até aos momentos mais dramáticos de novembro de 37 a maio de 38, em que conhecemos os homens, um a um, as fraquezas de uns, as traições de outros, a miséria de muitos e a grandeza de alma de poucos. Tudo isso nos ligou muito porque nada mais liga um homem ao outro do que o conhecimento mútuo e este torna-se absoluto nos supremos instantes do sofrimento.[56]

> [He worked alongside me in the most difficult crises of national life, with rare discretion, following everything that happened in 1937 and 1938, from the elaboration of the Constitutional Charter, discussed and crafted in my home, until the dramatic period from November 1937 to May 1938, in which we got to know the men, one by one, the weaknesses of some, the treacheries of others, the wretchedness of many and the greatness of soul of a few. All this connected us because nothing connects a man to another more than mutual understanding, and this becomes absolute in the supreme moments of suffering.]

---

[54] Gilberto Felisberto Vasconcellos, 'Presentation', in Gonçalves and Simões (eds), *Entre tipos e recortes*.
[55] See Gonçalves, *Entre Brasil e Portugal*.
[56] Correspondence from Plínio Salgado to Ribeiro Couto, 28 February 1940 (Casa de Rui Barbosa Foundation/ Personal files of Brazilian writers -Pop: 28177).

There is no doubt of his participation in the coup of 1937, despite his stating all his life that: 'o golpe de Estado de 1937 foi dado inteiramente à minha revelia' [the coup of 1937 was performed entirely without my knowledge].[57] His support for the new regime was not by chance. He wanted something in return — the agreement appointed Plínio Salgado as Minister of Education — but treason was a sentiment that marked all political relations of Integralists in the year of 1937, especially their leader. President Getúlio Vargas tried with all his might to postpone an official decision. It was clear that he would not give Plínio Salgado power, but would just use the strength of the Integralist militants to help solidify the Estado Novo. By decreeing the new regime, Vargas dissolved all political parties, besides banning civil militias and restricting uniforms and symbols of such entities, like the AIB. The results and impacts of the Estado Novo were seen differently in the eyes of other Integralist leaders.

Miguel Reale allegedly did not take part in the process that ended with the attempted coup against the Estado Novo. Yet he exiled himself for a year in Italy, fearing political persecution. In this period, he articulated his understanding of a fascist model of corporation, which was politically inviable and rather bureaucratic.[58] On one hand, his criticism helped Reale to sway from historical fascism, on the other hand, it revealed that he somehow viewed a certain similarity between a supposedly fascist practice and the model proposed by Integralism in Brazil.

Returning to Brazil, Miguel Reale withdrew from Integralist activism and their other leaders, and devoted himself to academic and intellectual activities. In 1940, he published *Fundamentos do Direito* and *Teoria do Direito e do Estado*, seeking a chair in the Law School of São Paulo. During the selection process, his enrollment was denied for alleged moral issues. This rebuttal was resolved only through the direct intervention of Getúlio Vargas, in 1941.[59] This moment marks the public relation between Reale and Vargas, resulting in the collaboration and insertion of the Integralist in the Estado Novo. Between 1942 and 1945, Miguel Reale joined the Administrative Board of the State of São Paulo, while also publicly advocating for the regime he was a part of.

Gustavo Barroso, on the other hand, did not exercise any institutional political activity after separating from Integralism. The end of his Integralist trajectory also marked the end of his intense antisemitic activity. The breaking point was his imprisonment, after the attempted Integralist *putsch*. However, Barroso was freed for lack of evidence — and stayed in Brazil.

Integralism, antisemitism, and corporatism, in Barroso, go through a

[57] Plínio Salgado, 'Presença do integralismo na vida política brasileira e raízes da crise contemporânea (15-4-1959)', in *Discursos parlamentares*, ed. by Gumercindo Rocha Dórea (Brasília: Câmara dos Deputados, 1982), p. 85.
[58] See Odilon Caldeira Neto, 'Miguel Reale e o integralismo: entre a memória militante e as disputas políticas', *Revista Espaço Acadêmico*, 126 (2011), 178–86.
[59] Rodrigo Maiolini Rebello Pinto, 'Miguel Reale: política e história (1931–1969)' (unpublished masters dissertation, Pontifícia Universidade Católica de São Paulo, 2008), p. 29.

systematic process of oblivion or explaining, seeking to understand his Integralist experience as a hiatus.[60] After that, Gustavo Barroso returned to his previous activities, especially in literature and museology. He remained director of the National Historical Museum, a role he kept until his death and, despite not having established political relations with Estado Novo, the regime's influence was noted in the organization, just as in many similar institutions. In a certain way, Gustavo Barroso was near the higher political and cultural circles of the Estado Novo.

By analysing the Constitution of 1937, Integralists identified themselves as visible elements of the corporatist proposition and practice in their theoretical framework. While establishing a legal analysis of the law, Anor Bluter Maciel highlights the sharply economical function of the union as a State body and delegate of functions of public power. There is no criticism of the proposition, but there are mentions that the AIB had a wider programme in organizing the Corporative State, which assigned to unions three other functions besides the economic: political, cultural, and moral, establishing unions for the Integral labourer, as recommended by the AIB.[61]

Even with the previous denial, due to frustration and political defeat at the moment of implementing the Estado Novo, the constitution which represented corporatism politically in Vargas's proposition was celebrated by Integralists, who identified an influence and a certain victory of the movement in an ideological concept, recalled, in 1937, with Plínio Salgado's words in the AIB's *Manifesto de outubro de 1932*: 'Um governo que saia da livre vontade das classes é representativo da Pátria' [A government based on the free will of the classes is representative of the Nation],[62] that in order to meet national needs, the AIB proposes a corporative State.[63]

Final Considerations

The issue of corporatism in the AIB can provide answers to a few questions. First of all, it is clear that there was a divergence of substantiations, propositions, and ends regarding what the Integral State should be. Apart from Miguel Reale's corporatism being more technical, due to his role as a fundamentalist on this issue in the movement, he also assumed a character that differs from the other two leaders.

Thus, corporatism turns out to be a matrix and a variant of the specificities of each author, who also included internal currents, as can be seen in the spiritual aspect established with Plínio Salgado and the profoundly antisemitic basis in Gustavo Barroso.

[60] See Odilon Caldeira Neto, 'Gustavo Barroso e o esquecimento: integralismo, antissemitismo e escrita de si', *Cadernos do Tempo Presente*, 14 (2013), 44–56.
[61] Anor Butler Maciel, *Subsídios*, pp. 8–9.
[62] Ibid., p. 10.
[63] Anor Butler Maciel, *O Estado Corporativo* (Porto Alegre: Edição da Livraria do Globo, 1936), p. 132.

More than internal currents of a political movement, such divergences evidence the diversity of Integralism itself, resolved in theory by the head and their deliberations. Despite the existence of disputes, this unity showed strength during AIB's lifespan, even though it turned out to be incapable after the end of the movement. Despite viewing the difference between an Integral corporatist model and a fundamentally economically supported tendency, some Integralists looked to insertion in the Estado Novo, the regime responsible for the movement's dilution. A possible way to success (the adoption of a supposedly Integral model for the Brazilian State) became the exact opposite for Integralists.

The Technical Councils of the Brazilian Government Structure: Corporatism, Authoritarianism and Modernization (1934–1945)

Cássio A. A. Albernaz

Pontifícia Universidade Católica do Rio Grande do Sul

In the 1930s, Brazil's economic growth, progressively, shifts from an export-led agricultural production to a state-led industrialization. Thus, it was necessary to create the structural conditions for the establishment of industrialization in order to overcome the economic backwardness compared to other industrialized countries.[1] At the beginning, this process was marked by a strong nationalist and authoritarian ideological content, through which the Government began to centralize and concentrate its power in various sectors of the economy in order to promote the industrialization process.[2]

Moreover, the Government sought to reform its structure and to incorporate new strategic functions in the political system, laying foundations, which gave them the role of an inductor, and in some cases, a development process inductor. In this respect, the strengthening of the centralization mechanisms in the Executive were gradually expanded and diversified, either with greater centralization or with greater fragmentation of the institutional structure. As a result, the interventionist and corporatist mechanisms joined the industrializing development project, defining and implementing a state interventionist institutional model in the economy.

This pattern of growth, in which industrialization and development became synonyms, also promoted a *material framework* in the government, through the multiplication and the overlapping of different bureaucratic-administrative bodies — centralized and national — thus allowing the intervention (even in a limited way) and development planning by the Brazilian Government.[3] This is how the Technical Councils are seen in the statist structure when they were created as important channels of definitions and general guidelines of

---

[1] On this subject see: Celso Furtado, *Formação econômica do Brasil*, Coleção Biblioteca Básica Brasileira (Brasília: Editora Universidade de Brasília, 1963); João Manuel Cardoso de Mello, *O capitalismo tardio* (São Paulo: Brasiliense, 1982); Annibal V. Villela and Wilson Suzigan, *Política do governo e crescimento da economia brasileira, 1889–1945* (Rio de Janeiro: IPEA/INPES, 1973).
[2] Eli Cerqueira Diniz: *Empresários, Estado e capitalismo no Brasil, 1930–1945* (Rio de Janeiro: Paz e Terra 1978).
[3] Sônia Miriam Draibe, *Rumos e Metamorfoses: um estudo sobre a constituição do Estado e as alternativas da industrialização no Brasil, 1930–1960*, 2nd edn (Rio de Janeiro: Paz e Terra, 2004).

development economic policies and that declare themselves as important spaces of power.

This paper, therefore, aims at analysing the emergence of the Technical Councils as the state economic planning bodies, between 1930 and 1945, seeking to identify the main organs. This analysis will provide an understanding of some political, social and institutional dynamics of the Brazilian Government history, its relations with the representation of interests, the paths, and the main bodies for the orientation and definition of development guidelines.

Thus, it will be possible to map out the main centres of the decision and planning of the Brazilian economic and industrial development in this period. Also, it will be possible to identify the roots and nature of these organs, their duties, their effective period of influence, their composition, and the criteria for recruiting members through legislation.

The Construction of Planning Bodies (1934-1945)

As previously mentioned, the implementation of an industrial policy by the Brazilian Government demanded a bureaucratic-administrative structure of intervention, regulation and control of the economic system, and, at the same time, it provided an emerging corporatist structure from the Estado Novo (New State), 1937-1945.[4] Hence, the Brazilian Government, during the 1930s and 1940s, experienced an expansion that, apart from the quantitative structure through the specialized organs, also involved a qualitative expansion of regulatory powers in the Brazilian economy. The bodies that were created in the institutional structure provided opportunities for an emerging number of organs (departments, technical councils, commissions, institutes, etc.) and that served as privileged spaces for those with 'expertise in economics'.[5] These organs were important decision-making and definition centres of economic guidelines policies of the Brazilian Government, as well as serving as privileged spaces for the representation of interests.[6]

---

[4] Several studies emphasize the corporatist character of the post-1930 Brazilian government, and especially post-Estado Novo. In this regard see: Diniz, *Empresários, Estado e capitalismo*; Draibe, *Rumos e Metamorfoses*; Vanda Ribeiro Costa, *A Armadilha do Leviatã: a construção do corporativismo no Brasil* (Rio de Janeiro: UERJ, 1999); Evaldo Vieira, *Autoritarismo e corporativismo no Brasil*, 3rd edn (São Paulo: Ed. Unesp, 2010). About the corporatist government see Philippe C. Schmitter, 'Still the Century of Corporativism?', *The Review of Politics*, 36 (1974), 85-131, online at <http://journals.cambridge.org/action/displayAbstract?fromPage=online&aid=5321652>, and Alfred Stepan, *Estado, corporativismo e autoritarismo* (São Paulo: Paz e Terra, 1980).

[5] Octávio Ianni, *Estado e planejamento econômico no brasil (1930-1970)* (Rio de Janeiro: Civilização Brasileira, 1971); Draibe, *Rumos e Metamorfoses*; Ângela de Castro Gomes, *Engenheiros e economistas: novas elites burocráticas* (Rio de Janeiro: Ed. FGV, 1994); Maria Rita Loureiro: *Os economistas no governo: gestão econômica e democracia* (Rio de Janeiro: Ed. FGV, 1997).

[6] Luciano Martins, *Politique et développement économique: structure de pouvoir e système de décisions au Brésil (1930-1964)* (Paris: Université de Paris, 1973); Luciano Martins, *Pouvoir et développement économique: formation et évolution des structures politiques au brésil* (Paris: Ed. Anthropos, 1976); Sérgio H. Abranches, 'The Divided Leviathan: State and Economic Policy Formation in Authoritarian

In addition to the demand for professionals with some expertise and knowledge in the area of economics, these bodies also played a role as training centres for specialized agents in economic planning.[7] Thus, these bodies defined development guidelines, elaborated studies, suggested general and sectoral policies, guided and directed investments, representing an important element by creating decision/influence spaces that were occupied, gradually, by 'technicians and experts' in economic planning issues.

In this context, the process of renewal of the state ruling elites took place, or, more specifically, the process of those elites devoted to a 'new' political competence that was being institutionalized, based on economic knowledge, and in particular, on Brazilian economic development. The emergence of these agents, in 1930, arose through the government, which became a privileged arena by controlling the access to new 'competitors' in the political area, since the democratic ways were restricted over the greater part of the period.

It is worth mentioning that the creation of the National Technical Councils happened through the debates in the Constituent National Assembly, between 1933 and 1934, and they were presented by a group of deputies connected to the Centre of Industries and the Federation of the Industries of São Paulo State (Centro das Indústrias do Estado de São Paulo — CIESP / Federação das Indústrias do Estado de São Paulo — FIESP)[8]. The proposal of the Technical Councils arose as a counterpart of the industrial groups to the debates on the formal representation of the professional associations in Parliament aimed at a better articulation of interests.

The 1934 Constitution incorporated the Technical Councils, in Article 103. However, their approach did not reach that initially expected by the industrial leaders from CIESP / FIESP in the Constituent Assembly. In this respect, despite the format approved by the 1934 Constitution suggested by the industrial leaders — councils formed by mixed members bringing together Government experts and professional association representatives — the functions approved in the constitutional text were basically consultative, aiming at qualifying

---

Brasil' (unpublished PhD dissertation, Cornell University, 1978); Diniz, *Empresários, Estado e capitalismo*; Renato Raul Boschi, *Elites industriais e democracia: hegemonia burguesa e mudança política no Brasil* (Rio de Janeiro: Graal, 1979); Adriano Nervo Codato, 'Estrutura política e interesse de classe: uma análise do sistema estatal no Brasil pós-1964. O caso do Conselho de Desenvolvimento Econômico' (unpublished MA thesis, UNICAMP, 1995); Maria Antonieta P. Leopoldi, *Política e interesses na industrialização brasileira: as associações industriais, a política econômica e o Estado* (Rio de Janeiro: Paz e Terra, 2000); Draibe, *Rumos e Metamorfoses*.

[7] According to the testimony of Jesus Soares Pereira on the Foreign Trade Federal Council, 'Para mim, uma grande escola técnica [...], a minha grande escola ativa no trato dos problemas econômicos nacionais, pois [no Brasil] não havia nessa época escola de economia' [For me, a huge technical school [...], my great school active in dealing with national economic problems, because [in Brazil] there was no school of economics at that time]. Jesus Soares Pereira, *Petróleo, energia elétrica, siderurgia: a luta pela emancipação (depoimento)* (Rio de Janeiro: Paz e Terra, 1975), p. 46.

[8] There were five members connected to CIESP / FIESP in the 1933/1934 Constituent Assembly: Roberto Simonsen, Horacio Lafer, Alexandre Siciliano Jr., Pacheco and Silva, who were elected by the class of employers, and Ranulpho Pinheiro Lima, chosen by the self-employed professionals.

parliamentary and ministerial activity. Thus, these councils presented features that were more technical than deliberative, as originally expected in the 779th Amendment.[9]

Nevertheless, through the Technical Councils, industrial representatives participated in consultative instances, providing opinions and proposing projects on strategic aspects of political, economic and social legislation. If, at first, they had no power of deliberation, either defining or blocking the agenda of debate and decision, they eventually ended up taking some deliberative functions, functions beyond answering a simple query, or transmitting and exchanging technical information. Thus, for the industries, the Technical Councils would represent the guarantee of a space to represent their interests, enabling them to intervene in the decision-making process. They could also organize and define their interests for further negotiation and reformulation through an interactive process with other interests.

It was between 1934 and 1945 that the bodies focused on the economic and industrial development planning.[10] It is possible to identify five bodies that were linked to the implementation of the general planning of the economic and industrial development policies: the Foreign Trade Federal Council (Conselho Federal do Comércio Exterior — CFCE), created in 1934; the Economic and Finance Technical Council (Conselho Técnico de Economia e Finanças — CTEF), created in 1937; the Coordination of Economic Mobilization (Coordenação de Mobilização Econômica — CME), created in 1942; The National Council of Industrial and Trade Policy (Conselho Nacional de Política Industrial e Comercial — CNPIC), created in 1943; and the Economic Planning Commission (Comissão de Planejamento Econômico — CPE), established in 1944.[11]

---

[9] See Section III — Technical Councils — Article 103 of the 1934 Constitution. In §4 it states that 'é vedado a qualquer Ministro tomar deliberação, em matéria da sua competência exclusiva, contra o parecer unânime do respectivo Conselho' [no Minister is allowed to take decisions on matters of their exclusive competence, against the unanimous opinion of the respective Council].

[10] It is not my purpose, here, to list all the moments and all the institutions that dealt with industrial development in Brazilian history. The periodization adopted is according to the studies of: Mário Wagner Vieira da Cunha, *O sistema administrativo brasileiro* (Rio de Janeiro: Centro Brasileiro de Pesquisas Educacionais, 1963); Jorge Vianna Monteiro and Luiz Roberto Azevedo Cunha, 'Alguns aspectos da evolução do planejamento econômico no Brasil (1934–1963)', *Pesquisa e Planejamento Econômico* (Rio de Janeiro), 4.1 (Feb. 1974), 1–24; Paulo Roberto Almeida, *A experiência brasileira em planejamento econômico: uma síntese histórica*, online at <http://pralmeida.org/05DocsPRA/1277HistorPlanejBrasil.pdf> (2004).

[11] These bodies, along with the Public Service Administration Department (Departamento de Administração do Serviço Público — DASP), are appointed by historiography as centres for economic planning and for Brazilian industrial development in the 1930s. Regarding this, see: Robert T. Daland, *Estratégia e estilo do planejamento brasileiro* (Rio de Janeiro: Liador, 1969); Jorge Gustavo da Costa, *Planejamento governamental: a experiência brasileira* (Rio de Janeiro: Editora FGV, 1971); Ianni, *Estado e planejamento econômico*; Martins, *Politique et développement économique* and *Pouvoir et développement économique*; Jorge Vianna Monteiro and Luiz Roberto Azevedo Cunha, 'A organização do planejamento econômico: o caso brasileiro', *Pesquisa e Planejamento Econômico* (Rio de Janeiro), 3.4 (Dec. 1973), 1045–64 and 'Alguns aspectos'; Algenyr dos Santos Correia and Rosa Maria Esteves Nogueira, 'A intervenção do Estado no domínio econômico: o caso da Coordenação da Mobilização

However, critics have pointed out that, despite the centralizing tendencies of the Vargas period, there would not be a unique central body, in this period, focused on planning with legal competence to centralize these actions.[12] Thus, the activities of the planning organs, emerged in the government structure of this period, marked by overlapping the attributions and functions, by the structural deficiencies, the parallelisms, and the conflicts of competence.[13]

It is fundamental to highlight, however, that the decisions were taken, often, at the level of bodies other than the planning, which indicates the nature of the state organization, particularly in the period of a hypertrophied executive. Thus, these 'dysfunctions' cannot be analysed only by the lack of coordination and lack of decision-making power from certain bodies, but the political determinants for such a statist model should be also taken into account.

Anyhow, if in the period between 1934 and 1945 there was no central planning agency with wide decision-making powers, it did not mean that the different state bodies were beyond the definitions of the guidelines for an economic and industrial development model, especially regarding the justification for the need to industrialize the country with the statist support.

Thus, this first post-1930 planning experiment was aimed, through the creation of statist bodies dedicated to planning, at economic and political purposes related to the concrete challenges in this period. So, it seems too much to expect that, at that time, the statist planning structure arose through a body ready to centralize and coordinate economic development, since the theme was presented in an unfinished form as suggested by the agenda for discussions in the period.[14]

Econômica', *Dados*, 13.2 (1976), 134–50; Diniz, *Empresários, Estado e capitalismo*; Boschi, *Elites industriais e democracia*; Ricardo Bielschowsky, *Pensamento econômico brasileiro: o ciclo ideológico do desenvolvimentismo* (Rio de Janeiro: Contraponto, 1996). With reference to DASP, the body created by the 1937 Constitution and established by Decree-Law No. 579 of 1938, according to Monteiro and Cunha and even though it was understood as the 'early focus of initial efforts in the Brazilian planning' it was more important as a body of public service and staff administration, in the universalization of procedures, besides preparing the government's budget proposals. Their importance for developmental planning is linked, at first, to the formulation of short-term plans, such as the Special Plan (Plano Especial), 1939, the Plan of Works and Equipment (Plano de Obras e Equipamentos), 1943, and SALTE Plan, 1949, limited to budget elaboration. Further, during the Dutra Government, DASP underwent great changes and its functions were restricted only to budget elaboration. Due to the difficulty in the implementation of the SALT Plan, which was coordinated directly by DASP, other sources of investment were created and used, reducing the importance of DASP in the economic area.

[12] Martins, *Politique et développement économique* and *Pouvoir et développement économique*; Diniz, *Empresários, Estado e capitalismo*; Draibe, *Rumos e Metamorfoses*.

[13] This discussion would be reviewed in the 1950s through the preliminary draft of the Administrative Reform submitted in 1952 by Getúlio Vargas to the Nacional Congress that aimed at 'the creation of a general body of coordination and planning'; Draibe, *Rumos e Metamorfoses*, p. 214.

[14] It is important to highlight that the concept of economic planning was not applied in a clear and complete way during the 1930s and 1940s, and then it was mistaken for the concept of *economic planification*, or for their own governmental plans, considering that these notions were very often used indistinctly. A significant historical comprehension can be gained through the debates held during the Brazilian economy planning period, between Eugenio Gudin and Roberto Simonsen. As Martins points out, it is only in the 1950s, through the press and through the development of the discussions of USA–Brazil Economic Commission (COMBEU) and the Economic Commission for Latin America

According to the institutional engineering of the period, the Technical Councils played important key roles, especially in the area of economic policy, by promoting space for a technical bureaucracy and for the representation of different economic interests, particularly industrial ones. As indicated by the 1934 Constitution, Article 103, its basic purpose was to help the government formulate policies and make decisions.

The objective of this organizational pattern involved serious political consequences, as it focused on reducing the embarrassments of successive interventions of the Ministry of Finance in the decisions and economic guidelines. In a centralized and interventionist government, it was, therefore, up to the Technical Councils to mediate in the relationships between the Ministries and the President of the Republic.

However, the political purpose of these bodies, within a statist structure, goes beyond opening up room for a technical bureaucracy to overcome the limitations and lack of knowledge of the political elites about the Brazilian reality. That is, it goes beyond approximation, decision and interaction between the administrative and bureaucratic centralization of a strong and centralizing government and the 'economic classes', as the authoritarian intellectuals of the period suggested.[15] It is understood that the Technical Councils also served as important spaces for planning and defining guidelines for the modernization and the development of the Brazilian Government, and therefore, they played a decisive role to guide and to define the path of the Brazilian Government.

The Foreign Trade Federal Council (O Conselho Federal de Comércio Exterior — CFCE)[16]

Within the broad political and institutional reforms of the first Vargas Era (1930–1945), whose objectives reflected a more general political and

---

(CEPAL), that these terms are better adjusted in debates; Luís Carlos dos Passos Martins, 'A grande imprensa "liberal" da capital federal (RJ) e a política econômica do segundo governo Vargas (1951–1954): conflito entre projetos de desenvolvimento nacional' (unpublished doctoral thesis, PUCRS, Porto Alegre, 2010). However, through historiography, it is common to observe planning analysis that did not advance the description and analysis of government plans, such as: Daland, *Estratégia e estilo*; Costa, *Planejamento governamental*; Ianni, *Estado e planejamento econômico*; Betty Mindlin Lafer, *Planejamento no Brasil* (São Paulo: Perspectiva, 1975). Criticizing this kind of approach, Monteiro and Cunha, state that 'It is an additional error to name Plans several documents that have no common characteristics. This aspect is very relevant in the analysis of the 1934/1945 period when most of the so-called Plans then presented were only budget reinforcement of the government [...]'.Otherwise, 'the major feature of the planning would be in the economic policy administration, especially in the organizational form of decision-making. The plan would not be a necessary or sufficient condition for the assessment of the planning' (Monteiro and Cunha, 'Alguns aspectos', p. 2).

[15] Argumentation proposed mainly by Oliveira Viana and Azevedo Amaral.

[16] The body was in existence between 1934 and 1949. However, the most effective period of its activity as an economic and industrial development planning body, even incipiently, was until 1945. Many authors highlight the CFCE as the first governmental planning body, considering the broad scope of its activities. In this regard see: Pereira, *Petróleo, energia elétrica, siderurgia*; Monteiro and Cunha, 'Alguns aspectos'; Diniz, *Empresários, Estado e capitalismo*; Draibe, *Rumos e Metamorfoses*.

administrative centralization and the strengthening of the government's powers of intervention, both in the economic and in the political control, the Foreign Trade Federal Council (Conselho Federal de Comércio Exterior — CFCE) was created, by Decree No. 24429 of 20 June 1934. Thus, the body was created as an important part of a complex administrative engineering provided by the 1934 Constitution, Article 103, through an intervenor system and the creation and improvement of institutions, autarchies and technical councils, was able to materialize a new institutional design.

In the beginning, the purpose of the CFCE aimed to centralize, to rationalize and to expand the foreign trade policy of the country according to a system through which they sought to formulate the economic policies, focusing on reducing their external dependency. As was defined by Decree No. 24429, of 20 June 1934:

> a solução racional dos problemas do comércio internacional exige combinações, acordos, favores, trocas e operações que são da iniciativa ou da alçada do poder público; considerando a oportunidade e a urgência de ser criado para esse fim um órgão coordenador de todos os departamentos federais e estaduais de produção do país e das suas classes produtoras, como têm feito as grandes nações.
>
> [the rational solution to the problems of international trade demands agreements, arrangements, favours, exchanges and operations that are on the initiative or within the jurisdiction of the government; considering the opportunity and urgency of creating, for this purpose, a coordinating organ of all federal and state departments of the country's production and its producing classes, as the great nations have done.][17]

In the early years, the CFCE focused on the elaboration of studies and on reports relating to tariff policy, foreign exchange, and foreign trade. However, over time, its responsibilities expanded beyond common foreign trade policy and started focusing on resolutions, economic policy coordination, and on the definition of planning guidelines of the industrial and economic development.

Hence, the CFCE arose as an instrument to expand state control of economic activities, its function being to help the Government to formulate political guidelines and to make decisions. The CFCE proposed measures aimed at the development of national production in order to increase Brazilian exports.

Concerning the CFCE representation, it was nominally chaired by the President himself, but in fact that role was performed by an executive director. The council originally consisted of thirteen members, as follows: four members indicated by the ministries (Ministry of Foreign Affairs, Ministry of Finance, Ministry of Agriculture, Ministry of Labour, Industry and Trade); a representative member of the Bank of Brazil; and a representative member of the Trade Association; three representatives with expertise in Foreign Trade;

---

[17] Presentation of Decree No. 24.429 of 20 June 1934.

and four technical consultants. All the members had to be selected directly by the President.[18]

It is worth highlighting that in the beginning the government ministers did not participate directly in the composition of the CFCE. The only members who participated were the representatives of the ministries, even though the government ministers would be at the plenary meetings. The members of the CFCE were people who had some influence on the economic policy guidelines, whereas the technical consultants participated in the plenary sessions, but they could only vote when the other members were prevented from voting.

The Foreign Trade Federal Council was divided into three chambers: the chamber of advertising and credit; the chamber of production, tariffs and transport; and the chamber of trade and negotiation. These chambers served to promote proposals and opinions for consideration by the council. Then, if they were approved, they were directed to the President of Brazil. Only after the approval of the President could they pass into law.

Between 1934 and 1937, 170 ordinary sessions were held during which studies and opinions related to the foreign trade policy, tariffs and exchange rate policies were promoted, and thus industrial policy measures were suggested. Gradually, the role of the CFCE started expanding, to include advising the government on foreign trade and giving opinions on any issues concerned the economic interests of the country, when addressed by the President.

In 1937, given the political condition of the Estado Novo, the CFCE expanded its range of actions even more, by becoming the government advisory council for any matter related to the economy. Thus, according the amendment of Decree-Law No. 74 of 16 December 1937, the CFCE developed a new organization, with the establishment of the National Economic Council (Conselho Nacional de Economia — CNE) required by the 1937 Constitution. According to its Article 2, it was determined that the council must consist of fifteen members, among which ten were directors and five were technical consultants. The distribution comprised of: one member representing the Ministry of Finance; one member representing the Ministry of Agriculture; one member representing the Ministry of Labour, Industry and Trade; one member representing the Ministry of Transport and Public Works; one Member of the Ministry of Foreign Affairs; one member representative of the Bank of Brazil; three class representative members: agriculture, industry and trade, respectively, out of a three-nominee list submitted to the President of the Republic by the Brazilian Rural Confederation (Confederação Rural Brasileira — CRB), the Brazilian Industrial Confederation (Confederação Industrial do Brasil — CIB) and the Brazilian Trade Federation (Federação das Associações Comerciais do Brasil — FACB); and one member chosen from among those with expertise in financial and economic studies and affairs. However, the five technical consultants had to be

---

[18] According to Article 3 of Decree No. 24.429 of 20 June 1934.

chosen from among those with expertise in customs duty; statistics; transport; rural economy and commercial law.[19]

This first reorganization of the CFCE, to include a representative member of the Ministry of Transport and Public Works (Ministério da Viação e Obras Públicas — MVOP) and one more technical adviser, was necessary to formalize a dynamic of the first period of the existence of the council, since they were already including the ministry informally. The reorganization also aimed at greater prestige by expanding the representation of the ministries and their technical skill. This reformulation met their objective of boosting the political intermediation of interests between the ministries and the Presidency. The great feature of this period was to promote a central economic coordinating and development planning body.

In the second phase, between 1937 and 1939 — during the reorganization — the CFCE held sixty ordinary sessions, analysing and developing opinions on several economic issues, whose greater prominence was the creation of the Petroleum National Council (Conselho Nacional do Petróleo — CNP).

The CFCE was once again reorganized by Decree-Law No. 1.163, of 17 March 1939, and as Diniz pointed out, 'it, in fact, represented the recognition of the evolution of the body over the previous year, specifically trying to make a reality of the idea of a central body of an economic coordination'.[20] The 1937 Constitution foresaw the creation of the National Economic Council (Conselho Nacional de Economia — CNE), but it was only established later. Thus, the CFCE started shaping up along the lines of what the CNE would be, and it played roles of coordination and promotion of production, becoming the advisory council to the Presidency for economic affairs.[21]

Concerning the composition of the council, according to Decree 1.163, the number of directors increased to sixteen, including three class representative members: agriculture, industry and trade. Each one was chosen from among three retired people, respectively from CRB, CNI and the Brazilian Trade Association Federation. The remaining members were chosen from among persons of 'recognized competence'.

Thus, with the amendments made in 1937 and 1939, respectively, the council achieved additional functions, occupying a distinctive position as the government's economic advisory body, becoming a consultative body of the Presidency of Brazil for economic issues and fulfilling the role of economic planning and coordination of other economic policy bodies. As Diniz has stated, 'the CFCE reflected such effort, a distinctive feature of the centralizing

---

[19] According to Decree Law No. 74 of 16 December 1937.
[20] Eli Diniz, 'Foreign Trade Federal Council', entry in *Dicionário Histórico-Biográfico Brasileiro* (hereafter DHBB).
[21] The 1937 Constitution foresaw the creation of the National Economic Council (Conselho Nacional Econômico — CNE), which would be chaired directly by a Minister of State, and that the Council would act as a centralizing body for economic issues.

experience of the period, in order to test embryonic forms of economic planning'.[22]

According to the testimony of Jesus Soares Pereira, 'the CFCE was a deliberative and even a legislative machine of the Estado Novo. The real creator body of an economic legislation for the country'.[23] During its existence, the CFCE stood out as one of the most important organs and reflected the centralizing efforts of the Vargas Era, starting from an untested model of economic and industrial development planning. In fact, the CFCE outlined important solutions for some of the priority issues of that time, for example, matters relating to steel production and to oil. Thus, the CFCE can be considered the first planning body for economic activities in Brazil.

As the CFCE started being institutionalized as an economic planning body, its class-base representation started increasing and it began to hire more and more members with 'recognized competence', making their selection process more flexible, and their plenary sessions relied on wide participation of the ministries (which were no longer formally part of the body) and class representatives. The CFCE underwent several changes in its institutional design until December 1949, when it was dissolved and replaced by the CNE, envisaged by the 1937 Constitution but only established by the 1946 Constitution.

The Economics and Finance Technical Council (CTEF)[24]

As part of the Estado Novo's project of political and administrative centralization, the Economics and Finance Technical Council (Conselho Técnico de Economia e Finanças — CTEF) was created, by Decree-Law No. 14 of 25 November 1937. The CTEF was conceived as a technical body with an advisory capacity, connected to the Ministry of Finance in order to study and gather information from different Brazilian states, to monitor and control the state and municipal finances, aimed at 'correcting the distortions resulting from the prevailing excessive autonomy of the Brazilian states in the previous regime'.[25] Thus, the CTEF aimed to centralize in the federal executive the regional financial operations to control the internal and external debt of the states and municipalities. It was up to the CTEF to issue opinions on various aspects of economic and financial policy (taxation, banking and monetary law, tax incentives, fuel use and energy policy, industrial policy).[26]

With regard to its composition, the CTEF was chaired directly by the Minister of Finance and consisted of eight advisers and a technical secretary, appointed directly by the President of the Republic. As a criterion for recruitment, it

---

[22] Eli Diniz, 'Foreign Trade Federal Council', entry in DHBB.
[23] Pereira, *Petróleo, energia elétrica, siderurgia*, p. 49.
[24] The CTEF existed between 1937 and 1971.
[25] Eli Diniz, 'Economics and Finance Technical Council', entry in DHBB.
[26] According to Decree-law No. 14, of 25 November 1937.

emphasized the need for people with 'remarkable knowledge' in the field of economics and finance.[27]

According to Diniz, 'obeying the dominant orientation at the time, the corporatist principle of representation of the business community within the State apparatus would be reflected in the systematic appointment of representatives of the industrial, financial and commercial business in the board composition'.[28] Thus, it is suggested that the CTEF would have been an important means of expression and articulation of the private sector within the structure of the Estado Novo.

As regards its internal organization, the council was composed of a deliberative and an executive body. In its deliberative body, the council was formed by the president, the advisers and the technical secretary. In its executive body, it was subdivided into four divisions (administration, control and monitoring of external debt, financial studies, and economic studies) and a technical secretariat, besides subsidiary bodies (special commissions and economic and financial conferences).[29]

The CTEF, as an advisory body of the Ministry of Finance, played an important role in the reorganization and rationalization of the Brazilian tax system during the Estado Novo to standardize the state and municipal budgets.[30] Additionally, it played an important role in the planning of Brazilian industrial development, especially in discussions involving steel and oil policies.[31] At the same time, the CFCE advocated the need to draw up a law regulating the organization of industrial credit banks to deepen the process of industrialization in the country.

However, with the end of the Estado Novo, the CTEF began concentrating its activities in the areas of tax and budget policy. Decree No. 63 abolished the agency on 14 January 1971 and it was absorbed by the Sub-secretariat for Economy and Finance, a new body established in the Ministry of Finance.

The Coordination of Economic Mobilization (CME)[32]

The outbreak of the Second World War, in 1939, accelerated the intervention

---

[27] Idem.
[28] Eli Diniz, 'Economics and Finance Technical Council', entry in DHBB.
[29] With the reform of the CTEF's internal structure in 1953, its executive body began to operate through the establishment of four chambers: a chamber of external and domestic debt, consolidated and floating; a chamber of economy and finances in general; a chamber of exchange supervision, transfer of funds abroad and exchange rate policy; and finally, a chamber of banking organization and monetary system in order to cover the wide area of the body's activity. According to Decree No. 34791 of 16 December 1953.
[30] This standardization is given by Decree No. 1804 of 24 November 1939, and supplemented by Decree No. 2416 of 17 July 1940.
[31] Boschi, *Elites industriais e democracia*.
[32] Despite not being strictly a body of the state structure, the Coordination of Economic Mobilization (Coordenação de Mobilização Econômica — CME) served as one during the War scenario, coordinatingthe joint committee of ministers. Its existence coincided with the period of Brazil's participation in World War II, between 1942 and 1945, with the CME was created for this

process of the Brazilian Government in the economic domain, in terms of economic nationalism — the defence of 'national interests' — and military defence. Thus, the coordination of economic activities, through planning as an instrument of state economic policy, became the centre of political discussions, especially as regards the organization of information, analysis of problems, decision-making, and control and implementation of economic development policies.

The impact on International Business resulting from this war scenario led the Brazilian government, through the CFCE, to create the Supply Commission (1939) and the National Defence Commission (1940), which consisted of representatives of several government departments and which were appointed by the President himself.[33] However, both committees were limited to the establishment of a price control system, not exercising effectively the coordinating activity that they had been assigned.

Even before Brazil's entry into the World War, there had been debates on the need to create a clearinghouse for economic decisions. However, with the declaration of war against the Axis powers made by the Brazilian Government in August 1942, a 'body of a more comprehensive character' was provided for, according to Article 180 of the 1937 Constitution, which was to replace the two committees.[34] Thus, by Decree-Law No. 4750, of 28 September 1942, the Coordination of Economic Mobilization (Coordenação de Mobilização Econômica — CME), which aimed to coordinate the functioning of the economy in the context of the emergency generated by Brazil's entry into the war, was created.

The CME was a body subordinated directly to the President of the Republic and in charge of the control and supervision of bodies, state enterprises and private companies related to 'strategic sectors' of the national economy.[35] In addition to responding to the emergency nature of the war, the CME had, as an underlying goal, the institutionalization of state control over the Brazilian

purpose. See in this regard Correia and Nogueira, 'A intervenção do Estado no domínio econômico'.
[33] Despite its initial neutrality, Brazil was affected by the fall in exports of its agricultural products, especially coffee, and the difficulty in importing machinery, industrial raw materials and fuels. In addition, there was the demand for ordnance made by the nations involved in the conflict.
[34] In addition to the Article 180 of the 1937 Constitution, the Public Service Administration Department (Departamento de Administração do Serviço Público — DASP), through the *Explanatory Memorandum*, number 1811 of 31 July 1942, also points to the need for a body of 'broader scope' due to the war scenario. Thus, according to this document '[...] before the international events, the internal difficulties arising from it, the undeniable need to extend the presence of the State action in this serious situation, to accelerate by all means the preparation of the economic and social structure of the nation to face the crisis, it is imperative to give the Government the necessary support to address the situation. A body under single direction must be created, with its own personality and administrative autonomy, with jurisdiction within and outside Brazil, armed with broad powers over administrative bodies and private entities, to coordinate, under the guidance of Your Excellency, the economic mobilization of the country.'
[35] The Coordination of Economic Mobilization had its administration centralized in the Federal District (Rio de Janeiro City, at the time) and had regional offices in the main capitals of the country, chiefly in the states of São Paulo, Rio Grande do Sul, Santa Catarina, Paraná and Minas Gerais.

economy. Thus, it represented a major effort of coordination and planning, confirming, despite its emergency nature, the trend of that time towards centralization and State intervention in the economy.

Stimulating agricultural and industrial production, supplying the domestic market, fixing the prices of essential food products, improving the transport system and fighting inflation were some of the CME's main functions. Thus, the agency acted as a 'super ministry' with broad powers to intervene in economic activities, especially in the setting of prices and wages, in supply and transportation problems, and in the establishing of production targets aimed at reducing the effects of war on the national economy. Thus, the CME absorbed much of the power of the Foreign Trade Federal Council.

The wide CME summit structure had a general coordinator, chosen directly by the Brazilian President, an advisory board, a planning sector, an information sector, research bodies and a secretariat, linked directly to the coordinator. Below this structure, there were a large number of sectoral executive bodies of coordination and direct action divided into three departments (Industrial Production Sector, Supply Services Sector, and Pricing and Imported Products Licensing Sector) and specific bodies of distribution and production, which were created according to the demand.[36] The Members of the CME structure were recruited from other bodies of the state structure (mainly from the ministries, boards, commissions, and autonomous bodies) and also from different states.

Consequently, the CME used the existing administrative structure in Brazil from before the war, and sought to guide this structure according to the new requirements, but it also created new bodies of direct action. At this point, the criticisms in the literature on the role of CME emerge due to the overlap of direct bodies of action, when there were already bodies able to perform such duties.[37]

The Industrial Production Sector (Setor da Produção Industrial — SPI) stood out within the CME structure, mainly regarding the discussions about the steel industry, pointing beyond the supplies needed for an effective planning of industrial production in Brazil. In this sense, the SPI was responsible for encouraging and creating new industries in order to produce goods for import substitution. The SPI was, therefore, important to the war effort and for the development and systematization of Brazilian industrial development, incorporating more accurately industrial policies to economic policy.

The CME was abolished in December 1945, just months after the end of the war, but almost all its departments were absorbed by the various ministries and the coordinator's duties passed to the Executive Director of CFCE.[38]

---

[36] D.O.U. [Diário Oficial da União] of 2 December 1942, Section 1, p. 17495. According to an interview with João Carlos Vital, CME coordinator in 1944, the CME once had two thousand employees; see Correia and Nogueira, 'A intervenção do Estado no domínio econômico'.
[37] This critique appears in Diniz's work (*Empresários, Estado e capitalismo*).
[38] On the extinction of the CME see D.O.U. from 28 December 1945, Section 1, p. 19201.

The National Council of Industrial and Trade Policy (CNPIC)[39]

The National Council of Industrial and Trade Policy (Conselho Nacional de Política Industrial e Comercial — CNPIC) was established in 1944 by Decree-Law No. 5982, of 10 November 1943, as an advisory body connected directly to the Ministry of Labour, Industry and Commerce (MTIC). Its goal was to study the industrial and commercial policy for a post-war scenario, and to propose planning guidelines for the national economy. The creation of CNPIC aimed at better coordination among many sectors of public administration, taking into account the various studies of the councils, of several public departments, and class representation entities already established, and that were involved in industrial and commercial activities.[40]

When highlighting the urgent need to define an industrial and trade policy for the post-war period it is worth mentioning the importance of the Ministry of Labour, Industry and Commerce (MTIC), during Alexandre Marcondes Filho's administration, for the creation of CNPIC. The body was composed of representatives appointed by four ministries: the Minister of Labour, Industry and Commerce in person (as the president of CNPIC); a representative of the Ministry of Finance; a representative of the Ministry of Agriculture; and a representative of the Ministry of Transport and Public Works. Also belonging to the composition were two industrial representatives, and two representatives of trade (indicated by the respective bodies), and five members with 'remarkable knowledge', directly appointed by the President himself.[41]

Regarding the role of the CNPIC within the state structure, one of its members, Rômulo Almeida says that this 'represented an attempt at a government partnership with the industrial sector which, through its most important leaders, was pressing for greater involvement in the formulation of alternatives in economic policy.'[42] For Diniz's part,

> among the advisory bodies created during the Estado Novo as part of the corporate project implemented over the period from 1930 to 1945, the National Council of Industrial and Trade Policy (Conselho Nacional de Política Industrial e Comercial — CNPIC) is among those most clearly committed to the view of transposing the conflict between different dominant groups of the state bureaucracy through self-representation in the technical bodies, of the main conflicting interests.[43]

However, according to Monteiro and Cunha, the creation of the CNPIC implied, in a sense, a duplication with the CFCE's tasks, which limited its importance as an economic decision-making body.[44] It is worth mentioning

---

[39] The CNPIC existed between 1944 and 1946. However, its most effective action ended in 1945.
[40] According to Decree-Law No. 5.982, from 10 November 1943.
[41] Article 1 Decree-Law No. 5.982, from 10 November 1943.
[42] Rômulo Almeida, *Experiência brasileira de planejamento orientação e controle da economia* (Rio de Janeiro: Edição de *Estudos Econômicos*, 1950).
[43] Diniz, 'Conselho Nacional de Política Industrial e Comercial (CNPIC)', entry in DHBB.
[44] Monteiro and Cunha, 'Alguns aspectos', p. 8.

the importance of the CNPIC for the seminal debate generated around the idea of creating a central body for coordination and planning of the economic and industrial development.

If, as a formal body, the CNPIC's functions overlapped with the CFCE's, the body also represented an arena for confrontation between different economic projects; hence the importance of the discussions developed within the CNPIC around the paths that the Brazilian economy should follow. This was evident in the famous *controversy over planning* between Roberto Simonsen, the CNPIC's rapporteur and the advocate of expanding the practice of protectionist measures in the Brazilian industry, and Eugênio Gudin, rapporteur of the Economic Planning Commission (Comissão de Planejamento Econômico — CPE), which pointed to the limitations of state *dirigisme* and protectionist policy.[45]

The debate on planning arose in the very first meeting of the Council when the President of the Council, Alexandre Marcondes Filho, asked members to study 'the fundamental principles that should guide the industrial and commercial development of Brazil in the future'.[46] As a result of this discussion, there were proposals for the organization and institutionalization of 'national planning' as a project submitted by the industrial representative, Roberto Simonsen, aiming at executives and governing bodies to enable this function, and that gave a new character to the interventionist state action, which was approved by the Council after discussions and amendments in the Council plenary. The approval of this proposal provoked strong reaction and criticism from the CFCE and the CPE, also created in 1944, and subject to the National Security Council, and they sought to undermine the CNPIC project. The person chosen as the CPE and the CTEF rapporteur on the CNPIC project, Eugênio Gudin, criticized and vehemently rejected the project, denouncing the inappropriate use of concepts and economic arguments, and suggesting a gradual reduction in state intervention mechanisms in the economy.

This debate went beyond the limits of state economic bureaucracy, since it constituted a significant element of the institutionalization of a space for a state planning elite, to promote and recognize economic planning as an important element in the definition of development guidelines, and therefore as an element in dispute in the political game.

With the end of the Estado Novo, and the closure of the project, CNPIC was extinguished by Decree-Law No. 9083, of 22 March 1946. Thus, its action was limited to the preparation of this project of the 'national economy planification' and it was unimpressive in terms of influence in the decision-making process. However, the debate generated was of great importance in the definition of an industrialization project, whose viability would depend on the strengthening of the state capacity to intervene in the economic field.

---

[45] The debates were published in Roberto Simonsen and Eugênio Gudin, *A controvérsia do planejamento na economia brasileira: coletâneas da polêmica Simonsen X Gudin* (Rio de Janeiro: IPEA/INPES, 1977).
[46] Indication number 09, according to ordinary meeting, 5 April 1944.

The Economic Planning Commission
(A Comissão de Planejamento Econômico — CPE)

While the discussions on planning in the CNPIC were developed, the Economic Planning Commission (CPE) was created by the Federal Government, in 1944, linked directly to the National Security Council, but it was soon extinguished, in 1945. Hence, like the CME, its goal was the adjustment of the national economy in the post-war scenario, making studies on the economic activities of general and military interest.

Among its duties was 'economic planning, in addition to the problems related to agriculture, industry, national and international business [...]'.[47] Concerning the composition of the CPE, despite the presence of names committed to the idea of strengthening the industrial sector, it is clear there was a preference for the non-interventionist trend that increasingly gained momentum in the country as the end of the war approached.

> O Planejamento Econômico Brasileiro assentará na conjugação de esforços entre o Estado e particulares, cabendo ao Estado criar e manter a ambiência indispensável ao surto e à expansão da iniciativa particular, complementando-a onde esta se mostrar deficiente.[48]
>
> [Brazilian Economic Planning will be based on joining together efforts between the State and private interests, with the State being responsible for creating and maintaining the environment necessary to the emergence and the expansion of private enterprise, supplementing it where it shows itself to be deficient.]

In its first paragraph, the *regimento* states that

> O Planejamento Econômico Brasileiro deverá orientar o aproveitamento dos fatores de produção — recursos naturais, mão-de-obra, capital e capacidade técnica — no sentido da maior eficiência da produção nacional e da melhoria do padrão de vida do povo brasileiro.[49]
>
> [The Brazilian Economic Planning must guide the use of the factors of production — natural resources, labour, capital and technical capacity — towards greater efficiency in the domestic production and improving the standard of living of Brazilian people.]

Among other matters, the CPE was also responsible for the development of general or special plans for the use and gradual development of the country's economic resources and the centralization and coordination of plans and projects for the national economy, prepared by any agencies, commissions and federal, state and municipal public councils.[50]

With regard to its composition, it was not connected to the ministry. The

---

[47] Article 1 § 2 from the Rules of the CPE, September 1944.
[48] Article 1 from the Rules of the CPE, September 1944.
[49] Article 1 § 1 from the Rules of the CPE, September 1944.
[50] Article 4 from the Rules of the CPE, September 1944.

commission consisted of seventeen members of the Advisory Board under the chairmanship of the General Secretary of the National Security Council, and all chosen directly by the President of the Republic.[51] The body was structured by the Advisory Board, an Executive Secretariat which had the task of coordinating the Special Sections which were divided into two sections, general and military affairs.[52]

However, the creation of the CPE seems to have resulted from the attempt to establish the experience of the CME on a permanent basis. Alternatively, as shown by Monteiro and Cunha ('Alguns aspectos') from Eugênio Gudin's interview, the creation of the CPE would have as a political motivation the objective of limiting and creating a counterpoint to the proposals of the CNPIC, under the guidance of Roberto Simonsen.

Conclusions and Final Remarks

The new organization, therefore, introduced by the Brazilian Government through the Technical Councils' economic apparatus, would promote the industrialization and the maintenance of the state space examined throughout this whole article. Thus, if the industrial and economic development process required state coordination, this *élan* State Coordinator was in the development model itself, which had as a goal Brazil's industrial development, as the coordinating central body failed to materialize.

It is interesting to highlight that by creating the Technical Councils, the Government catered to a multiple frame of interests that started to internalize within the State itself. Alternatively, it can be said that sectoral interests were enrolled in the very structure of the State in its economic apparatus, in its multiple control bodies of regulation and intervention. This is explicit in the process for recruiting members and in their composition.

Hence, the Technical Councils remained in the Brazilian Government structure for subsequent periods by setting not only an institutional model geared to the guidelines of the economic and industrial development, but also as a model of political interaction with a corporatist and authoritarian character among the Government, the sectoral demands of society, and private interests. Thus, the Technical Councils acted as political intermediaries legitimizing the direct involvement of the different economic interests within the State. This 'elites' instrumental corporatism',[53] also draws attention to the self-representation of interests, from state bodies, making use of technical and theoretical arguments for its legitimation through the legitimization of economic knowledge.

[51] Although the Decree-Law No. 6.476, of 8 May 1944, talks about seventeen members for the Advisory Board, Article 5 from the Rules of the CPE, of September 1944, talks about 'an unlimited number of members'.
[52] Article 4 and 5 of the Decree-Law No. 6.476, of 8 May 1944.
[53] This concept is introduced by Maria Lúcia Teixeira Werneck Vianna, *A administração do milagre: o Conselho Monetário Nacional (1964–1974)* (Petrópolis: Vozes, 1987).

The experience gained after the seminal attempts between 1934 and 1945 to establish a central organ for planning and economic coordination, and the discussions involving the Brazilian State development subject, are fundamental to the understanding of the direction of the Brazilian industrialization process post-1945 and its interaction with the state structure.

Reviews

Alexandra Curvelo, *Nanban Folding Screen Masterpieces: Japan-Portugal XVIIth Century* (Paris: Chandeigne, 2015). 175 pages, numerous colour illustrations. Print. Also available in Portuguese and French translations.

Reviewed by Jeremy Roe (Faculdade de Ciências Sociais e Humanas — Universidade Nova de Lisboa, Centro de História d'Aquém e d'Além-Mar / Portuguese Centre for Global History (CHAM))

Nanban Folding Screen Masterpieces provides a concise and lavishly illustrated introduction to a corpus of artworks that offers a visual testimony to Portugal's trading and missionary activity during the sixteenth and seventeenth centuries. Ninety-one folding screens, each measuring around a metre and a half in height and over three in length, depicting the Portuguese or *nanban-jin* [barbarians from the south], have been catalogued by Japanese researchers, although another screen appeared on the art market in 2015. Curvelo comments that this 'is an impressive number denoting the importance and popularity of this pictorial theme' (p. 7), and her book focuses on thirteen screens to chart the development of this subject matter succinctly.

The book opens with an introduction to the artistic, social and political context that shaped the representation of the *nanban-jin* as subject matter for these screens. Curvelo addresses the unification of early modern Japan before turning to discuss the development of the Kanō school of painting, whose painters are considered to have produced the most significant *nanban* folding screens. She explains how the Kanō school grew thanks to their ties with a succession of powerful patrons. Evidently, both the artists and their patrons developed a taste for what could be termed scenes of everyday life, and the arrival of Portuguese traders and missionaries provided a stimulus for a new facet of this subject matter. Detailed discussion of the function and reception of these paintings goes beyond the scope of Curvelo's introduction, which instead concludes with a reflection on how to read these artworks, but throughout her text she alerts the reader to the critical issues and concerns that remain to be addressed by scholars.

Curvelo continues by setting out a series of issues to be considered when studying these images, such as the superimposition of Japanese symbolism of the ship as bearer of good fortune onto the depiction of Portuguese caravels, a central motif. Trade is a key theme of these images and in relation to this Curvelo discusses how these screens are also testimony to the 'hybridity' of the

Luso-Asian encounter and later she examines a number that depict the world beyond Japan.

In the first of three groups of *nanban* screens discussed by Curvelo the arrival and unloading of the *Nau do trato*, or black ship, appears on the left-hand screen, and, on the right-hand screen, the elaborate parade of Portuguese traders bearing clearly identifiable commodities amongst Japanese buildings and people. Curvelo's painstaking selection of details enables close study of these complex images. It is clear how the rigging of the Portuguese ships fascinated the artists, with their eye for intricate depiction of detail, yet such alien elements were incorporated into their concern to hone the decorative potential of all the visual elements from natural phenomena, such as sea and trees, to the human figures and their garments. Curvelo traces the development of this first group of screens and comments on their many protagonists, along with their place in the social hierarchy of this rich cultural encounter. The depiction of the Jesuit and Franciscan missionaries is an intriguing component as they are shown integrated into Japanese society, with their religious houses and rites. Given that the missionaries would be expelled from Japan in 1614 it is all the more striking that such scenes of integration became decorative motifs.

In the second group of screens the left-hand screen shows the black ship being loaded and setting sail from a foreign land, while the right-hand screen shows its arrival in Japan and its cargo being unloaded. In this second group of paintings, with their contrasting depiction of both Japan and the barbarian world, there is a still richer wealth of details, including the depiction of Africans and elephants. The final image discussed by Curvelo offers a form of epilogue, as it is dated to after the expulsion of the Portuguese and they are notably absent from the seafaring and trade depicted; the merchandise, whose attentive depiction is a recurring feature in all these paintings, is in this case identified as traditional Japanese commodities. Thereby it is clear that the encounter between Japan and Portugal was a crucial dynamic to the production of these paintings and not mere subject matter.

Further research into these paintings remains to be undertaken. Curvelo comments that some of the frames of these screens have been found to be filled with old documents, whereby these paintings, as objects, may themselves contain valuable clues to their historical significance. However, whatever they may come to reveal, learning how to read these images is a crucial point of departure. Curvelo's book with its eloquent visual essay of details provides a valuable insight into how to engage with this corpus of *nanban* imagery.

PAULO DE MEDEIROS, *Pessoa's Geometry of the Abyss: Modernity and the 'Book of Disquiet'* (Oxford: Legenda, 2013). 134 pages. Print.

Reviewed by RUI MIRANDA (University of Nottingham)

With this very welcome monograph dedicated to the *Book of Disquiet*, Paulo de Medeiros accepts the challenge of addressing a complex text in very clear, straightforward language; and yet, the author is only too aware of the trap of falling into an explanation of the text or a definition of a 'Pessoan' method.

The various chapters of the book trace key textual operations and draw from signs, images or instances in the text, insightful meditations and timely extrapolations. Throughout the book, Medeiros issues several warnings against immanent, traditionalist readings; this does not mean, however, that the author overlooks the text. In fact, the author starts by addressing the intricacies and particularities of a work that never was an oeuvre as such: the *Book of Disquiet*, composed of 'texts without limits and without a possible end'. Published posthumously in the 1980s, some five decades after the death of Fernando Pessoa, it has since then been added to, complemented and reworked in the several published versions as a result of several delvings into Pessoa's (in)famous trunk. The author resists going transcendental, which so often has undermined the most well-intentioned approaches to the Pessoan text. On the contrary, the theoretical extrapolations and critical meditations developed are anchored in a close attention to the extracts.

The lucidity of the arguments and the clarity of the exposition throughout *Pessoa's Geometry of the Abyss* will undoubtedly assist those who may feel overwhelmed by an initial contact with the *Book of Disquiet*'s diversity of topics, range of references as well as variations in style and tone; the reader familiar with the Pessoan text will gain insight into different textual dimensions teased out from a careful reading, the re-situating of the text vis-à-vis close contemporaries and fellow 'modernists' (Franz Kafka, James Joyce), or the theoretical gains of a selective application of the thought of Walter Benjamin, Jacques Derrida and Alain Badiou.

Each chapter delivers a powerful meditation from which the following chapter can be seen to build. The first, with the self-explanatory title 'Protocols of Reading', sets the coordinates and the tone of the approach from a methodological as well as a critical perspective. Medeiros's discussion of the 'fragment' enters into dialogue with a rich critical tradition and is of interest for Pessoa's work as a whole. It should be read carefully by critics who too often make use of any text whatsoever, whenever, at the service of a given pretext. To be contemporaries of Pessoa (Badiou's challenge which is evoked by Medeiros) implies coming to terms with the text, not necessarily on — but nevertheless without ignoring — its terms.

'(Un)Seeing Pessoa' follows on the discussion of modernity by tackling the quintessentially modern medium of photography. It features an exemplary discussion which displays the intellectual dexterity at work throughout the book, featuring Bernardo Soares's writings on seeing, embracing the ability to blur borders, the notion of photographic writing, and an insightful analysis of iconic photographs and visual representations of Pessoa *qua* author. The discussion of (in)visibility provides an effective transition to the ensuing discussion in 'Phantoms and Crypts' which, among other things, analyses the spectrality underwriting and undermining the possibility of selfhood in writing. Those familiar with the thought of Derrida which punctuates this approach to the Pessoan text will welcome the analysis of João Botelho's adaptation of the *Book of Disquiet* (*Film of Disquiet*, 2010).

'Dreams, Women, Politics' takes on the oneiric allusions constantly at play in the Pessoan text and, while acknowledging Pessoa's misogyny, explores a complementary textual approach. The subsection on 'Disquiet as Resistance' is as incisive and balanced as one can hope for when the question of 'politics' in Pessoa's text is at stake. Medeiros's meditation on the politics of the *Book of Disquiet*, which even as a dream offers a possibility for resistance against nostalgia for the past and a future which is not preordained, may very well signal a veering towards a more mature discussion of politics in the Pessoan text.

The final chapter, 'Infinite Writing', presents a fruitful reading of extracts of *Book of Disquiet* alongside Emily Dickinson's poetry and Kafka's prose — the thread is the discussion of the human and the animal — in close dialogue with Walter Benjamin. The chapter convincingly argues for the hypothesis of writing as search for the infinity, which offers as well a fittingly open-ended conclusion to the book as a whole. 'Envoi', a coda as much as a conclusion, is a helpful reminder of the elusive power of the disquiet and it takes a final opportunity to remind its readers that, contrary to a well-established myth, Fernando Pessoa was never a ghost.

The maturity of the approach, the freshness of insight, the rigorous close reading, the extremely well articulated discussions, the breadth and range of references: there are plenty of reasons to admire Medeiros's undertaking. It is, however, the combination of all of the above that makes this book an invaluable *compagnon de route*, a theoretically conscious, critically minded approach to the texts of *Book of Disquiet* which constantly reminds its readers of the 'power and the beauty' of the *Book of Disquiet*. Pessoa may still be ignored or overlooked as a key author of and in modernity, as Medeiros — understandably perplexed — notes. This book makes ignoring Pessoa just that little harder.

DIDIER PÉCLARD, *Les Incertitudes de la nation en Angola: aux racines sociales de l'Unita* (Paris: Éditions Karthala, 2015). 370 pages. Print.

Reviewed by IRACEMA DULLEY (CEBRAP — Brazilian Centre for Analysis and Planning)

This book addresses the relations between Christian missions, Portuguese colonialism, local societies, and the emergence of UNITA (National Union for the Total Independence of Angola) in the Central Highlands of Angola. The book starts with a puzzle: how could a movement that on the verge of Angola's independence had just a few thousand members and no significant international support manage to declare a rival government — together with the FNLA (National Front for the Liberation of Angola) — in Huambo in November 1975? The government was short-lived and unrecognized by any foreign country, but UNITA would continue to challenge the legitimacy of the MPLA (Popular Movement for the Liberation of Angola) until the end of the bloody civil war, in 2002. In Savimbi's retreat to Eastern Angola, he would be joined by a significant part of the Evangelical Congregational Church in Angola (IECA), known as the 'church in the bush'.

If UNITA's 'social roots' include the Congregational church, Péclard's analysis of the history of missionization in the Central Highlands outlines the conditions of possibility of this history, not its necessary causes. His examination of the architecture of the Congregational mission in the Central Highlands reveals both the introjection of an ethos in a long-term process of subjectification and the place of Christian missions as the only means of upward social mobility for the vast majority of Africans during Portuguese colonialism.

The first chapter discusses the role of colonial knowledge in Angola and argues that the African population was rarely the object of detailed investigation. For the author, lusotropicalist ideology would promote the ontologization of the colonizer, not of colonial subjects, in its advocacy of Portuguese affability. The second chapter deals with the long-term relationship between the church and the colonial state and portrays the Portuguese New State as 'Catholaicist', i.e., marked by a separation of church and state in which the Catholic church was awarded privileges and funding in exchange for providing health and education services to Africans and promoting their 'nationalization' and 'civilization'. Péclard relativizes the view according to which the Catholic Church is considered an extension of the colonial state by revealing the tensions that marked their relation; he also argues that while North American Protestant missionaries tended to be viewed as 'denationalizing', the Congregational mission's diplomatic relations with the colonial state could ease tensions.

The third chapter focuses on the implementation of the Congregational project from 1920 to 1950, a period in which the Highlands transitioned from caravan trade to agriculture. According to Péclard, the Congregational mission took advantage of the historical circumstances of sedentarization to build 'rural bastions' relatively isolated from urban colonial society and undertake its work of 'culturalist modernization'. The process of subjectification that ensued included transformations in agriculture, education, and the domestic space while retaining part of what was understood to be Umbundu tradition. The fourth chapter describes the challenges faced by Congregational missions from 1940 to 1960, a time of pauperization and proletarianization of the Highlands due to contract labour and the arrival of white settlers. The author describes the transformations in the Protestant project as a rural exodus and the inevitability of urbanization challenged its main pillars, rural life and relative isolation from the colonial world; he compares it with the Catholic missions, already inserted in urban areas and intimately connected to colonial society.

The last chapter dwells both on the delayed participation of the Highlands in the uprisings and movements that challenged the colonial state from 1961 and on the repressive apparatus in the region, whose main targets were 'assimilated' subjects, especially Protestant ones. Repression and prosperity went hand in hand, as the 'native statute' was abolished in 1961 and economic growth provided opportunities for educated Africans. Péclard argues that while the Christian elite benefited from the colonial system that granted it privilege and status, the main opponents of the regime would nonetheless come from their ranks, given that education and upward social mobility depended on the missions.

The book focuses considerably more on Protestant missions, which makes one wonder about the similarities and differences in the subjectification process that occurred in the more numerous Catholic missions. Nonetheless, the suggestion that the Protestant imagination of rural life would become one of the pillars of UNITA, whose leader came from a prominent Protestant family, is convincing. The conclusion argues that the ethnicization of Angola was an outcome of the civil war rather than its cause, for although UNITA's political project arguably shares the structure of Protestant 'culturalist modernization', the existence of a given imagination does not automatically engender its actualization in political practice. This is surely a book to be read by scholars interested in the relationship between religion and politics in colonial and post-colonial Lusophone Africa.

PAUL MELO E CASTRO (editor and translator), *Lengthening Shadows*, intro. by Melo e Castro, afterword by Augusto Pinto, 2 vols (Saligão, India: Goa 1556 & Golden Heart Emporium, 2015). 182, 189 pages. Print.

Reviewed by CIELO G. FESTINO (Universidade Paulista)

Lengthening Shadows is an anthology of short stories in the Portuguese language from Goa, India, a former Portuguese colony, covering a period of more than a century, from the 1860s to 1980s. It was edited and translated into English by Paul Melo e Castro of Leeds University, who painstakingly retrieved the stories from Goan newspapers, the Bulletin of the Institute Menezes

Bragança (IMB), and private libraries. Melo e Castro's research has contributed to the preservation of narratives that might otherwise have been lost forever. Therefore, while they are a novelty for the lay reader, they are a real treasure for literary scholars. A bilingual edition with the short stories both in English and in Portuguese would be welcome in future.

In the 'Afterword' Augusto Pinto, a Goan critic and translator, praises the book both for the quality of the translations — 'the stories feel like originals' (p. 184) — and the fact that though the stories have been written by different authors '…the anthology is more than the sum of the individual pieces. It reads like a compendium of the lives and mores of *Goa Portuguesa* in the last century or so of its existence' (p. 184). What also contributes to the reading of the anthology as a compendium is the scholarly 'Introduction' in which Melo e Castro deftly weaves the stories together in terms of their historical, political and cultural context, their form of publication in Goa's newspapers and literary journals, as well as their themes and literary style. In so doing, he sets out how Goan literary tradition in Portuguese evolved over the last century of its existence.

Melo e Castro explains that the name of the book, *Lengthening Shadows*, comes from the two-line epigraph to *Monção* (1963), a classic of Portuguese-language Goan literature by Vimala Devi, taken from the Sanskrit poet Kalidasa: 'The tree's shadow lengthens at sundown | without ever splitting from it' (p. 54). Pondering these lines, he wonders 'how far the shadow of Portuguese language literature has crept from the trunk of contemporary Goan reality' and 'whether some attachment persists between the mindset, concerns and style of the writers who appear [in the anthology] in English translation and the contemporary Goan literary scene' (p. 54). In order that they may judge that, he presents the reader with an annotated two-volume book, beautifully illustrated by Bina Nayak, which comprises fourteen writers and forty-six short stories that cover Goa's political scene before and after its integration with the Indian Union in 1961, as well its different literary periods. As he discusses themes, literary styles and political views, Melo e Castro establishes a counterpoint among the different authors compiled.

The process whereby a literary tradition forms can also be perceived in the references to literary genres. While most of the narratives in *Lengthening Shadows* are short stories, there are some *cronicas* by Walfrido Antao, very much in the Brazilian style, as well as short stories that were aired via a radio programme called *Renascença*, broadcast by All-India Radio. This transmission of written narratives, in a way, bridges the distance between the European-style short story of most of the writers in the collection and the typically Goan dramatic genre, the *tiatr*.

To better contextualize 'The Bitter Sap' by Maria Elsa da Rocha, Melo e Castro explains that 'it deals with subjects of female subjectivity, gender relations and class hierarchies, all told against a sensitively depicted Goan village backdrop — of colourful weddings, overpriced onions, sewing teachers raised in British India, and irritable parish priests' (p. 44). Comments like this make the reader smile and hanker for the reading of each one of the short stories in the anthology in order to get to know the 'sights, sounds, and smells of Goa Portuguesa', as Pinto writes in his Afterword (p. 185).

Abstracts

The Political and Ideological Origins of the Estado Novo in Portugal

Ernesto Castro Leal

Abstract. This article sets out to reflect on aspects of the ideological and political origins of the Estado Novo dictatorship in Portugal, rooted in the times of the Portuguese First Republic. It is based on the following points of departure: 1) the 'original ideological basis' was in Christian Democracy and Social Catholicism; 2) the 'competing ideological basis' showed itself in Integralismo Lusitano [Lusitanian Integralism], with transformations relevant to the Estado Novo; 3) the 'eclectic or syncretic ideological basis' owed much to the Cruzada Nacional [National Crusade] D. Nuno Álvaro Pereira. Analysis is directed towards the processes of circulation and transference of political notions of nationalism, organicism, corporativism and authoritarianism between ideological and political camps critical of the parliamentary system of government in force under the Portuguese First Republic.

Keywords. Portugal, First Republic, Estado Novo, nationalism, organicism, corporativism, authoritarianism.

Resumo. O presente artigo pretende reflectir sobre aspectos das origens ideológicas e políticas da ditadura do Estado Novo português, situadas no tempo da I República portuguesa. Estabelece-se estes pontos de partida: 1) a 'matriz ideológica original' foi a Democracia Cristã e o Catolicismo Social; 2) a 'matriz ideológica concorrencial' manifestou-se no Integralismo Lusitano, com conversões relevantes ao Estado Novo; 3) a 'matriz ideológica eclética ou sincrética' deveu muito à Cruzada Nacional D. Nuno Álvares Pereira. A análise dirige-se aos processos de circulação e transferência das ideias políticas de nacionalismo, organicismo, corporativismo e autoritarismo entre os campos ideológico-políticos críticos da versão parlamentarista do sistema de governo da I República portuguesa.

Palavras-chave. Portugal, I República, Estado Novo, nacionalismo, organicismo, corporativismo, autoritarismo.

Redefining the State in the Dictatorship of Salazar and Marcelo Caetano: The Changing Face of Parliament (1935–1974)

Paula Borges Santos

Abstract. This article analyses the role of parliamentary structures in the Portuguese authoritarian regime (1935–74), discussing their configuration in the framework of the project for a Corporative state, and noting the debates that ensued on the question of representation. It studies in particular the transformations that affected the political chamber, known as the National Assembly, in order to see if the changes that took place strengthened or weakened its position in the political system. Rather than employing theoretical approaches that explain the forms and evolution of parliaments under the dictatorships between the wars by way of the creation of regime parties or by corporativism, the article proposes an explanation of the Portuguese case that emphasizes the formulation of political and juridical doctrines and practices in a national context, and downplays the allegedly mimetic character of the Portuguese authoritarian experience in relation to foreign models.

KEYWORDS. Portugal, corporativism, authoritarianism, parliament, Salazar, Caetano, politics.

RESUMO. Neste artigo analisa-se o papel da organização parlamentar no regime autoritário português (1935-74), discutindo a sua configuração no quadro do projeto corporativo do Estado, e observam-se os debates travados sobre a questão da representação. Verificam-se, em particular, as transformações que afetaram a câmara política, designada Assembleia Nacional, de modo a perceber se as alterações registadas fortaleceram ou não a posição desta no sistema político. Sem se acompanharem posições teóricas que explicam as formas e a evolução dos parlamentos nas ditaduras de Entre Guerras por via da criação de partidos de regime ou pelo corporativismo, propõe-se uma explicação para o caso português que valoriza as formulações de doutrinas e práticas políticas e jurídicas nacionais e desvaloriza o alegado mimetismo da experiência autoritária portuguesa em relação a modelos estrangeiros.

PALAVRAS-CHAVE. Portugal, corporativismo, autoritarismo, parlamento, Salazar, Caetano, política.

Memory of Resistance and the Resistance of Memory: An Analysis of the Construction of Corporatism in the First Years of the Portuguese Estado Novo

FRANCISCO CARLOS PALOMANES MARTINHO

ABSTRACT. This article aims to analyse how Union leaders reacted to the construction of a corporative model for the labour world during the initial period of the institutionalization of the Portuguese Estado Novo (1930-34). At the same time it discusses the impact of the 'memory of resistance' built upon the events of 28 January 1934, both among the representatives of the public sectors involved and in the field of historiography.

KEYWORDS. Estado Novo, labour relations, trade unions, corporatism.

RESUMO. O presente artigo tem por objetivo analisar como a construção de um modelo corporativo para o mundo do trabalho durante o período inicial de institucionalização do Estado Novo português (1930-34) foi recebido pelas lideranças sindicais à época. Ao mesmo tempo pretende discutir o impacto de uma 'memória da resistência' construída a partir dos acontecimentos de 28 de janeiro de 1934, tanto entre os setores políticos envolvidos no episódio como também no campo historiográfico.

PALAVRAS-CHAVE. Estado Novo, relações laborais, sindicalismo, corporativismo.

Portuguese Origins and the 'True' Brazilian Nation: The Corporative Vision of Oliveira Viana

LUCIANO ARONNE DE ABREU

ABSTRACT. This study aims to understand the foundations and meaning of the 'true' Brazilian nation, as defined by Oliveira Viana, a prominent conservative intellectual of the generation of 1920-40, who believed that nation building and development were directly connected to Brazil's Portuguese origins and the task of creating a corporative society. The conclusion drawn is that the corporative and syndicalist model proposed by Oliveira Viana does not only have its eye on the future, but also on the past, taking a deterministic view that the nation is shaped by the country's own environment and its own history.

KEYWORDS. Portuguese origins, corporativism, nation, nationalism.

RESUMO. O presente estudo tem por objetivo compreender os fundamentos e o sentido da 'verdadeira' nação brasileira, conforme definia Oliveira Viana, um dos principais intelectuais conservadores brasileiros da chamada geração dos anos 1920-40, para quem a construção da nação e o desenvolvimento nacional estariam diretamente relacionados às suas origens lusas e à construção de uma sociedade corporativa no Brasil. A esse respeito, contudo, conclui-se que o modelo corporativo e sindical proposto por Oliveira Viana nos remetem não apenas para o futuro, mas também de volta ao passado nacional, por uma espécie de determinismo do meio e da própria história do país.

PALAVRAS-CHAVE. Origem lusa, corporativismo, nação, nacionalismo.

Brazilian Integralism and the Corporatist Intellectual Triad

LEANDRO PEREIRA GONÇALVES and ODILON CALDEIRA NETO

ABSTRACT. Through the implementation of an Integral State of corporatist jurisdiction, the Brazilian Integralist Action (Ação Integralista Brasileira — AIB) anticipated the solution for national problems and disputes, especially those originated by socialism and liberalism. This study analyses how the corporatist matter was depicted in the writings of the three main intellectuals and leaders of the movement (Plínio Salgado, Gustavo Barroso and Miguel Reale), and how Integralism interacted with the Estado Novo of Getúlio Vargas.

KEYWORDS. Integralism, corporatism, conservatism.

RESUMO. A Ação Integralista Brasileira previa, por meio da instalação de um Estado Integral de foro corporativista, a solução dos problemas e disputas nacionais, em especial aqueles oriundos do socialismo e do liberalismo. Este artigo pretende analisar de que forma a questão corporativa se delineou nos escritos dos três principais líderes e intelectuais do movimento (Plínio Salgado, Gustavo Barroso e Miguel Reale), assim como se deu a relação do Integralismo para com o Estado Novo de Getúlio Vargas.

PALAVRAS-CHAVE. Integralismo, corporativismo, conservadorismo.

The Technical Councils of the Brazilian Government Structure: Corporatism, Authoritarianism and Modernization (1934-1945)

CÁSSIO A. A. ALBERNAZ

ABSTRACT. This paper aims at analysing the emergence of the Technical Councils as the state economic planning bodies, between 1930 and 1945, seeking to identify the main organs. This analysis will provide an understanding of some political, social and institutional dynamics of the Brazilian Government history, its relations with the representation of interests, the paths, and the main bodies involved in planning and setting development guidelines.

Thus, it will be possible to map out the main centres of the decision and planning of the Brazilian economic and industrial development in this period. Also, it will be possible to identify the roots and nature of these organs, their duties, their effective period of influence, their composition, and the criteria for recruiting members through their foundational legislation.

KEYWORDS. Technical Councils, corporatism, authoritarianism, economic planning, Brazilian State.

RESUMO. O objetivo desse texto é analisar a emergência dos Conselhos Técnicos como espaços estatais de planejamento econômico, dentre os 1930 e 1945, buscando a identificação dos órgãos que foram centrais nesse sentido. Essa análise permitirá compreender algumas dinâmicas políticas, sociais, e institucionais da história do Estado brasileiro, suas relações com a representação de interesses, os caminhos, e os principais espaços para orientação e definição de diretrizes de desenvolvimento.

Nesse sentido, será possível traçar um mapa dos principais centros de decisão e de planejamento do desenvolvimento econômico e industrial brasileiro nesse período. Assim, será possível identificar: as origens e a natureza desses órgãos, suas atribuições, seu período efetivo de influência, sua composição, e os critérios para o recrutamento de membros através de sua legislação de criação.

PALAVRAS-CHAVE. Conselhos técnicos, corporativismo, autoritarismo, planejamento econômico, Estado brasileiro.

www.ingramcontent.com/pod-product-compliance
Lightning Source LLC
Chambersburg PA
CBHW070837020526
44114CB00041B/1944